D1094118

# FILMMAKERS SERIES
## edited by
## ANTHONY SLIDE

28. *William Desmond Taylor: A Dossier,* by Bruce Long. 1991
29. *The Films of Leni Riefenstahl,* 2nd ed., by David B. Hinton. 1991
30. *Hollywood Holyland: The Filming and Scoring of "The Greatest Story Ever Told,"* by Ken Darby. 1992
31. *The Films of Reginald LeBorg: Interviews, Essays, and Filmography,* by Wheeler Winston Dixon. 1992
32. *Memoirs of a Professional Cad,* by George Sanders, with Tony Thomas. 1992
33. *The Holocaust in French Film,* by André Pierre Colombat. 1993
34. *Robert Goldstein and "The Spirit of '76,"* edited and compiled by Anthony Slide. 1993
35. *Those Were the Days, My Friend: My Life in Hollywood with David O. Selznick and Others,* by Paul Macnamara. 1993
36. *The Creative Producer,* by David Lewis; edited by James Curtis. 1993
37. *Reinventing Reality: The Art and Life of Rouben Mamoulian,* by Mark Spergel. 1993
38. *Malcolm St. Clair: His Films, 1915–1948,* by Ruth Anne Dwyer. 1997
39. *Beyond Hollywood's Grasp: American Filmmakers Abroad, 1914–1945,* by Harry Waldman. 1994
40. *A Steady Digression to a Fixed Point,* by Rose Hobart. 1994
41. *Radical Juxtaposition: The Films of Yvonne Rainer,* by Shelley Green. 1994
42. *Company of Heroes: My Life as an Actor in the John Ford Stock Company,* by Harry Carey Jr. 1994
43. *Strangers in Hollywood: A History of Scandinavian Actors in American Films from 1910 to World War II,* by Hans J. Wollstein. 1994
44. *Charlie Chaplin: Intimate Close-Ups,* by Georgia Hale; edited with an introduction and notes by Heather Kiernan. 1995
45. *The Word Made Flesh: Catholicism and Conflict in the Films of Martin Scorsese,* by Michael Bliss. 1995
46. *W. S. Van Dyke's Journal: White Shadows in the South Seas (1927–1928) and other Van Dyke on Van Dyke,* edited and annotated by Rudy Behlmer. 1996
47. *Music from the House of Hammer: Music in the Hammer Horror Films, 1950–1980,* by Randall D. Larson. 1996
48. *Directing: Learn from the Masters,* by Tay Garnett. 1996
49. *Featured Player: An Oral Autobiography of Mae Clarke,* edited with an introduction by James Curtis. 1996
50. *A Great Lady: A Life of the Screenwriter Sonya Levien,* by Larry Ceplair. 1996
51. *A History of Horrors: The Rise and Fall of the House of Hammer,* by Denis Meikle. 1996
52. *The Films of Michael Powell and the Archers,* by Scott Salwolke. 1997

# The Divine Comic

## The Cinema of Roberto Benigni

Carlo Celli

*Filmmakers Series, No. 85*

The Scarecrow Press, Inc.
Lanham, Maryland, and London
2001

SCARECROW PRESS, INC.

Published in the United States of America
by Scarecrow Press, Inc.
4720 Boston Way, Lanham, Maryland 20706
www.scarecrowpress.com

4 Pleydell Gardens, Folkestone
Kent CT20 2DN, England

PN2688
.B44C45
2001

Copyright © 2001 by Carlo Celli

*All rights reserved.* No part of this publication may be reproduced, stored
in a retrieval system, or transmitted in any form or by any means, elec-
tronic, mechanical, photocopying, recording, or otherwise, without the
prior permission of the publisher.

British Library Cataloguing-in-Publication Information Available

**Library of Congress Cataloging-in-Publication Data**

Celli, Carlo, 1963–
    The divine comic : the cinema of Roberto Benigni / Carlo Celli.
      p. cm. — (Filmmakers series ; no. 85)
    Includes bibliographical references and index.
    Includes filmography.
    ISBN 0-8108-4000-6 (c : alk. paper)
      1. Benigni, Roberto. I. Title: Cinema of Roberto Benigni. II. Title.
III. Series.
PN2688.B44 C45 2001
791.43′028′092—dc21                                    00-054766

♾ ™ The paper used in this publication meets the minimum requirements
of American National Standard for Information Sciences—Permanence
of Paper for Printed Library Materials, ANSI/NISO Z39.48-1992.
Manufactured in the United States of America.

# Contents

# Preface

Roberto Benigni, the Italian comedian, actor, director, and writer, gained international fame when his film *La vita è bella/Life Is Beautiful* (1997) won three Oscars in 1999, including Best Foreign Film and Best Actor. Almost overnight Benigni entered the pantheon of Italian cinema legends that includes actors Sophia Loren, Anna Magnani, and Marcello Mastroianni, and directors Vittorio De Sica, Federico Fellini, Luchino Visconti, Michelangelo Antonioni, and Roberto Rossellini. However, Benigni has been a steady presence in Italian popular culture since the mid-1970s. This book will introduce Benigni's performances in film, stage, and television, little known outside of Italy, with an emphasis on the cultural and intellectual backdrops that characterize his films.

A focus of cultural studies examines artistic content in light of changes in areas as subjective as historical and social identity. Such studies may be pursued to gain an understanding of the conflict between dominant canons and dynamic forms of culture in the mass media. In this context, the tensions between high and low culture, between iconoclastic rebellion and hegemony, indicate how culture has changed and even been formed. Given Benigni's status as a popular Italian performer and his origins in the peasantry, a study of his career offers a unique opportunity to examine transformations in Italian culture and film history with a particular emphasis on his roots in Tuscan literary and theatrical traditions.

Benigni's humor and performances express the socioeconomic changes in Italy after the economic boom period in the late 1950s and early 1960s. The arrival of consumer culture and the migration of Benigni's own family in this period challenged Benigni's previous cultural formation in the communal lifestyle of Tuscan peasantry. Besides these geographic origins, Benigni's work has elements of the fragmentation of proletarian political identity and a subcurrent of nostalgia for peasant culture. Benigni's championing of cultural authenticity is further expressed in his rebellion against the intellectual classes supporting the dominant models of Catholicism, mafia, consumerism, and fascism, which are the hostile systems that his ex-peasant alter ego Mario Cioni confronts in his films. Comedy in popular culture and the mass media, as commonly identified with a performer such as Benigni, is rarely considered in relation to the canon of high culture. Yet because of his origins in the archaic Tuscan culture of improvisational poetry that was a source of the official Italian literary canon, Benigni does not treat the material of high culture as a threat to his identity. Besides an attentive study of Benigni's work in film, this book also offers an introduction to Benigni's readings of Dante and the Old Testament, which demonstrate how Benigni offers a populist message of the canon often lost in the rigidity of academic/educational formats.

This book also looks at the progression in Benigni's art, from its purely theatrical and oral origins in the improvisational traditions of Tuscany to his conquest of audiences in television and the cinema. Benigni has continued to perform as a stage comedian throughout his career, and the material from his monologues provides clues for understanding the themes that dominate his films, particularly in his religious parodies. There is a similar progression in Benigni's cinematic style. Beginning with *Il mostro/The Monster* (1994) and continuing with *Life Is Beautiful,* Benigni attempts a more ambitious use of the film camera to filter reality into his own artistic vision.

Finally, in my own conversations with Benigni and his colleagues, I was struck by the manner in which the international consumer media has been able to ferret out and disseminate the cultural authenticity that Benigni represents. It is a long trip from the boondocks of the Tuscan countryside to the Dorothy Chandler Pavilion and the Oscar ceremony in Los Angeles. Benigni is one of the very few, if not the only, foreign language comedians to conquer a mass audience in the English-speaking world. One explanation for his success is that his cultural signature in the improvisational traditions of archaic Tuscan poetry is an original format and the expression of a vibrant cultural identity.

However, Benigni is also well versed in numerous cinematic, literary, and cultural currents, which should be evident by the breadth of his responses in the interview in the appendix of this study. It is no accident that when Italy's most famous professor and renowned novelist Umberto Eco gathers guests for an evening of linguistic contests that Benigni is among those invited. After his commentary and recitation of Dante at the University of California at Los Angeles, Benigni was invited to give university seminars, a recognition not only of his popularity but also of his expertise in the material.

Given Benigni's interests in poetry and what may be called high culture, one may wonder what exactly is his relationship with the cinema. He has, after all, invented a clown persona that is arguably the heir to the great comedians of the silent film era, when performance relied more on pantomime than on verbalism. Given Benigni's versatility, his work in film is an extension of the storytelling capacity that he developed first in front of the hearth in rural Tuscany and later as an improvising poet, a *poeta a braccio*. As Benigni explains in my interview, the art of these poets is rooted in a sense of the epic—of characters in time with a sense of a story. Therefore, along with his noted comedic brilliance, Benigni's abilities are an expression of his background in these more traditional, even archaic areas.

# Acknowledgments

I would like to thank Roberto Benigni; Marcello Pezzetti of the Centro di Documentazione Ebraica Contemporanea Milan; Vanina Pezzetti; Saverio Zumbo at Edizioni Falsopiano for allowing a reprint of Vanina Pezzetti's interview with Benigni; Gianluigi Braschi; Alessia Jannece of Melampo Cinematografica; Emilio Canidio; the Celli family; Sergio Toffetti and Flavia Morabito of the archives of the Scuola Nazionale di Cinema Rome; Cinzia Pistolesi and Sandra Eichberg of the Rai Direzione Teche e Servizi Tematici/Educativi; Gianluca Farinelli; Anna Fiaccarini and Cesare Ballardini of the Cineteca del Comune di Bologna; Lori Repetti; Wendy Worth; Peter Wollen; Marga Cottino-Jones; Frank Tomasulo; Vincent Rocchio; Joseph Farrell; Millicent Marcus; the staff at the Hotel Sant'Anselmo Rome; Silvia Bruni and Salvatore Scali at the Biblioteca Rai in Rome; an anonymous reader at the University of Toronto; and my mother-in-law, Mary Ann, for editing the first draft of the work and inspiring the title.

At Bowling Green State University: Kausalya A. Padmaraj of the interlibrary loan department; Mark Gromko and the Speed Grant subcommittee of the Faculty Development Committee; James Pfundstein; Linda Meek; Terrilyn Meel; Henry Garrity; Joseph Cranny; Julia Mason; and Michael T. Martin.

An earlier version of a section of chapter 2 appeared as an article in *Italica* 77(2) (Summer 2000): 171–186; my thanks to editor Albert Mancini for allowing a reprint. An earlier version of chapter 11 appeared in *The Journal of Popular Film and Television* 28 (2) (Summer 2000): 74–79. I would like to thank Heldref publications, Martin Norden, Mary Jane Winokur, and Page Pratt for their help in allowing a reprint.

Benigni on the set of *Life Is Beautiful*. Photo courtesy of Melampo Cinematografica.

# · 1 ·

# Biographical Summary

$\mathcal{I}$n his acceptance speech for the Best Actor Oscar in 1999, Roberto Benigni joked that he wanted to thank his parents for giving him the greatest gift of all, poverty.[1] In fact, Benigni's first years were spent in a region where day-to-day life had remained largely unchanged since the eighteenth century, in a home that often lacked many modern conveniences.[2] The structure of Benigni's family and his position as the youngest child with three older sisters allows some insight into how his rebellious, mischievous, and joyful personality was formed.[3]

Roberto Benigni was born October 27, 1952, in Misericordia, a small agricultural settlement in the province of Arezzo in the Tuscan hinterland. His parents, Luigi Benigni and Isolina Papini, were married in 1942, at the height of World War II. The story of Luigi Benigni's military experiences and eventual internment in a Nazi labor camp later influenced Roberto's film *La vita è bella/Life Is Beautiful* (1997). Since his mother eventually worked outside the home, Roberto's sisters played a vital role in raising him. Roberto recalls living with forty or fifty people in the same house, just as people did in the 1800s. This communal arrangement was common for farmers and sharecroppers such as Roberto's father, who farmed lands owned by the local count.[4] Roberto was born into a rapidly disappearing agricultural world of subsistence farming.

In 1958 Luigi Benigni sold the two rooms he owned in the large, multifamily house. He loaded his family belongings onto a rented truck, and then squeezed his wife and children into the front cab. They left the small agricultural settlement of Misericordia for Vergaio, near the larger city of Prato. Moving to a regional industrial center to become a wage earner was a common occurrence during the period historians have defined as Italy's economic boom (1957–1962). Emigration was highest in areas where absentee landlords controlled most of the land, as in Benigni's home region near the town of Arezzo. Between 1950 and 1960

1

the national economy grew by nearly 47 percent, almost as much as it had during the entire first half of the century. By the early 1960s the number of industrial workers surpassed agricultural workers nationwide.[5]

Italy's economic explosion was an epochal event that transformed the nation from an economy that was primarily agricultural-based to one that was industrial- and consumer-based. Add to that the diffusion of television, and in the space of a few years a nationwide process of cultural homogenization began. Instead of local dialects, traditions, and songs, Italians began to identify more with a national language, game shows, and song festivals geared to mass audiences. Benigni's comedy is an expression of the cultural tensions and transformations of Italy in this period.

Despite the increase in Italy's gross national product, the Benigni family's economic situation in Prato was not much better than it had been in Misericordia. Roberto remembers that his family slept in one room attached to a horse stable. Roberto initially had trouble adjusting to his new school. Even though Prato was a part of Tuscany, to Roberto the local dialect sounded like a foreign language. Roberto's sense of estrangement indicates just how local and specific his culture was. He reacted to this new location and dialect by taking refuge in his family, where his earlier culture was preserved. This attachment to local identity was precisely what the process of industrialization would attenuate during this era.

Some of the most important influences on Benigni's artistic formation, such as the ability to improvise in verse, date back to his days as a youth in rural Tuscany, when he spent time among traditional troubadours, the *poeti a braccio*. Benigni's verbal skills are not a casual talent, but part of a highly sophisticated cultural whole that has deep roots in the Tuscan improvisational poetry tradition.

Although today Benigni is well-versed enough to recite Dante at university campuses, he did not have the advantage of a rigorous education. When Benigni gained the attention of the *poeti a braccio,* the local clergy also noticed him. A common destiny for a bright fellow in the peasant class, particularly after the arrival of compulsory education in Italy, was a career in the priesthood. After Benigni finished middle school, a priest noted his natural intelligence and invited his parents to enroll him in a Jesuit college in the regional capital, Florence.[6] Benigni may very well have completed religious training, had his seminary not closed when the Arno River flooded in 1966, an event that became famous as volunteers from around the world descended on Florence to help preserve the city's cultural treasures.

The peasantry admire the advantages, social and economic, that come with employment as a priest or white-collar worker. For a peasant family, a son in the priesthood promises an elevation of social status and economic expectations; Benigni has stated that economic concerns influenced his parents' decision to send him to the Jesuit seminary in Florence. Yet, the peasantry are also often skeptical and disdainful, and a bit envious, of the intellectual class.[7] Benigni demonstrates such attitudes in his irreverent monologues on Old Testament themes in his stage shows, later documented in the films *Tuttobenigni/Everything Benigni* (1986) and *Tuttobenigni 95/96.* The setting of a seminary also returns in Benigni's film *Il piccolo diavolo/Little Devil* (1988).

After the brief seminary experience, Benigni attended the Datini Institute, a technical school attended mostly by girls planning to become secretaries. As in his family of three older sisters, Benigni again found himself surrounded by women, this time in a school that was not very demanding. While at the Datini, Benigni became a fan of Italian pop and film star Adriano Celentano, perhaps best known abroad for his brief cameo, singing Elvis-style in Federico Fellini's *La dolce vita* (1960). In an era when Italy was producing numerous rock 'n' roll records for the mass youth market, Benigni tried to have his own songs recorded and to join Celentano's Clan of performers in Milan, a negative experience that ended when a crooked record company swindled his father.

By the early 1970s Benigni's family was fully integrated into the Prato economy, which had a growing textile industry. The bustling industrial life was based on the family unit, which caused many in the region to abandon school early in order to bring income to the family. Benigni's decision not to quit school and his family's support of this choice was unusual for someone of his family's economic class.

Benigni's formative years were also centered on performance. As did Federico Fellini, Benigni worked in a circus when he was thirteen or fourteen years old. He did not run away from home, but remained with the circus for a couple of weeks, performing as a straight man to a magician who would hypnotize him and light a fire in his hand. It is here that he learned some pantomime and gymnastics.[8] Benigni's first experience on stage was at the regional theater in Prato, the *Ridotto del Metastasio,* where he sang octets in the Tuscan tradition for an audience of friends. The success of his one-man show led to further opportunities in the theater. In 1972 Benigni was hired for his first professional theatrical role in *Il re nudo/The Naked King* by Eujenij Schwarz, directed by Paolo Maselli.

During this period Benigni met his traveling companions for the next few years: Carlo Monni, ten years Benigni's senior, another Tuscan peasant who became an actor after the industrial farms squeezed traditional pig herders like him out of business[9]; Donato Sannini, a Tuscan aristocrat whose grandmother had run an acting school with graduates including Giorgio Albertazzi, known for his recitations of Dante; and the director Franco Zeffirelli.[10] With his acting friends, Benigni traveled to remote parts of Tuscany to improvise public discussions in town squares. In the highly charged political period of the 1970s stages were already in place for frequent political rallies.[11] These impromptu performances would become the basis for Benigni's future television shows, such as *Onda libera/Free Wave,* and his stage tours around Italy.

In 1972 Benigni and his friends—Monni, Sannini, and Aldo Buti, a set designer—left Tuscany for the avant-garde theaters in Rome, including the Beat 72, the Satiri, and the Albericchio. Benigni began to perform regularly with his friends as part of the Phantom of the Opera Theater Company. He was directed by Sannini in works such as *I burosauri/The Burosauruses* (1972), *La contessa e il cavolfiore/The Countess and the Cauliflower* (1973), *La corte delle stalle/The Court of the Stables* (1974), and *Il mito della caverna/The Myth of the Cave* (1975). He also appeared as part of The Words, The Things Theater Group, with many of the same colleagues, in plays for children directed by Lucia Poli; they included *The Fables of Basile* (1972), Ovid's *Metamorphoses* (1974), and *The Party* (1974). He appeared in two plays written and directed by Marco Messeri: *Bertoldo Azzurra* (1973) and *Mi voglio rovinare/I Want to Ruin Myself* (1974).

Benigni encountered the avant-garde theater of such noted impresarios as Carmelo Bene, Giuliano Vasilicò, and Memè Perlini. He used the period to hone his performing skills and fill in gaps in his education. Benigni read voraciously and attended cinema clubs. This encounter with the avant-garde and Benigni's own intellectual curiosity was fundamental for his later development into a more sophisticated artist. Benigni could easily have become just another Italian regional comedian, successful on television and in the commercial cinema. Instead he developed interests in so-called serious literature (Dostoyevsky, Rabelais, Whitman), and in film (Chaplin, and surprisingly, Dreyer). (See interview in Appendix.)

The encounter of Benigni's heritage of oral poetry and the free-form experimentation of counterculture theater eventually resulted in the monologue *Cioni Mario di Gaspare fu Giulia/Mario Cioni Son of Gaspare and the Late Giulia* (1975). The piece, which Benigni co-wrote with Giuseppe Bertolucci, combines stories and voices from Benigni's Tuscan past with the influences of the avant-garde theater and his own readings, particularly Dostoyevsky and Rabelais. Benigni's performance was an archaic, primitive explosion of coarse invective that perhaps needed the climate of avant-garde experimentation to come to fruition. Benigni's first television shows, *Free Wave* (1976–1977) and *Vita da Cioni/Cioni's Dog Life* (1978), were based on the foulmouthed Tuscan bumpkin character Mario Cioni from the monologue. Benigni starred, under Giuseppe Bertolucci's direction, in the film version of the *Cioni Mario* monologue, *Berlinguer ti voglio bene/Berlinguer I Love You* (1977). The film's disappointing box office performance belied the difficulty in transposing a theatrical piece to the cinema and raised questions about how to adapt Benigni's talent to the screen.

Undeterred, Benigni spent the late 1970s appearing in film cameos for several renowned filmmakers, such as Bernardo Bertolucci, Marco Ferreri, and Costas Gravas. In the early 1980s Benigni took up projects that indicated the various directions that his career may have taken. After appearing as a cast member in jazz and showman Renzo Arbore's television program *L'altra Domenica/The Other Sunday* (1978–1979), Benigni costarred in Arbore's film *Il Pap'occhio/Pope in Your Eye* (1980), a prime example of the Italian commercial cinema of the time featuring television-based performers.

Benigni then accepted a year-long apprenticeship with Cesare Zavattini (1902–1989), the master of the neorealist style and author of some of the most important Italian films of the postwar period, such as *The Bicycle Thief* (1948) and *The Garden of the Finzi-Contini* (1970). Zavattini was then in his twilight years, preparing what was to be his last film, *La veritaaa'* (1983), for which he wanted Benigni in the starring role. Although Zavattini eventually decided to cast himself in the film, the period that Benigni spent with Zavattini influenced his later work in terms of its fabulist approach and simple cinematic style. In 1981 Benigni costarred in *Il minestrone* (1981), a film directed by Pier Paolo Pasolini disciple Sergio Citti. The screenwriter of *Il minestrone,* Vincenzo Cerami, had also been Pasolini's assistant director on his famed film starring Italian comic legend Totò, *Uccellacci e uccellini/Hawks and Sparrows* (1966).

Benigni's new influences—from Zavarattini and Pasolini—sought to challenge the formats and commonplaces of mainstream cinema. Like his earlier encounter with the vital atmosphere of the Roman avant-garde theater, Benigni's artistic sensibilities were fostered in an environment that would lead him to greater heights than may have been expected of a performer whose previous work and background had been in television and commercial film.

In 1983 Benigni was an ubiquitous presence in Italian theaters, appearing in Giuseppe Bertolucci's documentary of his national stage tour *Everything Benigni* and in a comedy directed by Arbore, *F.F.S.S.* (1983). He also tried his own hand at directing a feature film of shorts, *Tu mi turbi / You Bother Me* (1983). In his directorial debut, Benigni attenuated the graphic and provincial treatment of themes of sex, religion, and politics from the *Cioni Mario* monologue and the film version *Berlinguer I Love You.* Although the film was criticized for being overly grounded in Benigni's monologue performances, it marks a successful attempt by Benigni to marry the art house sensibilities and fabulist approach of Zavattini and Pasolini with the mainstream appeal of the commercial cinema.[12] *You Bother Me* is also the first film in which Benigni appears with his future wife and perennial costar, the classically trained actress Nicoletta Braschi, who has had an enormously positive influence on Benigni in both artistic and personal terms.[13]

Benigni codirected and costarred in his next film, *Non ci resta che piangere / Nothing Left to Do But Cry* (1984) with another future Oscar winner, Massimo Troisi. The film is a fabulist comedy in which the two travel back in time to the fifteenth century where they meet Leonardo da Vinci and attempt to stop Columbus from discovering the Americas. The film established Benigni as a box office draw and heir to the Italian comedians of previous generations such as Totò and Petrolini. In 1986, after meeting Ohio-born director Jim Jarmusch at a film festival, Benigni starred in Jarmusch's film *Down by Law.* The style, pace, and narrative of Jarmusch's films make him somewhat of an anomaly in U.S. filmmaking and he is often compared to European filmmakers. The collaboration, in which Benigni appeared again with Braschi and received a screenwriting credit, is another instance in which Benigni ventured into the sort of experimentation seen in his earlier theatrical period.

In 1988 Benigni directed *The Little Devil,* a film begun as collaboration with Giuseppe Bertolucci and completed with Vincenzo Cerami as screenwriter. The film is the first in a series in which the Benigni-Cerami tandem places the persona originated in the *Cioni* monologue into a variety of situations for comic effect, in this case as a Pinocchio-like devil tormenting a doubting priest played by Walter Matthau. In 1989 Benigni starred in what was to be Federico Fellini's last film, *La voce della luna / The Voice of the Moon.* With Fellini, Benigni was exposed to a more formalistic approach to the cinema, an experience Benigni would begin to elaborate in his most successful film, *Life Is Beautiful.* However, Benigni's next films were in a more commercial vein. He directed himself in a double

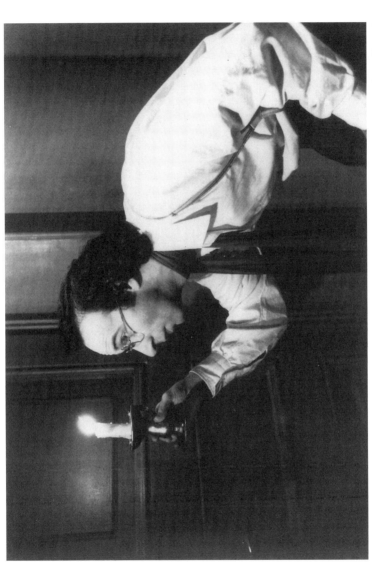

Benigni in Federico Fellini's *The Voice of the Moon*. Photo courtesy of the Museum of Modern Art/Film Stills Archive.

role as a bus driver-mafia boss in *Johnny Stecchino* (1991), the highest-grossing Italian film in Italian film history at the time. After an attempt to revive the Pink Panther series in director Blake Edward's *Son of the Pink Panther* (1993), a film incidentally more convincing in Italian than in English, Benigni directed himself as an urban scrounger mistaken for a serial killer in *Il mostro/The Monster* (1995).

Following the path set by Troisi's Oscar winning *Il postino/The Postman* (1994), Benigni's next film with Cerami, *Life Is Beautiful,* broke out of the art house circuit and gained the sort of popular audience that he already had in Italy. In the film, Benigni courageously placed his comic persona, the often obscene and mischievous Tuscan joker, in a film that explored themes of extraordinary complexity and potential thematic pitfalls. Aside from the tremendous commercial success and recognition that included awards at both Cannes and the Oscars, the film also marks a moment of artistic maturation for Benigni. His screenwriting collaboration with Cerami developed into a manner of filmmaking that combined the influences and lessons learned from his earlier cinematic experiences with Zavattini, the Pasolini school, and Fellini.

## ANCIENT TUSCAN ORIGINS

Benigni's origins in the Tuscan peasantry are the basis of his linguistic and cultural formation, which began in the stories and poetry he heard recited around the family hearth. In an attempt to account for the uniqueness of Benigni's talents, Italian critics have sought to render his origins as more noble, referring to Benigni's comedy as an echo of Etruscan heritage.[14] In the search for cultural substrata, Silvano Ambrogi noted the similarities between Benigni's performances and the harvest festivals where Etruscan clowns, or *fescennini* (lampooners), improvised crude verses, dances, and songs.[15]

The term *fescennini* derives from *fascinum,* meaning "phallus" or "witchcraft," and Fescennium, a town in ancient Etruria (modern Tuscany). Etruscan peasants performed comic improvisations during celebratory occasions to ward off bad luck and evil spirits; in contemporary times Tuscan revelers continue this tradition by gathering at birthdays or marriage feasts. Evidence of these *fescennini* in ancient times appears in writings by Roman authors, such as Horace (*Epist.,* II, I vv. 145 ff). Among funeral decorations in Etruscan tombs, archeologists have found depictions of multicolored suits named *phersu,* which became the Roman *persona* or "mask," later typified by the *commedia dell'arte* character of

Harlequin. Another character that is identified with the *fescennini* and that may have relevance for Benigni is *charun,* a demon with exaggerated and grotesque facial features that became the model for the medieval devil.[16] This is most notable in the film *The Little Devil,* in which Benigni is the playful devil Giuditta.

The Etruscan clowns also danced about and played the flute (Livy VII, 2), and were closely identified with death. It was their job in the Roman amphitheater to make sure the gladiators were dead by poking them with a hot iron, and then removing their lifeless bodies. Benigni's spry dances, his ode to excrement—*l'inno del corpo sciolto/Hymn of a Slippery Body,* which closes his *Tuttobenigni* monologues—and his guitar playing in *Free Wave* seem to echo these ancient formats.[17] The scatological humor of the ancients immediately brings to mind the traditions of carnival humor that mixed lower and upper body, official and unofficial references, in order to express a regenerative power of humor.[18]

As a child, Roberto enjoyed rhyming contests and linguistic games, such as improvising sentences using words in alphabetical order or with words beginning with the same letter, in the tradition of the *stornelli* and *corbellerie* of Tuscan improvisational poetry. Benigni recalls his entire family around the hearth enjoying word games and songs that often included personalized versions of poetry from works in the Italian literary canon, including those of Dante. Benigni's abilities as a verbal performer developed further with his introduction to traveling poets, or *poeti a braccio.* Luigi Benigni encouraged his teenage son to participate in country festivals with these improvising poets,[19] mostly elderly men. They performed at popular gatherings, reciting eight-line stanzas of hendecasyllabic verse with an ABABABCC rhyme scheme. In improvised exchanges on set themes, each poet continued the rhyme of his companion's last two lines (CC) in a display of wit and verbal acrobatics. Usually each contest featured seven stanzas total. Two poets would take turns improvising stanzas and then would collaborate on the seventh, alternating lines.[20]

The Tuscan *poeti a braccio* combine the oral tradition of the 1300s with the diffusion of high culture that came with the printing press in the 1500s. In fact, *the poeti a braccio* singers and troubadours think of themselves as the legitimate heirs of the chivalric court poetry tradition.[21] The *poeti a braccio* also call themselves the *bernescanti* in honor of Francesco Berni (1497–1535), a poet who mixed coarse, plebian expressions with sophisticated literary forms in a burlesque and satirical style. Some of Berni's works, such as *Capitolo dell'anguille, Capitolo dei cardi,* and *Capitolo delle pesche,* emphasize lower body themes. Like Berni, the *bernescanti*'s oral rhyming contests used vulgar humor that could grab the attention of an audience at a tavern or country fair. The contest themes also had an element of the carnival tradition—for example, the *donna grassa e donna magra* (the fat and thin woman)—in which an emphasis on physicality was used as a tool to defrock official culture.[22]

## BENIGNI AND DANTE

Despite their origins in peasant traditions, the *poeti a braccio* are quite sophisticated and their performances are the fruit of careful and detailed preparation. Many of these poets include references to poets such as Ariosto and Dante, whom they have studied in order to gain familiarity and dexterity with the hendecasyllable meter. Therefore, when Benigni appears at universities to recite cantos of Dante from memory, he is continuing an ancient oral tradition.

The scatological and sexually graphic nature of popular, barroom poetry is also evident in the more salacious of Dante's cantos, which every Italian schoolboy knows by heart.[23] Benigni has spoken of the manner in which the Tuscan dialect is considered to be the language of the upper classes, of Dante, art, and culture.[24] It is imperative to recognize that the national Italian language used in the media and in education is an invented tongue, an intellectual construct. In his recitations of Dante, Benigni's vibrant and subaltern Tuscan dialect revitalizes the sources of official national culture developed after Italian unification and further promulgated in the fascist era.

In 1993 Benigni performed a commentary and recitation by memory of canto 5 of Dante's *Inferno* for the RAI television program *Babele,* hosted by anchorman Corrado Augias.[25] *Babele* was RAI's attempt to emulate the format of highbrow, cultural programs such as the French *Bouillon di culture,* hosted by Bernard Pivot, in which authors and cultural figures would promote their latest books. Benigni appeared on *Babele* to publicize his book *Everything Benigni,* a collection of the theatrical pieces and film scripts cowritten with Giuseppe Bertolucci. On *Babele,* Benigni commented on canto 5 of Dante's *Inferno* before reciting it in front of an audience of high school students, Italy's Education Minister Luigi Berlinguer, and several Dante scholars. His appearance broke the barriers between high and low culture, between sanctified literature and Rabelaisian effusion. Benigni switched from one level of cultural discourse to another without any sense of affectation. In this context, Benigni has referred to himself as a modern *giullare,* or minstrel, who, according to tradition, must have a cultural background that is varied and sophisticated enough to reach any audience.[26] Benigni's efforts are similar to those of Nobel laureate Dario Fo, who has been involved in similar efforts to popularize seemingly dusty figures of Italian high culture. In 1999 Fo toured Italy with performances that presented such figures as Leonardo da Vinci and St. Francis as iconoclastic revolutionaries. Given Benigni's identification with Fo's political views, his reading of Dante is very much in this vein.

Benigni has stated that in his Dante recitation for television and in other public arenas, he has sought to communicate the oral origins of Dante's verses. Benigni, in the *poeti a braccio* tradition, presents a recited, declaimed verse, returning a contemporary audience to the origins of poetry. Dante's epic poetry, like the *Iliad* or the *Kalevala,* belongs to the tradition of poetry born as song, recited and even yelled by the evening fireplace. In his brief introduction to the fifth canto of the *Inferno* for Italian television, Benigni appealed to an everyman with stories about Dante's fame as a ladies' man, since the popular stories about Dante in Benigni's youth focused on these bawdy themes. Benigni also mentioned Dante's reputation for stubbornness. In Tuscany Dante is as famous for his difficult and dour disposition as for his writings.

The historical references that Benigni makes when introducing Dante's canto 5 are accurate. Dante did concentrate on the theme of love in a new form, the *dolce stil novo* (sweet new style), which featured an idealization of Beatrice, the "angelic woman," a figure who appears frequently in Benigni's films. Benigni also mentions Dante's first collections of poems that emphasize a sense of youthful exuberance in works such as *Guido vorrei . . .*, which supports Benigni's insistence on Dante's more hedonistic side. To this youthful appetite for life, Benigni adds the more tragic elements of Dante's love story with Beatrice, her death, and the fact that they never had much contact. Benigni also refers to the sexual reference in Dante's famous metaphor of flowers that reawaken and rise up from the night's cold to the warmth of the sun (*Inf.,* II, 127–133). Benigni is by no means the first to make this connection; however, he accurately explains the attitude change of Dante's character after the sexual metaphor of awakening and the realization of Beatrice's involvement in his journey.

When presenting the fifth canto of the *Inferno,* where the subject is physical love, Benigni jokes about Dante's reputation as a ladies' man. This focus allows him to break the barriers of high culture that separate the *sommo poeta* from a wider audience. Benigni presents Dante as a poet for the masses, and not the remote figure of scholastic philosophy. He is a *trom-batore* (screwer) whose womanizing was the motor of his intellectual life and whose stubborn curiosity allows the reader entry into the fascinating world of his invention.

There is also a carnivalesque, Rabelaisian essence to Benigni's Dante presentations. When he appeared at the University of Bologna to recite the thirty-third canto of Dante's *Paradise,* in which the subject is sublime contemplation of God, Benigni introduced the piece by referring to the stench of Dante's clothing after having made a trip through the beyond without bathing. With these physical references Benigni, like a carnival clown, reduces the austere and forbidding nature of the subject, render-ing Dante more human and, above all, more approachable. The conclu-sion to be drawn from Benigni's reading is that so-called serious literature endures a forbidding reputation as a remote and difficult subject due only to the manner in which it is taught. Benigni's performance demonstrates how high literature, poetry in particular, can thrive if presented as oral performance.

Benigni's command of a subject of such high cultural tone as Dante may seem surprising given the fact that he never had a rigorous formal education, and never received a university degree. His apprenticeship among the archaic singers, the *poeti a braccio,* may seem anachronistic amid the increasing cultural homogenization of Italy. However, Benigni's con-nection to a dialectical and oral tradition is also a reason for his cultural sophistication.[27] When Benigni presents Dante as an oral rather than a lit-erary subject, he transmits an undeniable sense of cultural authenticity. Benigni continues in the path of other Italian artists whose work is steeped in regional linguistic traditions. Previous examples are a "who's who" in Italian letters (Dante, Machiavelli, Goldoni), and in film (the neorealist tradition, Pasolini), to mention only very few of the numerous examples in which Italian regional expression eventually gained national and inter-national acclaim.

## NOTES

1. In his acceptance speech Benigni also drew from William Blake (1757–1827), "Does the winged life destroy; But he who kisses the joy as it flies, Lives in eternity's sunrise"; and Dante, "L'amor che move il sole e l'altre stelle (love that moves the sun and the other stars)" (*Par.* 33, 146).

2. Alessandra Levantesi, "Benigni e Troisi: due incontri d'epoca," in *Una generazione in Cinema. Esordi ed esordienti italiani 1975–1988,* ed. L. Micciché (Venice: Marsilio, 1988), p. 409.

3. Carla Nassini, *Benigni Roberto di Luigi fu Remigio* (Milan: Leonardo Arte, 1997), p. 45.

4. Stefania Parigi, *Roberto Benigni* (Naples: Edizioni Scientifiche Italiane, 1988), p. 158.

5. *Garzanti atlante storico* (Milan: Garzanti, 1982), p. 573.

6. Roberto Benigni, "A lezione da Benigni," *L'espresso* (June 24, 1999), p. 78.

7. Antonio Gramsci wrote about the manner in which each social class has historically created intellectuals who were adopted into the power structures of the ruling hegemony. A typical example of these intellectual categories, according to Gramsci, was the clergy, historically tied to the landed aristocracy. Antonio Gramsci, *Gli intelletuali e l'organizzazione della cultura* (Turin: Einaudi, 1949), p. 4.

8. Stefania Parigi, *Roberto Benigni* (Naples: Edizioni Scientifiche Italiane, 1988), p. 160.

9. Benigni reports that Monni carried a photo of his favorite pig in his wallet next to that of his girlfriend. See Silvano Ambrogi, "Le antiche radici di un comico moderno," in *Quando Benigni ruppe il video* (Turin: Nuova ERI, 1992), p. 9.

10. Massimo Martinelli, "Un uomo e una lampadina," *Benigni Roberto di Luigi fu Remigio* (Milan: Leonardo arte, 1997), p. 70.

11. There is a film documentary of one of Benigni's comic political rallies, *Il comizio* (1978). See filmography.

12. Tulio Kezich, *Dizionario del cinema italiano. I film dal 1980 al 1989 A/L,* vol 5, ed. R. Poppi (Rome: Gremese, 2000), p. 331.

13. Nicoletta Braschi has established herself as an actress in her own right, appearing in Bernardo Bertolucci's *The Sheltering Sky* (1991), Giuseppe Bertolucci's *La domenica specialmente/Especially on Sunday* (1991), Jim Jarmusch's *Mystery Train* (1989), and Marco Ferreri's *Come sono buoni i bianchi* (1987). She has also been sought out by members of the latest generation of Italian filmmakers, such as Marco Tulio Giordano in *Pasolini, an Italian Crime* (1995), by Paolo Virzì in *Osovodo/The Hardboiled Egg* (1997), and Roberto Faenza in *According to Pereira* (1998).

14. See, for example, Giulio Martini, "La grande depressione dell'Emilia e il trionfo della risata etrusca," in Giulio Maritini and Guglielmina Morelli, eds., *Patchwork Due geografia del nuovo cinema italiano* (Milan:

Il castoro, 1997), pp. 46–53. In the nineteenth century linguistics enjoyed developing so-called substratum theory, by which modern linguistic traits are traced back to ancient origins. An example is the allegedly Etruscan roots of the aspiration of the "c" in the Tuscan dialect, the *gorgia toscana*. Such themes have lost currency in contemporary academia. See Francesco Bruni, *L'italiano: elementi di storia della lingua e della cultura* (Turin: UTET, 1987), pp. 294–301.

15. Silvano Ambrogi, "Le antiche radici si un comico moderno," in *Quando Benigni ruppe il video* (Turin: Nuova ERI, 1992), p. 9.

16. Margrete Bieber, *The History of the Greek and Roman Theater,* 2nd ed. (Princeton, N.J.: Princeton University Press, 1961), p. 147.

17. Ambrogi, "Le antiche radici," p. 9.

18. See Mikhail Bakhtin, *Rabelais and His World* (Cambridge, Mass.: MIT Press, 1971). All subsequent references to this work from here on will be from the Italian translation, Michail Bachtin, *L'opera di Rabelais e la cultura popolare riso, carnevale e festa nella tradizione medievale e rinascimentale,* trans. Mili Romano (Turin: Einaudi, 1995).

19. For a collection of some of Benigni's participations in improvised poetry festivals, see Alessandro Bencistà, *I bernescanti* (Florence: Edizioni Polistampa, 1994).

20. Massimo Martinelli, "Un uomo e una lampadina," in *Benigni Roberto di Luigi fu Remigio* (Milan: Leonardo arte: 1997), p. 61.

21. See Andrea Cosentino, *La scena dell'osceno. Alle radici della drammaturgia di Roberto Benigni* (Rome: Oradek, 1998).

22. See Bencistà, *I bernescanti.* This work includes transcriptions of a few of Benigni's *poeta a braccio* style improvisation.

23. Perhaps the most obvious example is in *Inferno* (XXI, 139).

24. Parigi, *Roberto Benigni,* p. 174.

25. Corrado Augias, "Babele Benigni," directed by Belli, RAI 3, May 30, 1993.

26. Massimo Moscati, *Benigniaccio con te la vita è bella* (Milan: BUR, 1999), p. 46.

27. There has been a recent trend in the Italian cinema of movies, such as *La Gapa Gira* and *Sangue vivo,* that are filmed in dialect with Italian subtitles.

# • 2 •

# Benigni's Cioni Persona, from
# Theater to Film

$\mathcal{R}$oberto Benigni arrived in Rome in 1972 with Tuscan friends Carlo Monni and Donato Sannini to try his hand at acting. There he encountered a highly theoretical approach to the theater, steeped in the experimentation and iconoclastic mood of the period.[1] Benigni also found himself among people with far more formal education than he had. Unlike Benigni and Monni, the former pig farmer, many of the avant-garde performers and authors with whom Benigni worked came from the social classes that were more traditional providers of intellectuals. Lucia Poli, Benigni's director and colleague in the Phantom of the Opera Theater Group, had been educated as a schoolteacher. Sannini came from a noble Tuscan family that had run a theater school. Poli's then-companion, Giuseppe Bertolucci, was the brother of director Bernardo and son of the poet Attilio Bertolucci.

It was Giuseppe Bertolucci who noted Benigni's improvisational and linguistic abilities and suggested that if Roberto were interested in becoming more sophisticated he would do better to read the classics rather than experimental, avant-garde texts.[2] Bertolucci, who Benigni has recognized as a cultural father figure, suggested that he begin with Collodi's fable *Pinocchio.* After *Pinocchio,* Bertolucci suggested Ariosto's *Orlando Furioso,* a sixteenth-century epic poem in the octet rhyme scheme of Benigni's Tuscan troubadour friends. Benigni also read the German philosopher Arthur Schopenhauer, whose philosophy is featured in Benigni's 1997 film, *La vita è bella/Life Is Beautiful.* Bertolucci next suggested the semimythological, scatological classic *Gargantua,* by Rabelais, as well as the poetry of Walt Whitman. Of all these works the obscene, corporeal *Gargantua* seems to have been the text that Benigni identified with the most. This was an early clue that Benigni's comedy would revolve around lower body, Rabelaisian themes in which official culture and society are confronted by the grotesque and satirical effusion of often obscene humor.

When Bertolucci suggested that Benigni read the Russian classics, Benigni began to think about writing a monologue in the style of Dostoyevsky's *Notes from the Underground*. But Bertolucci so admired Benigni's stories about his hometown that he suggested that Benigni perform something about his past in a Rabelaisian style. Roberto recalled the stories he heard evenings as a bartender at his hometown's communist party cultural center, the *Casa del popolo*. In regions of the Tuscan hinterland left-wing politics is almost a birthright, especially among Benigni's class. Benigni reports having always belonged to a world where the left represented equality and the right was identified with order.[3]

Benigni's ear for local expressions and stories formed the basis of his monologue *Cioni Mario di Gaspare fu Giulia/Mario Cioni Son of Gaspare and the Late Giulia* (1975). The monologue is a combination of literary influences suggested by Giuseppe Bertolucci with Benigni's experiences after his family's emigration from Misericordia in the late 1950s. After a visit to Benigni's old stomping grounds in Tuscany, Bertolucci transcribed and organized Benigni's tales in the monologue, leaving ample room for Benigni's improvisational flourishes onstage. The title is taken from parish birth records that list a newborn's name by father and grandparent. This reference to lineage immediately places the monologue in a static cultural context where the relationship to origin and geography are fixed. Although he is a contemporary character, Mario Cioni is the heir of his forefathers and belongs to their centuries-old cultural and linguistic traditions.

For the monologue performance, stage instructions called for stark atmosphere and a single country-style lamp above Benigni's head. Benigni began the performance with his hands in his pockets and was supposed to limit his movements during the hour-long monologue.[4] Like the experimental works that influenced the 1970s Roman avant-garde theater, Benigni's first theatrical piece and even his later stage tours are devoid of any elaborate staging. The idea was that the shock from the reduction in artifice would lead to the increased critical consciousness of the spectators. In terms of staging, Benigni's piece retained the spirit of experimentation and iconoclasm of the Roman avant-garde. However, this influence did not extend to Benigni's verbal approach to the theater; an entirely verbal performance was contrary to the Roman avant-garde theater's imagery and style.[5] Benigni performed the *Cioni* monologue at a time when Poli's *Le parole e le cose* (The Words and the Things) Theater

Company had begun to reject the idea of the theater as the purveyor of a paradoxical form of academic antiacademics.[6] The inherent iconoclastic elements of Benigni's raw linguistic and improvisational talents also challenged the formalism of the Roman avant-garde theater.

The encounter with the highly theoretical Roman avant-garde was important in forming Benigni's intellectual outlook since it confirmed the traditional skepticism of his forefathers for the intellectual classes. The peasant class, despite performing a vital function in the economic life of a country, has never been able to create its own class of intellectuals.[7] The priests who singled Benigni out for religious vocation had been attempting to perform their traditional duty of removing a bright student from the roles of the peasantry for the benefit of the landed aristocracy. Rather than becoming a member of the intellectual class at the service of dominant societal forces, Benigni's eventual work allowed him to express the culture of his origins.

Like the protagonist in Dostoyevsky's *Notes from the Underground,* Mario Cioni, the main character in Benigni's monologue, confesses the hidden, often shameful aspects of his experiences. However, the monologue's resonance is deeper than a mere recounting of the particularities of Benigni's life in Vergaio. Silvano Ambrogi, the author of *I burosauri/The Burosauruses,* one of the pieces Benigni performed in his early theatrical period, has noted that the monologue cannot be understood without a grounding in the peasant world, especially in Tuscany.[8] In the monologue, Benigni transmits all of the anxieties, stupidities, and malaise of a generation abruptly uprooted from a traditional peasant culture. Benigni distills the voices of an entire village into his monologue, emphasizing the Tuscan peasantry's fixation with lower body humor, religion, and left-wing ideology.

In the *Cioni* monologue, the first word Benigni repeats is the last name of the secretary of the Italian Communist Party in the 1970s, Enrico Berlinguer. Benigni changes the accent on the name, which can change the meaning to include words within the name itself, such as *Ber* or *Per* (for), *lingue* (tongues), Berlin (the city in Germany), *re* (king), *guerre* (wars), and so on. The Berlinguer mantra is repeated four times in the published version of the monologue, dividing the different voices and segments and perhaps calming Cioni's verbal excesses.

The choice of Berlinguer as a motif in the performance obviously had a political subtext. Berlinguer was a controversial figure for the Italian left in the 1970s. He introduced a policy of rapprochement, the *compromesso storico,* with the Christian Democrat Party, out of fear that communist electoral gains would lead to a right-wing reaction similar to the coup against Chilean President Salvador Allende in 1973.[9] That the name of the Communist Party secretary could serve as a sort of incantation explains much about Benigni's peasant background, where left-wing politics were almost innate and the Communist Party was supposed to guarantee political representation and be the harbinger of a favorable revolution. The repetition of Berlinguer's name must be read as a challenge to the established party intellectuals who had moved the Communist Party toward a political compromise with the Christian Democrats.

The first segment of the monologue introduces a Rabelaisian, scatological-style of humor. Cioni is speaking to his father, who is on the toilet, where he has been spending much of his time since Cioni's mother died. Rabelais's *Gargantua* also begins when Gargantua's mother, Gargamelle, is on the toilet, having induced labor and diarrhea by overeating tripe, in a scene mixing maternity, scatology, and misogyny. Cioni's reaction to his father's habit of hiding in the toilet is a stream of excremental and graphic invective.[10]

After cursing at his father, Cioni speaks with his friend Gommone at a dance. Cioni details his sexual frustrations and tells his friends that he is going to the local prostitutes. Here we see the influence of the second section of Dostoyevsky's *Notes from the Underground* in which the unnamed narrator, the Underground Man, relates the melancholy and solitude that push him to search for company even where he is unwanted. Cioni's anger and frustration echo the feelings of Dostoyevsky's narrator, who also ends his fruitless and depressing evenings with prostitutes.

Cioni then returns to lambaste his father, still on the commode, with a long, seemingly incomprehensible stream of violent and hateful diatribe that is explained by the reference to fascists and to Palmiro Togliatti, one of the founding fathers of the Italian Communist Party.[11] One of the constants in the Tuscan hinterland where Benigni grew up was the role of the political left and the memory of the resistance movement against the Nazi-fascists during the final years of World War II. It is also necessary to recall that the 1970s were years of political terrorism in Italy, and the violent language was very much a product of the time. Many of the political parties on the extreme left presented themselves as the true heirs of the resistance against Nazi-fascism, and criticized the Italian Communist Party, Enrico Berlinguer, and his policy of compromise with the Christian Democratic Party. The cursing that Cioni's father endures ends only when Benigni returns to his opening incantation of the name, *Berlinguerre . . . Berlinguerre.*

From politics, the monologue turns to sex. The next voice is Cioni's mother, who warns against masturbation with a nonsensical repetition of the words for "quit it" in Italian. When Cioni returns to using his own voice, he vents his frustrations at Wanda, a barmaid who has rejected his advances. Cioni then takes up what seems to be his father's voice as he recalls being an Italian soldier in World War II and idyllically describes a Russia where everyone is kind and good, especially Stalin, another source of division in the Italian left. Stalin's reputation changed from that of a benevolent antifascist *Baffone* (Uncle Joe) of the World War II years, to the paranoid, genocidal tyrant alluded to in Khrushchev's secret speech to the Soviet Communist Party. The inclusion of a memory of the Soviet Union alludes to a unified left before the schisms caused by the invasions of Hungary and Czechoslovakia. From politics, Cioni turns back to his sexual frustrations with Wanda. Cioni is jealous that she has chosen Moreno over him, and he erupts into a virulent, misogynist imprecation.[12] Then the voice once again sounds like Cioni's mother. She takes Cioni to Amadeo, a sorcerer, complaining that Cioni cannot hold a job. The segment ends with Cioni contorting in pain from the magician's lotions.

From the peasant magic of the sorcerer's potions Cioni switches to the dream factory of the cinema. Cioni is at the movies, watching *The Seven Lovers of Dracula,* prohibited for viewers younger than eighteen because of sexual content. Cioni talks back to the screen in the theater, interjecting his own comments about the physical corruption and buggery of the film industry with the dialogue of the film. Cioni's angry and sarcastic comments reflect a frustration and boredom with cinematic culture in a period when many theaters in Italy screened pornographic films in order to survive the decline in spectators caused by competition with television.[13]

Cioni falls asleep during intermission. He awakes to realize that in his dreams Giorgio Almirante, the leader of the postwar Italian neofascist party, MSI (*Movimento Sociale Italiano*), had given him oral sex. Cioni is horrified to discover that he must have enjoyed the dream since he ejaculated. This provokes a stream of curses aimed at the neofascist Almirante with references to the slow death of the Spanish dictator Francisco Franco, the right-wing coup in Greece in 1967, and the concentration camps of World War II. Again the fears and diatribe, both sexual and political, end with the reassuring mantra of the name of the communist party secretary, Berlinguer.

In the penultimate segment of the monologue, Benigni returns to Cioni's mother's voice. She complains that at twenty-five Cioni cannot hold a job and is uninterested in marrying a neighborhood girl just because she is lame. Although seemingly comical, this section illustrates how adolescence became prolonged as part of the transformation of the Italian economy from agriculture to industry. As in all consumer societies, the economic boom in Italy brought an extension of the period in which children attended state schools and remained tied to their families.[14]

In the monologue's conclusion, Cioni expresses his immaturity and inability to form lasting relationships. Cioni bargains with a prostitute, asking her to explain why she charges less for one type of sex than for another. As in *Notes from the Underground,* Cioni unloads his frustrations on the only character weaker than himself. Unlike Dostoyevsky's Liza, the prostitute in *Cioni* is nameless and does not seek to redeem her client. She, like Cioni, is reduced to an animal existence devoid of noble sentiment. In the final moments of their coupling Cioni stares at the stars and warms himself as the light dims.

The importance of the material from the *Cioni* monologue in Benigni's career cannot be underestimated. It formed the basis of his first appearances on television (*Onda libera/Free Wave, Vita da Cioni/Cioni's Dog Life*) and his first film (*Berlinguer ti voglio bene/Berlinguer I Love You*). While the *Cioni* monologue has no explicit octets in the *poeti a braccio* tradition, there is a similarity to the octet format in the long series of curses against Almirante.[15] By the time Benigni performed the *Cioni* monologue, he had adapted the improvisational techniques of the *poeti a braccio* into a format accessible for an Italian audience.[16] In these performances the improvised rhyming, a format perhaps too sophisticated for a mass audience, is not as prevalent as the more childlike improvisations on suggested words or sentences in alphabetical order.[17]

In his performance Benigni challenged the hegemonic position of two intellectual elites. By a recursion to his original linguistic roots Benigni treated sexual and ideological themes in a manner that subverts the traditional linguistic domination of the Italian national language. With his emphasis on the verbal he subverted the formalism of the antiacademic academics of the Roman avant-garde theater. Benigni's tutoring sessions under Bertolucci reveal how his performances incorporate improvisational material into a narrative format. This approach would carry over into his film style that has roots more in the theatrical and narrative forms than in the use of photographic effects.

For the debut performance of the *Cioni* monologue, Benigni and Bertolucci decided to take the show to Tuscany. The first performance took place at Grignano, near Benigni's hometown of Vergaio, and was not well received. The next day the president of the theatrical club that sponsored the event was apparently forced to resign. When a performance was staged at nearby Incisa, some of the audience began to file out before Benigni had even finished the monologue. Eventually the monologue was taken to Rome in December 1975 and performed at the Albericchino Theater, in the lower section, which Benigni and friends were able to rent cheaply. The monologue became a tremendous success, to the point that Benigni did four and five performances a day, which was then followed by a national tour.

## NOTES

1. Franco Quadri, *L'avanguardia teatrale in Italia 1960–1976* (Turin: Einaudi, 1977), p. 640. Sannini, writing in 1976, gives an idea of the abstruse theoretical grounding of the Roman avant-garde theater of the early 1970s.
2. Parigi, *Roberto Benigni,* p. 165.
3. See interview with Roberto Benigni in appendix.
4. Roberto Benigni and G. Bertolucci, *TuttoBenigni, Berlinguer ti voglio bene, Cioni Mario di Gaspare fu Giulia* (Rome: Theoria, 1992), p. 143.
5. Giuseppe Bertolucci's statements regarding the style of the Roman avant-garde theater were made on the RAI television documentary *Benigni da Oscar,* RAI, March 20, 1999.
6. Lucia Poli's statement appears in Quadri, *L'avanguardia teatrale in Italia,* p. 649.
7. Gramsci, *Gli intellectuali e l'organizzazione della cultura,* p. 4.
8. Ambrogi, *Quando Benigni ruppe il video,* p. 12.
9. Enrico Berlinguer, "Riflessioni sull'Italia dopo i fatti di Cile," *Rinascita* 5 (October 9, 1973).
10. Benigni and Bertolucci, *Tuttobenigni,* p. 143.
11. Benigni and Bertolucci, *Tuttobenigni,* p. 145
12. Benigni and Bertolucci, *Tuttobenigni,* p. 147.
13. See Lorenzo Quaglietti, *Storia economico-politica del cinema italiano 1945–1980* (Rome: Editori Riuniti, 1980).
14. See Paolo Bianchi, *Avere 30 anni e vivere con la mamma* (Milan: Bietti, 1997).
15. Benigni and Bertolucci, *TuttoBenigni,* p. 153.
16. Andrea Cosentino, *La scena dell'osceno. Alle radici della drammaturgia di Roberto Benigni* (Rome: Oradek, 1998), pp. 50–55.

17. After his initial success in cinema and television in the late 1970s, Benigni returned to poetry festivals. There is a transcription of his appearance at a Festa dell'Unita near his hometown Misericordia, in which Benigni improvises with Libero Vietti on the theme of the fat and skinny woman. Alessandro Bencistà, *I bernescanti* (Florence: Edizioni Polistampa, 1994), p. 16. The collection also contains transcriptions of some of Benigni's other improvisations. See also Roberto Benigni, "Cavallo pazzo! Improvisazioni a Perugia, 1989," in Roberto Benigni, *E l'alluce fu monologhi e gag* (Turin: Einaudi, 1996), pp. 89–99.

# · 3 ·

# Cioni on Film

*BERLINGUER TI VOGLIO BENE/BERLINGUER I LOVE YOU*

*R*oberto Benigni's monologue and the Cioni character eventually made it to the silver screen with a film version, *Berlinguer ti voglio bene/Berlinguer I Love You* (1977). It was directed by Giuseppe Bertolucci, who was fresh from his experience as assistant director on his brother Bernardo Bertolucci's epic film, *1900*. For the film, Benigni and Bertolucci changed the set of Cioni's antics from the stark lighting of the Albericchino Theater, or the barnyard set of a RAI television studio, to Benigni's hometown in Tuscany. The film has extensive on-location shooting in the local Communist Party recreation centers, *Case del popolo* (the houses of the people) in Vergaio (Benigni's adopted hometown), as well as Quarrata and Capalle. Touches of local color include a cameo of an elderly man singing poetic, if slightly obscene, ditties in the *poeti a braccio* tradition.

When Benigni and Bertolucci turned the *Cioni* monologue into a feature-length film, they increased the number of characters that Benigni fished out of his past. The *Cioni* monologue had distilled an entire people into a stream of voices spoken by one performer. With *Berlinguer I Love You,* this process is reversed. Many of the characters from the monologue appear in flesh and blood, such as Gommone (Bozzone); the priest; Moreno, the bartender; and Wanda, the barmaid. In the film, Cioni's father, instead of being on the toilet, has died of cancer. In the monologue Cioni's mother is initially dead, and only appears in a flashback when she brings Cioni to be cured by a sorcerer and later to consult a priest. In the film the oedipal triangle between Cioni, his best friend Bozzone, and Cioni's Mammina becomes the focus of the plot. Mammina is played by the charismatic actress Alida Valli, an international star of films such as *Piccolo mondo antico* (1941), *The Third Man* (1949), *Senso* (1954), and *Strategia del ragno/Spider Stratagem* (1971). Valli was fifty-six years old when the movie was filmed, and she dominates the film. As the

23

central figure in Cioni's oedipal drama, she is bartered as a marker in a gambling debt. The film further inscribes the oedipal trajectory by casting Benigni's actual father as Martini, the farmer who wants to arrange a marriage between Cioni and his lame daughter, Adelina, and break apart Cioni's oedipal household.

For the film, Benigni and Bertolucci gave Cioni an entourage in the tradition of Boccaccio's pranksters in the *Decameron*. The immediate identification of Cioni with a male gang is important for the misogynist theme developed in the film. Cioni's gang has the sort of nicknames typical in the Tuscan countryside: Ignorante (Fool), Buio (Darky), and Bozzone (Lumpy). Like Boccaccio's group of Calandrino and Buffalmacco, Cioni's friends play cruel tricks on him. They have the dance hall singer announce that Cioni's mother is dead in order to spoil his chances to have sex with a woman he met there. Later Cioni is forced to allow Bozzone into his house in order to have sex with Mammina, much to her initial consternation, in order to settle a card-playing debt.

In the *Cioni* monologue the mantralike repetition of Berlinguer's name divided the segments and was a point of reference in a storm of verbal chaos. In the film, Berlinguer is reduced to a scarecrow in a field where Cioni goes to contemplate, but not to work. By placing Berlinguer in a field as a lifeless puppet, completely separate from Cioni's day-to-day life, Benigni and Bertolucci seem to point to the attenuation of the revolutionary mandate of the Italian Communist Party. Many of Cioni's soliloquies in front of the Berlinguer scarecrow from the script do not even appear in the final film.[1]

In the mid-1970s, during the decline of U.S. political popularity after the Vietnam War, the Italian Communist Party reached a political and electoral high point, but was never able to enter a governing coalition. The party had an ambiguous political stance on issues such as NATO and its own role as a revolutionary organization. In the 1970s Berlinguer's opening to the Christian Democrats, the *compromesso storico,* alienated the radical elements of the Italian left.[2] In the film, one of Cioni's gang members, Ignorante (Fool), complains that Berlinguer has slowed down in his revolutionary activities. Cioni rebuts that all Berlinguer has to do is to give the masses the go-ahead, simply appear on television at nine in the evening, and calmly state "Good evening, comrades. . . . Go!" Ignorante then asks Cioni why Berlinguer hasn't given the go-ahead. Cioni responds awkwardly that Berlinguer must be busy, and after all he has a family to consider.[3]

Ignorante's criticism of Berlinguer reprises the traditional peasant skepticism and mistrust of intellectuals who are supposed to be the working class's political allies as leaders of the Communist Party. The inference is that the party has lost contact with the working class and the party apparatus has been transformed into another mechanism to retain the status quo. Cioni's response that Berlinguer just has to say "*Via* (Go)" on television is an ironic recognition of the changes in party activities from previously open revolutionary politics.

The final explanation that Cioni gives for Berlinguer's inactivity reflects the fact that part of the postboom transformation of the Italian economy was that ex-peasants like Bozzone and Cioni could aspire to the consumerist model of a middle-class lifestyle. In Italy, increasing segments of the populace became not only economically part of the middle class, but also culturally. Cioni and his friends are no longer farmers or peasants, even if their earthy language hints at their origins. They have entered the world of salaried employees and are no longer dependent on a harvest for survival. In one of the last scenes in the film, after Bozzone declares his conversion to Christianity and middle-class aspirations, Cioni performs a dance while the soundtrack plays a worker's protest chant: *Il potere dev'essere dell'operaio* (Power must belong to the workers). But the protest song is a distant echo that mixes with the sounds of wind blowing through trees and the roar of cars on a freeway. The old culture of left-wing certainty and class identity is evaporating.

If the traditional left of the Tuscan peasants is waning, with a leader who is reduced to a scarecrow and is unwilling or unable to lead his forces in revolution, then in what do Cioni and his friends believe? For Cioni, the only certainty is the body, a fixation with a long history in Tuscan literature. But rather than a strictly Tuscan source, Cioni's worldview reflects a Rabelaisian physicality. Of the texts that Benigni read on Bertolucci's instruction, Rabelais's *Gargantua* made the deepest impression. The body in *Berlinguer I Love You,* as in Rabelais, is positive, an expression of universality that lowers all that is spiritual, ideal, or abstract onto a corporeal plane. Cioni's discussions with the priest, with the two feminists who give him a lift, and even with his mother, revolve around a desire to have sex. In the film, Cioni explains everything in terms of physical experience, including communism, which he says is like a wet dream, existing and arriving without knowledge or awareness.

The most graphic example of a physical worldview is the long soliloquy of curses Cioni delivers when he has been tricked into thinking that his mother is dead.[4] A mother's death provokes an obscene anger at all of the possible orifices in the world subject to human baseness. But in Cioni's billingsgate, his vulgar and abusive language, one also senses a survival of the peasantry's physical relationship to the natural world, since the curses are largely bucolic, based on bodily secretions and cows. When Cioni begins the soliloquy, the soundtrack accompanies him with a crescendo of nature sounds: crickets, frogs, and howling dogs.

*Berlinguer I Love You* received a rating prohibiting viewers younger than eighteen due to the coarse language and numerous references to sex and sacrilege. Yet the obscene content of the film is entirely verbal, without visually explicit scenes. This obscene language has an element of innocence and is not unique to Cioni and his gang, but common to every character in the film, young, old, and even the priest, Waldemaro. In a rare moment of tenderness between Cioni and Mammina, Cioni asks his mother to tell him the fable of the man without a penis, a fable party to a long tradition in Italian and Tuscan literature, particularly by authors who followed the *novellistica* tradition of Boccaccio, Firenzuola, or Straparola.

Obscene language in these traditions has been identified as a form of popular speech in which the negation of the rules of physical and grammatical propriety allow for the creation of an opposite reality.[5] While writing about Rabelais, Bakhtin wrote that in medieval comic traditions obscenity and swearing actually had a regenerative function. However, Bakhtin also noted that these ancient traditions of swearing had been obfuscated by what he calls a "contemporary cynicism" in which swearing, rather than denying the power of official authoritative culture, has digressed into banal insulting. Perhaps a reason why *Berlinguer I Love You* does not communicate the comic vitality of Benigni's later films is that he uses obscenity in an archaic sense that is lost on contemporary sensibilities. In fact, in Benigni's subsequent films swearing and obscene language are progressively attenuated to the point of their exclusion from *La vita è bella/Life Is Beautiful.*

The script of *Berlinguer I Love You* makes a determined effort to reverse the verbal emphasis of the original *Cioni* monologue by introducing slapstick sequences. Benigni even performs a series of harlequinesque dances, such as the scene with his lame fiancée, where he makes a show of his legs in order to humiliate her. Cioni performs a similar dance after Bozzone proclaims faith in God. This dance ends in a Keatonesque routine with an oil barrel, where Cioni, viewed from above and in profile, acts like a puppet. However, despite the attempts to increase the cinematic aspects, the film still communicates the verbalism of Benigni's *Cioni* monologue. Bertolucci's original instructions to Benigni for the *Cioni* monologue had been to perform motionlessly with his hands in his pockets, to emphasize the words of the performance.[6]

Like the *Cioni* monologue, the film has references to religion. Part of the film's materialistic message is rooted in the Catholic belief that the world is inherently evil and sin is inevitable. When Cioni laments his mother's death, he reduces the Catholic afterlife to the betting schemes of the national football lottery. To play, one must guess a game's final result by putting a mark next to the names of the competing teams: 1 for the first team; 2 for the second team; X for a tie. Given the arbitrary and continuous repetition of the weekly soccer games, Cioni sees little difference between the teams playing: 1 for Paradise; 2 for Hell; X for Purgatory. A nihilistic and bored Cioni even questions God about his motives in an imagined dialogue about masturbation in Paradise. Cioni complains that, according to Catholic teachings, masturbation should be avoided. In this imaginary dialogue Cioni impersonates the voice of God, who retorts that masturbation is only done in Hell and that Cioni should have masturbated when he was alive. An angry Cioni feels that he has been cheated out of physical pleasure and announces that he made a mistake: he would rather be in Hell.[7] The combination of betting and masturbation is another example of Cioni's physical philosophy and a prime example of Benigni's Rabelaisian comic method of emphasizing lower bodily existence in order to call into question through grotesque imagery the authority of official culture. Besides anger at the indifference of God to the physical urges of his subjects, there is an admiration at the Devil's ability to provide earthly pleasures. Cioni follows his imagined conversation with God by musing on whether his mother went to Hell or Heaven. His conclusion is that his mother is in Hell, where the Devil now enjoys her physical company. Cioni is jealous of the Devil's appropriation of Mammina's body and he angrily curses God's indifferent silence.[8]

The one character that might be expected to give a spiritual rebuttal to Cioni's hedonism does nothing of the sort. Don Waldemaro, the village priest, has a name that sounds like "valley of the sea," implying that any understanding of the Earth is foreign to him. He echoes Cioni's extreme materialism and hedonism. Waldemaro's reasoning against masturbation is not spiritual but pragmatic and physical, and he abuses Cioni in very coarse language.[9] Other references to religion come from Cioni's friend and rival for his mother's affection, Bozzone. When Bozzone first speaks about God, he is an angry atheist who insists that the only cleverness about the God business is that he does not exist. After daring God to prove his existence, Bozzone expounds on the dictatorship of the prole-

tariat in the jargon of dialectical materialism. But Bozzone's tune changes
after he couples with Cioni's mother, a sexual experience he takes as proof
of God's existence.[10] A transformed Bozzone restates a scholastic argument about the existence of God, although in Bozzone's version the
"prime mover" becomes the "prime builder." Bozzone in a continuation
of the oedipal plotline answers Cioni's questions about who was the father
of the father of the builder of their house, which concludes with a declaration that God was the first builder and, in effect, also the first father.[11]

Bozzone later makes a statement about how his sexual encounter
with Mammina is the proof he needed of God's existence. His sexual passion for her is evident even at the most solemn moment of mass, the raising of the host. Bozzone concludes that as long as he can sleep, screw, eat,
and touch such a woman, then there must be a God.[12] Bozzone's statement demonstrates how nothing is a match for the power of physical
desires. Even old age submits to the sexual impulse. Ignorante makes the
proverbial statement *trombata anziana, trombata sana* (the elderly screw, the
healthy screw) before they head to the tango dance hall frequented by
middle-aged couples. Mammina's sexual encounter with Bozzone rein-
vigorates her. The morning after, she is the image of a woman half her
age, and Cioni remarks that she looks like the good fairy from *Pinocchio*.

In the film's emphasis on sex, interestingly enough, there is never any
mention of pragmatic arguments against promiscuity, such as venereal disease. The only threat to the physical impulses in Cioni's world comes from
cancer. Cioni's father and sister died from cancer, and the only ill character in the film, Gelone, complains not so much that he has cancer but that
his condition has caused his stomach to swell. Yet the fear of cancer paradoxically reaffirms the supremacy of the physical since cancer is a disease
in which the body attacks itself. So even in illness, the body rules the spirit
in confirmation of Cioni's worldview. Bozzone's attitude toward medicine and doctors is illuminating. He never takes medicine when sick, reasoning that if an illness has disturbed the body's equilibrium, then the body
must find its own remedy.[13]

The emphasis on sex and physicality is also developed through female
characters, many absent in the original monologue, who humiliate Cioni.
The film continues the theme of anger at women from Cioni's outburst
at the barmaid Wanda in the *Cioni* monologue.[14] In the opening scenes
at a movie theater, there are placards advertising films in which women
are either threatened by violence or sexually submissive. Titles include *La
supplente/The Substitute* and *I sette violentatori delle donne anziane/The Seven
Rapists of Elderly Women*. There is even an affront to motherhood. The

baby of the theater owner or projectionist sleeps in a crib under a poster advertising the film *Lo strangolatore delle gestanti / The Strangler of Expectant Mothers*. In traditional Italian society motherhood had been sacred, whereas in the behavior that Cioni's countrymen see on the movie screen, women, including mothers, are subject to barbaric violence.

The behavior of Cioni's Mammina helps to explain his trouble with women. Mammina is anything but a stereotypical Italian mother. Her harsh words crush Cioni's self-esteem. She calls him a toad and a worm— an interesting choice of metaphor. The worm's constant ingesting and defecating locomotion corresponds to Cioni's very physical worldview. Worst of all, Mammina tells Cioni how she tried to abort him but failed, and she curses his insistence on being born. There is a naturalistic subtext to her statements. According to Mammina, Cioni is unworthy of life. He is a physical anomaly, destined to a solitary, sterile existence. This senti- ment is reinforced in the cold calculations of Martini, the father of the lame Adelina, whom Mammina wants Cioni to marry. Martini, played magnificently by Benigni's father, Luigi Benigni, lists the cruelly practical reasons why Adelina should accept a marriage with the unstable and unat- tractive Cioni. By Martini's cold calculation, Cioni's physical weakness will lead to his early demise and material gain for Martini, who can expect his daughter to inherit Cioni's field.

This cruel naturalism carries over into all of Cioni's encounters with women. Like the lame Adelina, many of the women Cioni meets are phys- ically damaged, such as the two women at a disco who have casts on their injured limbs. But Cioni is unable to speak to women, even when they show interest in him. In one scene two feminists pick up a hitchhiking Cioni and take him to the *Casa del popolo* for a debate on women's rights that further reveals the province's ignorance and its resistance to debates about cultural, sociological changes of the period. At the debate the feminists cannot pen- etrate the dialect of the local crowd. One of the feminists seems sexually receptive to Cioni and gives him a seashell and her telephone number, later obliterated by his oedipal rival, Bozzone. Yet Cioni is unable to respond to her invitation without using the formal form of "you," *lei,* signaling distance rather than availability.

The town homosexual, Furio, nicknamed *Signorinaaa* (Little Miss), lays out the new paradigm for sexual relationships in the postpeasant world. Cioni complains to Furio about his dilemma as an *omo moderno* (modern man). Furio responds that there is no modern man. Furio explains that, as the town homosexual, he has a role, just as the town idiot and town priest had a role in the past. But Cioni, the modern man, simply does not count. Despite the economic and cultural changes brought by the postpeasant economy, Cioni and his companions remain tied to the mentality of their forefathers and have not adapted as easily as women have. Convinced by Furio's argument, Cioni decides to act on Mammina's curse against him by eating a poisonous mushroom. But even in his attempt to kill himself Cioni fails.

Benigni and Bertolucci's film did not present an idealized view of the peasantry or working class in the tradition of Marxist ideology, where the proletariat was the ultimate arbiter of taste and social justice. Cioni's world is a rural Tuscany ripe with obscenities and references to incest, bestiality, and a dull materialism, a combination of ignorance and vitality. After the boom years the old order of the peasant world and the certainties of religion, the Communist Party, and sex are in flux. The party is no longer the revolutionary presence leading the working classes to a Marxist paradise. The Communist Party leader, Enrico Berlinguer, despite having his name featured in the film's title, is a marginal scarecrow in a field. God is blamed for his infuriating indifference to Cioni's physical predicaments and the inadequacy of traditional religious formats in postboom reality.

Finally, the film blames women for being better able to adapt to a postpeasant reality. Although the film is set in the provinces, there is not a single female character playing a traditional family role. Cioni's Mammina is a merry widow who tried to abort him and then breaks generational taboos by coupling with his friend Bozzone to pay Cioni's gambling debt. For Cioni and his gang, the postboom world means an increasing alienation from the land, from women, and from God. In an often-cited scene, Bozzone recites a fatalistic lament in verse. Despite the cultural and economic changes brought by the economic boom, the subalternity of Tuscan ex-peasants is doomed by a cruel, almost Darwinian determinism to remain subjugated to other classes and regional identities.[15]

In terms of cinematic style, *Berlinguer I Love You* fits into a current of the Italian films in the 1970s that reexamined Italy's peasant roots, such as *Padre padrone* (1977), *1900* (1976), and *L'albero degli zoccoli* (1978). Giuseppe Bertolucci's direction of Benigni's first film displays a mannerism and style that attempts to echo Pasolinian/Zavattinian elements. The fact that Italian directors would be interested in themes of peasant culture is a reflection of the political struggles of the Italian left, which Benigni and Bertolucci emphasize in the political references to Enrico Berlinguer in their film.

Unfortunately, unlike Bernardo Bertolucci's *1900,* Giuseppe

Bertolucci's *Berlinguer I Love You* did not enjoy wide distribution and was not well received by the public, despite relatively warm reviews. Benigni gained a reputation as a comic actor suitable for television but not the cinema. In fact, the film communicates a fatalistic melancholy about the changes in the provinces rather than the comic immediacy and vitality that characterize Benigni's television appearances (examined in chapter 4), many of which were aired after the theatrical release of *Berlinguer I Love You*. Nevertheless, the film today can be seen, along with Nanni Moretti's debut *Ecce bombo,* as a film that was part of the affirmation of Benigni and a new generation of Italian filmmakers.[16]

## NOTES

1. For example, Benigni's retelling of the Cain and Abel story in front of the Berlinguer scarecrow is cut from the film. Roberto Benigni and G. Bertolucci, *Tuttobenigni, Berlinguer ti voglio bene, Cioni Mario di Gaspare fu Giulia* (Rome: Theoria, 1992), pp. 80–82.
2. Douglas J. Forsyth, "The Peculiarities of Italo-American Relations in Historical Perspective," *Journal of Modern Italian Studies* 3(1) (1998): 10.
3. Massimo Moscati, *Benigniaccio con te la vita è bella* (Milan: BUR, 1999), p. 48.
4. Stefania Parigi, *Roberto Benigni* (Naples: Edizioni Scientifiche Italiane, 1988), p. 16.
5. Michael Bachtin, *L'opera di Rabelais e la cultura popolare riso, carnevale e festa nella tradizione medievale e rinascimentale,* trans. Mili Romano (Turin: Einaudi, 1995), p. 21.
6. Benigni and Bertolucci, *Tuttobenigni,* p. 143.
7. Benigni and Bertolucci, *Tuttobenigni,* p. 71.
8. Benigni and Bertolucci, *Tuttobenigni,* p. 72.
9. Benigni and Bertolucci, *Tuttobenigni,* p. 93.
10. Benigni and Bertolucci, *Tuttobenigni,* p. 140.
11. Benigni and Bertolucci, *Tuttobenigni,* p. 132.
12. Benigni and Bertolucci, *Tuttobenigni,* p. 140.
13. Benigni and Bertolucci, *Tuttobenigni,* p. 138.
14. Benigni and Bertolucci, *Tuttobenigni,* p. 148.
15. Parigi, *Roberto Benigni,* p. 9.
16. Massimo Giraldi, *Giuseppe Bertolucci* (Milan: Il Castoro, 1999), p. 8.

# Cioni on Television

## ONDA LIBERA/FREE WAVE, VITA DA CIONI/CIONI'S DOG LIFE

$\mathcal{S}$ince its inception, the RAI (Italian state television) has been aligned with the cultural policies of the Christian Democrat Party, the conservative political force that guided Italian politics in the Cold War period. The fact that the decidedly leftist, obscene, country bumpkin Cioni could get his own show was a complete subversion of RAI's conservative policies. The change in RAI programming came partly in response to the social upheavals that began in the late 1960s. Another decisive factor was the 1976 decision by the Italian Corte Costituzionale (High Court) to open the airwaves for private television stations, ending the state television monopoly. The Italian public gained increased access to U.S. films and serials for broadcast from private television stations such as those owned by media mogul and later prime minister and Benigni target, Silvio Berlusconi.

In the Italian television industry, the period following the court decision became known as *televisione selvaggia* (wild television).[1] As the term implies, there were opportunities and room for experimentation. Benigni had the luck, repeated in later phases of his career, to be in the right place at the right time. After his success in the Roman theater in 1975 with the monologue *Cioni Mario di Gaspare fu Giulia,* RAI producer Massimo Fichera invited Benigni and his companions to participate on the newly instituted second state television channel, RAI 2, with a television program of their own.[2] The result was a series of television programs, *Onda libera/Free Wave* and *Vita da Cioni/Cioni's Dog Life,* in which Benigni brought his Cioni persona to television.

Benigni and Bertolucci wrote and recorded three half-hour episodes in 1976, adapting the original *Cioni* monologue material into *Cioni's Dog Life.*[3] However, these efforts were shelved for years until finally broadcast on RAI's channel 2 on October 13 and 20, and November 3, 1978.[4] From the beginning of his television career, Benigni would have difficulty with the censorship codes of Italian television, which would not be liberalized until the 1980s.

Perhaps because the network functionaries considered *Cioni's Dog Life* unsuitable for immediate broadcast, they asked Bertolucci and Benigni to collaborate with journeymen professionals from RAI who would help to write a new program, hoping to use Benigni's Cioni character in a more controlled setting. The result was originally titled *Televacca/Cow TV,* later changed to *Free Wave* after the network rejected the original title.[5] *Free Wave* aired in four episodes (December 19 and 26, 1976, and January 2 and 9, 1977) on RAI 2. As with many television shows that are run on deadline and that have many authors, *Free Wave* was not always carefully written. The shortcomings with the scripts are obvious when compared to Benigni's later collaborations with Vincenzo Cerami.[6]

As might be expected, when Benigni's Cioni character finally appeared on television, protests from conservatives led to drastic cuts in the show, such as the elimination of Don Giordano, a priest who bore the brunt of Benigni's religious jokes.[7] In the *Cow TV* or *Free Wave* programs, Benigni and Bertolucci expanded Cioni's central theme of sexual angst in the wake of the cultural and economic changes to peasant life. But the program also included new material that would appear in the *Cioni's Dog Life* program, with routines on the United States, China, television, political violence, and class tensions.[8]

*Free Wave* begins in the style of RAI state television, with a close-up of a well-dressed female announcer. In very correct Italian, she invites the spectators to enjoy a lighthearted musical program titled *The Fabulous Years of the Preboom,* which promises a nostalgic musical review of the years preceding the economic boom of 1957–1962. A resonating, flatulent Bronx cheer interrupts this standard and predictable opening. Benigni, as Mario Cioni, appears in a barn filled with straw, cows, pigs, and chickens, playing the guitar and shouting out in his heavily accented Tuscan a song called *La marcia degli incazzati* ("The March of the Pissed Off").[9]

The song immediately challenges official culture, attacking the stalwarts of the Christian Democratic, Catholic ideology with antifamily and anti-Catholic tones. Cioni sings that if he finds a priest he will eat him alive. Monna, played by Benigni's cotroubadour Carlo Monni, runs in after Cioni, carrying a camera that he wobbles while stumbling among the animals' stalls. Cioni makes an appeal for spectators to send donations to an address in Poggibonsi, the heart of the Tuscan countryside, to help the barn-

yard team continue to pirate the network frequency. The audio switches to
the network's off-camera agents, who try to reacquire control of the pirated
transmission. Throughout the program, audio and video control shifts
between the two sides.

After Cioni's song, the network regains control of the transmission
and a sign appears apologizing for the temporary suspension of programming due to technical difficulties. Cioni tears the sign apart and reads the
news. But instead of the usual reports on Italian politics, international
events, and sports, the news is from the microcosm of the *Casa del popolo,*
the Communist Party community center. Cioni announces that Giuliano
has quit smoking and that Valentini started a fight with the bartender
because he was served a beer instead of a coffee. Cioni then moves to the
police blotter. Franceschina, a four-year-old girl, the youngest of twelve
brothers and sisters, has murdered some members of her family by trick-
ing them into looking at the ground and then hitting them over the head
with a large spoon. Cioni reports that she is still on the loose, spoon in
hand, and the public is advised to do their hoeing looking up.

When an Alpine chorus interrupts Cioni with a rendition of
Giuseppe Verdi's slavery lament *Va' pensiero,* Cioni explains that music
increases the milk yields. The joke is a parody of the scientific methods
of the new industrial farms that had pushed traditional farmers, such as
Cioni, and pig herders, such as Monna, out of business. While the barn
interior remains on the screen, the soundtrack cuts to the voices of famous
Italian newscasters whose voices comment off-camera that if someone like
Mario Cioni can take over the network, then the television monopoly is
doomed. These functionaries begin to plot Cioni's assassination.

When the network retakes control of both video and audio, it
broadcasts the interrupted documentary on the music of the preboom, a
theme with several subtexts. The early 1950s was a period of high con-
formity, when political control of Italy was solidly in the hands of the
pro-American Christian Democrats. The well-manicured format of the
network program and the music are actually more American than Italian
in origin, with music by Italian-American crooner Perry Como. The preboom years were also the last period in which the traditional agricultural
economy was still intact. (As mentioned in previous chapters, the Italian
economy's transformation in the boom years affected Benigni's family
when they emigrated from their ancestral home of Misericordia to Prato
(Vergaio) in 1958.) When Cioni interrupts the network transmission of
preboom nostalgia, he brings the real preboom culture to the screen: the
peasant reality of barns, livestock, poverty, vulgarity, excrement, and

heavy dialect. Between each song and vignette, the principal characters in the barn (Cioni and Monna) change the hay, sweep out the barn, and feed the animals on camera.

Mentions of the United States are not limited to Perry Como's crooning. Cioni satirizes Columbus's voyage. This theme is repeated in the film *Non ci resta che piangere/Nothing Left to Do but Cry* (1983), codirected by Benigni and Massimo Troisi, where the characters are magically transported back to 1492. In that film, the Benigni character, Saverio, becomes obsessed with the idea of stopping Columbus from discovering America so that his sister will not become involved with a U.S. soldier. In *Free Wave,* we see the roots of this comical wishful thinking. In a series of Socratic dialogue with Monna, Cioni points out, quite correctly, that Columbus was not interested in discovering America but was searching for China. In Cioni's version of history, some crafty Americans offered themselves for discovery first and deliberately sidetracked Columbus. The American appropriation of Columbus had been tried earlier on Marco Polo, when a group of Americans disguised as Russians tried to give Polo directions to America instead of to China. Luckily, Cioni states, Polo was too clever for them and was able to reach China.[10] These routines seem to be spoofs on history but they have an undercurrent of protest against the U.S. domination of Europe's collective imagination, first as the Promised Land for emigrants of the early 1900s and later as a hegemonic power.[11]

The snippets of *The Fabulous Years of the Preboom* between Cioni's interruptions also feature a montage of U.S. films. But the most obvious reference to the United States in *Free Wave* is the character Prudence Livingstone, described as a beautiful Italian–American girl, dressed in a colonial outfit with an enormous tape recorder on her shoulders. Prudence is fascinated with Cioni's preboom, peasant culture and remarks that he has the eyes of Harlequin or the Tuscan comic character Stenterello. As part of her study of Italian folklore, Prudence asks for a typical peasant song. The chorus, which had previously sung Verdi's *Va' pensiero* to increase milk production, sings *Tripoli bel suol d'amore* ("Tripoli, Beautiful Land of Love"), a hymn to the Italian colonization of Libya in the early 1900s. Prudence mistakenly admires it as a peasant song when in fact it is a nationalist song later absorbed into fascist culture. The physically attractive but ignorant Prudence typifies the struggle between the ex-peasant Cioni and U.S. cultural paternalism. Prudence announces that she has just taken a course with pop artist Andy Warhol. When Prudence asks Cioni if he is familiar with Warhol, Cioni responds brusquely that he has never heard of him. Cioni's stinking barn and heavy regional humor and dialect are the antithesis of Warhol's repetitive silk screens of celebrities.

Despite the program's comic tone, the episodes end violently when the off-camera network functionaries end Cioni's intrusion on their airwaves by killing him. Given the intense political terrorism in Italy between 1968 and the early 1980s, these gags have a tragic subtext and continue the violent tone in the original *Cioni* monologue. At the end of the first episode, a network functionary disguised as Cioni's mother stabs him. At the end of the second episode, a functionary in a blond wig, who pretends to be Cioni's cousin Clementina, shoots him. After each Cioni murder scene, the screen cuts to the logo of RAI state television. The off-camera voices from the network lament about having to stoop to violence, but agree that Cioni's elimination was vital.

In the death scene ending the first episode, Cioni points out the cultural changes brought by television. He describes the airborne waves of television signals as a virus that infects people and reduces their individuality.[12] Everyone becomes sick after contact with the signals. Eventually the television signals go underground, where they contaminate agriculture and become part of the grain and ham that people eat. By ingesting the waves, the mind of the nation is reduced to parroting phrases heard on television. An agonizing Cioni gasps that either the signal must stop or man will stop.[13]

With the liberalization of RAI programming in the late 1970s, debates raged over television's role as a promoter or a destroyer of Italian culture. Umberto Eco even noted a schism among intellectuals concerning the cultural influence of television, which he called the *apocalittici* and *integrati*.[14] Thus, despite his barnyard setting and coarse jokes, Benigni was already handling themes of great sophistication in his early television shows. The shows continued his challenge to intellectual hegemonies in Italy, in this case the linguistic and cultural commonplaces of Italian state television. When Cioni asks if he is a man or a signal as he lies dying, he warns of the disappearance of indigenous culture in the face of economic changes and mass media culture. Benigni's reassertion of the peasant roots of Italian culture reveals a romantic nostalgia for the simplicity and solidarity of the agricultural lifestyle, a theme that echoes Pasolini's recognition of the disappearance of indigenous culture in the face of consumerism.[15] With his parody of RAI programming methods, Benigni continues the challenges to cultural elites that were first expressed in the Roman avant-garde theater.

## LATER TELEVISION APPEARANCES

Benigni's television appearances did not stop with his adaptation of the *Cioni* monologue for television. With his rural accent and oversize dark gray suit of "the peasant comes to town," Benigni's Cioni persona eventually became a sort of Italian national clown or, more appropriately, a modern *giullare* or minstrel. Given Benigni's abilities in storytelling, songwriting, and performing, it is possible to see him in the tradition of the vagabond medieval performer.

In medieval times the *giullari* often performed on the run from ecclesiastical or governmental authorities because of their openly sacrilegious or iconoclastic performances. The *giullare* tradition was incorporated into the standardized formats of the *commedia dell'arte,* in which the actors wore masks and improvised on themes of class inequality and regional stereotypes but without the subversive element that authorities found unacceptable in independent, medieval *giullari*. Like a Shakespearean fool, or in an Italian context, a medieval *giullare,* Benigni is a devastating political comedian. Benigni has explained his desire to test the patience of the political elite in Italy as a throwback to the medieval buffoon and as part of the paradoxically reactionary nature of the clown, the expression of a subaltern cultural essence that intrigues and intimidates the powerful.[16]

In the 1980s Benigni's television appearances reduced Italian politics to jokes about the sexual and physical handicaps of Italy's leaders. On the debut of the television show *Fantastico,* October 1, 1988, Benigni lampooned Italy's political elite by making a parallel between the drug testing of athletes and the private parts of former Italian prime ministers Giulio Andreotti, Fanfani, Giovanni Spadolini, Bettino Craxi, and Ciriaco de Mita. Benigni's solution for the terrorist problem of the 1970s and 1980s was to encourage terrorists to focus on how to prevent Italy's leaders from being born by giving their mothers birth control pills on the night of conception, rather than killing them.[17]

In the 1980s and 1990s, just as television became more willing to accept material previously considered obscene or blasphemous, Benigni reduced the number of his appearances. This decision may have been a result of his success in the cinema. However, once censorship no longer interfered with Benigni's verbal excesses, he began to emphasize physical comedy by kissing, spanking, straddling, and performing stripteases.[18] Examples of Benigni's antics include his improvisation on synonyms for the female reproductive organ, derived from the poet Belli, while asking the well-respected television hostess, Raffaella Carra, to lift her dress. Benigni chased recently married television host Pippo Baudo around the RAI television studio before pinning him to the ground and kissing him on the mouth. In another appearance, Benigni convinced the much taller Baudo to exchange pants. Benigni began to perform mock stripteases on programs such as Enzo Biagi's usually sedate news magazine, *Il fatto*. Benigni even realized his dream of being the buffoon of the new king, consumerism, when he cohosted RAI's channel 1 national news broadcast at 8 P.M., long the official organ of ruling coalition governments. Benigni ended the broadcast by jumping on the anchorman's table and straddling him.[19]

Benigni's best-known and most-discussed political satire was on the television program *Numero Uno,* hosted by Pippo Baudo, on October 25, 1994, a period in which the ruling coalition government headed by Silvio Berlusconi[20] was embroiled in the *mani pulite* (clean hands) political corruption scandal. Benigni appeared on RAI 1 with a routine that fiercely criticized Berlusconi's government, with Baudo as straight man. It is important to note, once again, how Benigni used his improvisational skills in this performance. Baudo reports that the script consisted of a bar napkin on which Benigni had scribbled some notes at the RAI cafeteria only hours before the show.[21] In the routine Benigni feigns ignorance of recent political events in Italy in order to lampoon the powerful, who had little choice but to allow themselves to be ridiculed.[22] Benigni's method is to declare the most outrageous and insulting things about Italy's political leaders by prefacing his attacks with declarations of goodwill.[23]

When asked about his practice of relying on physical humor in his later television appearances, Benigni explained that his appearances in the different media of film, theater, and television are conditioned by the time allowed for communication to the audience in each format. For his theatrical monologues, Benigni may give full vent to his verbal abilities and improvisational talents. Benigni as film director adopts a straightforward cinematic style in order to heighten his comic body with pantomime routines that are reminiscent of performers from the silent era. Television, however, so reduces the attention span of the audience that the clown must strike for a laugh, whether verbally or in pantomime, in the least amount of time possible, as conditioned by the setting and requirements of the medium.[24]

## NOTES

1. See A. Grasso, *Storia della televisione* (Rome: Garzanti, 1992).
2. The story of Benigni's struggles with the RAI network appear in

Giorgio Simonelli and Gaetano Tramontana, *Datemi Un Nobel!*
*L'opera comica di Roberto Benigni* (Alessandria: Falsopiano, 1998), pp.
41–81.

3. *Vita da cani* is also the Italian translation for one of Charlie Chaplin's
   first films, *A Dog's Life* (1918). References to Chaplin will become
   more frequent in Benigni's work, particularly in his film *La vita è bella*
   (1997).
4. For a list of Benigni's performances on television between 1977 and
   1988, see Stefania Parigi, *Roberto Benigni* (Naples: Edizioni Scientifiche Italiane, 1988), pp. 121–126.
5. In Italian *vacca* means "cow" but can also mean "whore."
6. According to interviews, Benigni has never been too satisfied with
   the final transmitted program. See Parigi, *Roberto Benigni,* p. 167. It
   must also be stated that Benigni's films have been collaborative efforts.
   His first works were completed and coauthored with Giuseppe
   Bertolucci and his later films with Vincenzo Cerami. In this respect
   he is like another accomplished performer/director in the Italian cinema, Vittorio de Sica, who relied on the theoretical vision of the guru
   of neorealism, Cesare Zavattini. As a critic I have always noted the
   relative scarcity of books in English on De Sica in comparison to his
   Italian director colleagues who could be approached as directors only,
   such as Fellini and Rossellini.
7. There were also protests against the broadcast of Dario Fo's plays in
   1978. Radiotelevisione italiana, *Storia della RAI I. 30 anni di televisione
   Date Momenti personaggi 1954–1983* (Rome: Rai Documentazione e
   studi, 1983), p. 60.
8. See Roberto Benigni, *Quando Benigni ruppe il video* (Rome: Theoria,
   1992). The routine on China appears on page 94; the local count and
   his new shoes, page 102; and television as a virus, page 110.
9. Benigni and Bertolucci, *Quando Benigni ruppe il video,* p. 22.
10. Benigni and Bertolucci, *Quando Benigni ruppe il video,* p. 31.
11. Benigni has described his own sense of confusion and marvel at his
    first visits to the United States as a sense of déjà vu, since when he
    arrived he had already been exposed to everything about America via
    the media. Parigi, *Roberto Benigni,* p. 68.
12. Benigni and Bertolucci, *Quando Benigni ruppe il video,* pp. 48–50.
13. Benigni and Bertolucci, *Quando Benigni ruppe il video,* pp. 48–50.
14. Umberto Eco, *Apocalittici e integrati* (Milan: Bompiani, 1984).
15. See, for example, Pier Paolo Pasolini's comments in "La scomparsa
    delle lucciole," *Corriere della sera* (February 1, 1975).

16. See interview with Roberto Benigni in Appendix.

17. Roberto Benigni and G. Bertolucci, *Tuttobenigni, Berlinguer ti voglio bene, Cioni Mario di Gaspare fu Giulia* (Rome: Theoria, 1992), pp. 27–28.

18. Massimo Moscati, *Benigniaccio con te la vita è bella* (Milan: BUR, 1999), p. 32.

19. Roberto Benigni, "Roberto Benigni . . . Fare il buffone oggi . . . meglio il medioevo," *L'Unita'* (January 15, 1981), p. 15.

20. In 1994 Berlusconi's right-wing political party Forza Italia led the Pole of Liberty coalition in a defeat of the ex-communist Olive Branch Coalition of the PDS (Partito Democratico della Sinistra), which was supported by Benigni.

21. Baudo's comments are recorded on the RAI television documentary, *Benigni da Oscar, 1999,* March 20, 1999.

22. Moscati, *Benigniaccio,* p. 39.

23. Giorgio Simonelli and Gaetano Tramontana, *Datemi un Nobel! L'opera comica di Roberto Benigni* (Alessandria: Falsopiano, 1998), p. 78.

24. Moscati, *Benigniaccio,* p. 102.

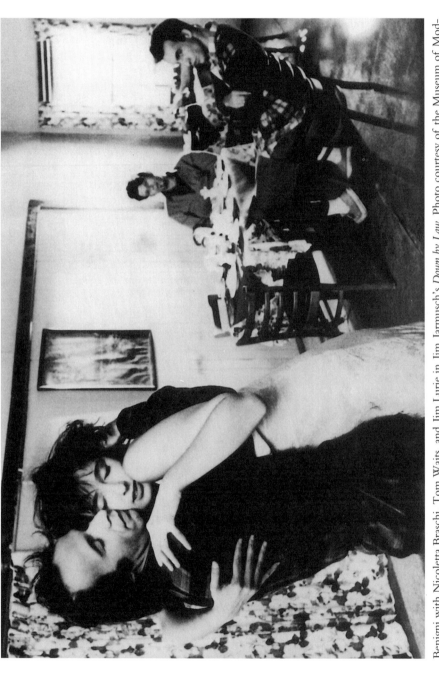

Benigni with Nicoletta Braschi, Tom Waits, and Jim Lurie in Jim Jarmusch's *Down by Law*. Photo courtesy of the Museum of Mod-

# · 5 ·

# Film Apprenticeships and
# Cameos, 1979–1989

## FOUR CAMEOS IN 1979

After his experiences in Italian television in the late 1970s and his film debut with *Berlinguer ti voglio bene/Berlinguer I Love You,* Benigni became somewhat of a fixture as an actor in the Italian cinema, appearing in five films released in 1979 alone. In *Clair de femme* (1979), by Constantin Costas-Gravas, Benigni plays a bartender who speaks a mixture of French and Italian. Benigni's jocular approach to the ridiculousness of linguistic difference would appear in some form in all of his later films. In *I giorni cantati* (1979), directed by Paolo Pietrangeli, Benigni is a law professor who sings a Schubert song with a female colleague as they reminisce about the counterculture and its glory days in 1968. This was the first time that Benigni appeared as a teacher or educator, a role he would often repeat.

In *Letti selvaggi/Tigers in Lipstick* (1979), directed by Luigi Zampa, Benigni is again cast as an educator, this time as a principal in the episode *Una mamma* with Monica Vitti. The story, cut from many prints, including the North American release, is about a child who leads the school principal to believe that his mother is a prostitute. The story is rooted in the traditions of the Italian short *novella,* in which physicality and the power of nature overturn artificial social barriers. Benigni also had a cameo in *La luna* (1979) by Bernardo Bertolucci, as an upholsterer who descends from a rope into the heroin- and incest-ridden lives of the protagonists.

## RENZO ARBORE

After working in these small roles for various directors in 1979, Benigni returned to television when radio disc jockey and jazz musician Renzo

43

Arbore invited him to participate in his television program *L'altra domenica/The Other Sunday*. Benigni appeared in a variety of roles as a Tuscan outsider, out of place among Arbore's cast of Roman show business veterans. Benigni's best-known role in the program was as a reluctant cinema critic. Arbore filmed the skits from his own home, putting Benigni in an oversized chair and provoking him with personal references to his sex life. Benigni was able to bring some of the Rabelaisian material from his improvisational monologues to the program, such as *L'inno del corpo sciolto/The Hymn of the Slippery Body*, a scatological song about the joys of defecation.[1]

The success of *The Other Sunday* brought opportunities for Arbore's troupe to appear in films. These films, with television personalities in quickly produced and distributed comedies, were a common format in the Italian cinema of the 1970s. In this same period many comedians made the transition from television to film: Carlo Verdone in the Sergio Leone produced *Un sacco bello* (1980); Paolo Villaggio in the *Fantozzi* series directed by Neri Parenti; and others, including Massimo Troisi. Benigni's first film, *Tu mi turbi/You Bother Me* (1983), was originally destined for television, as was the documentary of his 1983 stage tour, *Tuttobenigni/Everything Benigni* (1986). Even Sergio Citti's *Il minestrone* (1981), which stars Benigni, would eventually appear in an expanded format on television in three episodes.

In the film *Il Pap'occhio/Pope in Your Eye* (1980), Arbore's troupe from *The Other Sunday* is hired to produce the first television program for a fictitious Vatican television network. The show, *Gaudium Magnum,* is mock-directed by Isabella Rossellini's then-companion, Martin Scorsese. Benigni plays a leftist character referred to as Judas, who, as his name indicates, eventually betrays the troupe for thirty telephone tokens. Arbore's film pokes fun at Catholic culture on location in the Vatican. In one sequence, Benigni does a pantomime and dance in the papal apartments. Benigni's character Judas repaints Adam's hand in the Sistine Chapel as a clenched fist in the style of proletarian protest. Arbore filmed this sequence as a nine-minute-long take, during which Benigni performed a monologue on the Last Judgment. Eventually the Supreme Being sends a giant wrecking ball and earthquake so that Arbore's cast and set are swallowed by the earth, in a homage to Fellini's film *Prova d'orchestra/Orchestra Rehearsal* (1979). Besides his religious monologue, Benigni also leads the troupe in a quiz show of riddles that gives an idea of the word games that he enjoyed as a child and as a *poeta a braccio*. During the game, a rhyme leads contestants to believe they must respond with an obscene word, when in fact there is another less vulgar answer.

After an attempt to repeat the formula of *Pope in Your Eye* with a sequel, *Il resto del Pap'occhio,* Arbore reassembled the cast for a film of short comic skits: *F.F.S.S.—Federico Fellini Sud Story ovvero che mi hai portato a fare sopra Posillipo se non mi vuoi più bene?* (1983). (FFSS are the initials of the Italian state railway system.) In the film's opening sequences the camera follows papers blown from Federico Fellini's desk that are picked up by Arbore's collaborators, who decide to pass off Fellini's work as their own. Benigni's role of the beige sheik is a parody of Alberto Sordi's white sheik in Fellini's film *Lo sceicco bianco / The White Sheik* (1952). Benigni also performs a parody of the Arab tongue with repetitions of the word "harem." In advertisements the film was hyped as the first Arab film produced entirely in Italian.

## MARCO FERRERI: *CHIEDO ASILO / SEEKING ASYLUM*

The 1979 film in which Benigni made the greatest contribution is Marco Ferreri's *Chiedo asilo / Seeking Asylum* (1979). Benigni played the starring role and received a writing credit. In the film, Benigni reprises themes developed in the *Cioni* monologue and *Berlinguer I Love You,* regarding the alienation from nature and the disappearance of traditional culture. Roberto, Benigni's character, is cast as a kindergarten teacher who attempts to foster the innocence of his charges. Benigni's character expresses the contradiction between his innocent pupils and the alienating presence of the industrialized world. He pushes the limits of a Montessori educational system that encourages the independence of the child by speaking to his charges as equals, and sparks their curiosity by bringing a donkey to class and pretending to be pregnant. The plot revolves around the conflict between Benigni's character and the bureaucratic system that harasses him because of his alternative approach to teaching. He becomes romantically involved with and impregnates the mother of one of his students. The film ends when the teacher takes his charges to Sardinia to commune with nature.[2]

With Ferreri, Benigni was exposed to a style of filmmaking that was heavily influenced by the French New Wave and its rebellion against costume dramas and traditional literary adaptations. Ferreri's film was a "slice of life" without traditional plot formats. This experience with Ferreri was important for Benigni's future films, as his improvisational abilities were certified and encouraged by an established director.

## CESARE ZAVATTINI

Among the many directors/screenwriters that Benigni met in what may be called his formative years in the cinema was Cesare Zavattini, the chief screenwriter and theorist of Italian neorealism. Zavattini's collaborations with actor/director Vittorio de Sica, from the 1930s to the 1970s, produced some of the most important works in film history, including *The Bicycle Thief* (1948), *La ciociara* (1960), and the Holocaust drama *The Garden of the Finzi-Contini* (1970). Zavattini wrote of an ideal cinema with unfiltered long takes as the means to communicate the phenomenological essence of reality.[3] Because of the high level of planning and the set narrative format in his later films, Benigni may seem far from Zavattini's fly-on-the-wall school of cinema. Yet within his previous reliance on theatrical forms and narrative structure, Benigni allows himself the freedom for improvisation that was at the heart of Zavattini's concept of the cinema. Benigni and Zavattini also share the courage to approach potentially tragic subjects in the format of a fable. A spirit of jocularity is part of the Zavattini/De Sica repertoire in films such as *Miracolo a Milano/Miracle at Milan* (1951) and *Il giudizio universale/The Last Judgment* (1961).[4]

When Benigni met Zavattini, the aging screenwriter was attempting a comeback after a period of inactivity following the death of long-time collaborator De Sica in 1973, a year during which Zavattini produced the screenplay for De Sica's last film, *A Brief Vacation*. Zavattini had singled out Benigni to star in what was to be Zavattini's last film, *La veritààà/The Truth* (1982). In the film, the eighty-year-old Zavattini escapes from a mental hospital in order to announce to the world that there is only mendacity in their way of thinking. He visits the pope and appears on television, but then realizes that all efforts are futile, and he holds his breath until he dies. Unfortunately, the Zavattini-Benigni collaboration never went past the discussion stage. Zavattini eventually decided to play himself in the film. Given Zavattini's insistence on the elimination of barriers between actor and character, perhaps Benigni had difficulties in impersonating Zavattini to the latter's satisfaction. However, their year-long collaboration gave Benigni a crash course on Zavattini's ideas on the cinema and was an important influence on his future work.[5] Nevertheless, the importance of Benigni taking a year-long period to learn a style and school of filmmaking from Zavattini cannot be underestimated. Benigni states that he went to Zavattini's house each day, where the aging master (who died in 1989) taught him how to write a treatment and a screenplay.

It must be mentioned that the late 1970s was a time of decline for the Italian cinema in both artistic and commercial terms. The heroes of post-war Italian film styles, such as neorealism or the *commedia all'italiana* (comedy Italian style), were aging, and television was becoming the entertainment choice of many in Italy. At the time Benigni was a television star who had also appeared in small roles in several artistic films. He might have been expected to continue working in the commercial route offered by the films of Renzo Arbore. With Zavattini, Benigni came into contact with a prime representative of an Italian film culture that had prospered and developed between the 1940s and 1960s as an alternative to the dominant Hollywood model. In thematic terms Benigni followed the fabulist approach of the lesser-known De Sica/Zavattini collaborations such as *The Last Judgment* or *Miracle in Milan*. In the screenplays for these films, Zavattini's humble protagonists impart didactic lessons on the nature of human existence and behavior. Zavattini's reliance on lower bodily humor to communicate a universal theme has at its roots a Gramsican interest in developing an art that highlights nonbourgeois themes, such as the squatters in *Miracle in Milan* who fly into the sky on broomsticks in search of a more sincere world. The protagonists in Benigni's later films are heirs to the Cioni country clown who live outside society and express the type of social contrast that is a set theme in the films penned by Zavattini.

With Zavattini, Benigni also encountered a film style dominated by what Italians have called the *piano americano,* or three-quarters shot. This was the primary camera shot used by silent comedians such as Charlie Chaplin because it communicates the stagelike authenticity of performance. De Sica, who directed many of Zavattini's screenplays, was one of the more consummate theatrical performers in Italian history. He also relied on simple camera techniques such as long takes and the *piano americano,* particularly in his famed neorealist period—from *I bambini ci guardano/The Children Are Watching Us* (1943) to *Il tetto/The Roof* (1956). Benigni's adhesion to a filmmaking style that emphasizes the authenticity of performance is a constant of his directing style. Benigni has stated that as a director he avoids close-ups of a comedian's face, or mask, in order to preserve its communicative power. (See interview in appendix.)

## CITTI AND ECHOES OF PASOLINI: *IL MINESTRONE*

Between the collaborations with Arbore, Benigni also starred in *Il mine-strone* (1981), an allegorical film that returns the Benigni persona to the themes of the alienating effects of contemporary consumer culture, a subtext of his *Cioni* monologue and *Berlinguer I Love You*. *Il minestrone*'s plot involves the pilgrimage of three beggars—Benigni again a teacher—who wander around Rome and then Tuscany in search of a meal to fill their perpetually empty stomachs. The film evokes the historical memory of the Italian underclass's fixation with the immediate gratification of physical and sexual hunger.

Through the film's director, Sergio Citti, Benigni was exposed to the Pasolinian school of filmmaking. In Citti's *Il minestrone* the beggars' search for a meal works as a parable to express Pasolini's concerns about the extinction of peasant culture. Such themes were also the focus of Benigni's first film, *Berlinguer I Love You,* directed by another Pasolini student, Giuseppe Bertolucci. The film features such Pasolini troupe regulars as Franco Citti, who had debuted in the Italian cinema in Pasolini's *Accattone* (1960), and Ninetto Diavoli, who had appeared in Pasolini films featuring legendary Italian comic actor Totò—*Uccellacci e uccellini/Hawks and Sparrows* (1966) and an episode in the film *Le streghe/The Witches (La terra vista dalla luna/The Earth Seen from the Moon)* (1968). The film was written by Vincenzo Cerami, another Pasolini disciple and Benigni's future screenwriter from *Il piccolo diavolo/The Little Devil* (1988) to *La vita è bella/Life Is Beautiful* (1997). Cerami, like Citti, entered the cinema under the tutelage of Pasolini as assistant director on Pasolini's two films with Totò: *Hawks and Sparrows* and *The Earth Seen from the Moon.*

Like Zavattini and De Sica, Pasolini also relied on simple techniques, with camera shots dominated by long-take medium or the three-quarters shot. And again like Zavattini, Pasolini's films and the films of his disciples, such as Citti and Cerami, explored fabulist themes. Pasolini made film versions of pre-Enlightenment, preindustrial works such as *The Decameron* (1971), *The Canterbury Tales* (1972), and *Arabian Nights* (1974) to decry what he saw as the disappearance of the peasant culture. Pasolini also mixed the humble physicality and lower body of his characters with the sublime elements in iconography or music. Examples include *La ricotta/Cream Cheese* (1962), in which an extra starves to death while playing one of the thieves in a film depicting Christ's passion, and the use of Bach's "St. Matthew Passion" to accompany the sordid demise of a Roman thief in *Accattone* (1961). Benigni's interest in combining themes of high and low culture in his readings of Dante, mentioned in chapter 1, or in his use of Offenbach's music in *Life Is Beautiful,* echo this thematic and ideological current.

With Pasolini, as with Zavattini, Benigni was exposed to a strategy of filmmaking that sought to counter the dominant cinematic culture with an alternative based in artistic forms that have at their heart a Gramsican search for nonbourgeois sources. These influences on Benigni would become more evident when, as director and screenwriter, he confronted his comic persona with a series of hegemonic adversaries, such as the Catholic Church in *The Little Devil,* the mafia in *Johnny Stecchino,* and urban consumer society in *Il mostro / The Monster.*

## JIM JARMUSCH: *DOWN BY LAW* AND *NIGHT ON EARTH*

Benigni's next acting experience was also his first introduction to the U.S. film industry and the English language. In 1986, Benigni came to the United States to work with director Jim Jarmusch, then a new figure of the U.S. independent cinema. Jarmusch and Benigni met at a film festival in Italy, where both were on the jury. Despite not sharing a common language, the two became fast friends and Jarmusch decided to include a Benigni-like character in a jailhouse script he had originally planned for John Lurie and Tom Waits. Jarmusch plans his films with actors in mind for specific roles, and is thereby able to accommodate an actor's penchant or reticence to improvise. This provided a perfect forum for Benigni's abilities.

Jarmusch was attracted to themes of petty criminality and alienation in a postindustrial world with characters living at the periphery of society. Jarmusch's films also seek to break convention in terms of plot and time sequences for an approach to the cinema that is akin to a musical sensibility. In *Down by Law,* Tom Waits plays a disc jockey and John Lurie, a pimp. Benigni appears as a hapless Italian tourist/immigrant, who ends up sharing a jail cell with the two Americans, although he is the only one actually guilty of a crime, having committed a murder in a pool hall. Benigni plays a Cioni-like country bumpkin who makes constant references to his mother and is armed only with his wits. In the jail cell he needles his cellmates with references to Walt Whitman and Dante, and is able to make the threesome communicate and cooperate, and eventually organize their escape.

The film is a study of language and improvisation, two of Benigni's great strengths. Benigni, who could not speak English properly at the time of shooting, improvises a form of English and plays with double meanings in words and phrases as seen in his riddles in *Pope in Your Eye.* Benigni's improvisations are a sort of semiotic game in which he writes new words in English on a notebook and then plays with their meanings, to the discomfort of his morose cellmates. Roberto even recites a bit of American poet Whitman and is able to break the linguistic divisions with a children's rhyme *I scream, you scream, we all scream for ice cream,* which reduces the cultural and personal differences among the three prisoners. Like his experiences with other filmmakers, Benigni took the lessons from Jarmusch to his later films. The cinematographer on *Down by Law,* the Wenders-trained Robbie Müller, worked on Benigni's film *The Little Devil.* Benigni's role in *Down by Law* also brought him to the attention of an international audience, which reacted with delight to the contrast between Benigni's joyful unpredictability and the subdued gloom that opens the film. Benigni's dynamic vitality provides the shock needed for the two more fatalistic characters played by Lurie and Waits to react against the injustice perpetrated against them.

Jarmusch and Benigni collaborated again in the feature *Night on Earth* (1991), an episodic film in which Jarmusch follows taxi drivers around the planet from Los Angeles, New York, Rome (featuring Benigni), Paris, and Helsinki (featuring world-class Finnish actor Matti Pellonpaa). The taxi driver is a perfect metaphor for Jarmusch's themes of alienation, since he lives on the outside, connected to society only by the tales of his passengers and the scratchy voices of radio dispatchers. In the Rome episode, which Benigni cowrote, Benigni plays Gino, a Cioni-like Tuscan who works as a cab driver in the wee hours of the Roman night. The film was released nearly twenty years after Benigni's original emigration from Vergaio to Rome. Had Benigni's acting career failed, his destiny might have been to become a taxi driver.

Benigni's Gino lives on the fringes of society, rebelling against normality and nature by wearing dark glasses at night, driving the wrong way down streets, and consorting with transsexual prostitutes. The physical themes of Gino's monologue confession to his passenger, who is a priest, have clear references to the *Cioni* monologue from 1975, as does his irreverent treatment of a class intellectual, the priest. The peasant physicality of Benigni's Cioni character again takes center stage with Gino's stories of his copulation with pumpkins, a lamb named Lola, and his sister-in-law. When Gino asks the priest (Paolo Bonacelli) for absolution he is not really penitent and states that even if his experiences need to be confessed, they are still beautiful. When the passenger/priest dies of a heart attack, Gino carries his corpse to a bench and complains that the priest weighs enough to be a cardinal. As in the *Cioni* monologue and the film *Berlinguer I Love You,* in Cioni's world, even in death, the physical is supreme.

Benigni's experiences with Jarmusch, like his earlier episodes with Zavattini and the Pasolinian school, were immensely important for his artistic development. Like Pasolini and Zavattini, Jarmusch's films emphasize the concerns of lower-class characters, such as the thieves and pimps in *Down by Law*. Jarmusch's films also have a fabulist element such as the semimagical manner in which Nicoletta Braschi appears with food and lodging to save the escaped prisoners in *Down by Law*. Finally, Jarmusch expresses his themes in a dry and unaffected style that is a signature of a "counter cinema" in order to lead the audience to question the commonplaces of commercial cinema.

## FEDERICO FELLINI: *LA VOCE DELLA LUNA/ THE VOICE OF THE MOON*

In film cameos, Benigni was always able to retain an allusion to his comic persona. Thus every film in which he appeared, even with Ferreri, was a vehicle for the expansion of his reputation and prestige as a comic phenomenon. The exception to this rule was Federico Fellini, who was the only director able to control Benigni and adapt him to a director's vision of a film. Benigni starred in the famed director's last film, *La voce della luna/Voice of the Moon* (1989), based on the novel *Il poema dei lunatici/Lunatic's Poem* by Ermanno Cavazzoni, who also collaborated on the screenplay. Benigni took the role after he had already established himself as a director on the Italian market with the box office successes of *Non ci resta che piangere/Nothing Left to Do but Cry* (1984) and *The Little Devil*.

Fellini's later films are self-referential not only in their study of his personal history but also in their focus on the interior, spiritual life of characters who are isolated from the noise of contemporary culture and society. When Fellini and Benigni worked together on *The Voice of the Moon*, Fellini was again interested in the nostalgic themes popular with international audiences in his 1974 film *Amarcord*. In *The Voice of the Moon*—as in *La città delle donne/The City of Women* (1980), *Ginger and Fred* (1985), and *Amarcord* (1974)—Fellini criticizes the dehumanizing confusion of the modern lifestyle. In *The Voice of the Moon,* the protagonists are marginal figures who live a life of poetic mystery and memory. Benigni's character, Ivo Salvini, is a recently discharged mental patient. He hears voices in wells, some of which quote from the nineteenth-century Italian poet, Giacomo Leopardi, whose verses are also featured in *Amarcord*. The other main character is a paranoid ex-prefect, Adolfo Gonella, played by comedian Paolo Villaggio. Gonella is also a marginal figure, having lost his job due to mental instability. Fellini questions the contemporary definition of normalcy under the yoke and cacophony of modern consumer culture.

For Fellini, these characters, whom society labels as insane, have retained a sense of their connection to the natural world and their local culture.[6]

Fellini, like Benigni, was a product of a rural, provincial Italy who made his fortune in Rome, eventually becoming an international star. The similarity in their work lies in the contrast between their origins and contemporary culture, which Fellini heavily criticized in his later films. The similarities actually go deeper in their filmographies than one might expect. Fellini's *I vitelloni* (1953) is about the boredom in the 1950s in Fellini's hometown, Rimini. Provincial alienation is also the theme of Benigni's *Berlinguer ti voglio bene,* set in the Tuscan countryside in the 1970s. In Benigni's *The Little Devil,* the gruff priest Maurizio learns how to enjoy physical existence from the devil, Giuditta. In Fellini's *La strada* (1954), the brutal circus strongman Zampano' learns about spirituality from the angelic Gelsomina.

Fellini has an anti-intellectual current in his films as does Benigni; particularly those films made before the mid-1960s. In a typical Fellini plot, *La dolce vita,* for example, an intellectual character leads a protagonist on a futile life-discovery journey. The film ends after the intellectual is either killed or emarginated, and Fellini's famous circular plot structure leaves social and economic roles among characters unchanged.[7] Benigni's suspicions of intellectuals stem from his roots in the peasantry. The villains in his films are the intellectual representatives of hostile hegemonic systems such as the mafia *(Johnny Stecchino)*, consumer society *(The Monster)*, or Nazi/fascism *(Life Is Beautiful)*.

The ultimate debt that Benigni owes to Fellini is an introduction to a cinema that eschewed the realistic current in Italian filmmaking for a more fantastic approach. Fellini's influence would be decisive in Benigni's Oscar-winning film, *Life Is Beautiful,* for which Benigni hired Fellini's cinematographer Tonino delli Colli and his set designer Danilo Donati. The collaboration between Fellini and Benigni was to continue after *The Voice of the Moon;* Fellini hoped to feature Benigni in a film version of *Pinocchio,* for which he had already made drawings.

While Benigni's early film roles included stints with directors such as Bertolucci, Ferreri, Citti, Fellini, and what may be called an apprenticeship with Zavattini,[8] he also had a taste of the U.S. independent style, yearning for the simplicity and angst of the glory days of Hollywood B movies with Jarmusch. The exposure to these filmmakers provided Benigni with a rich background in filmmaking styles and techniques that he would combine with his original culture and improvisational schooling in the Tuscan oral tradition. Given these numerous influences, it is important to note that

Benigni does not follow any one film style or school but has been able, particularly in his last films, *The Monster* and *Life Is Beautiful,* to incorporate the influences of his previous acting experiences into his own films.

## NOTES

1. Roberto Benigni and G. Bertolucci, *E l'alluce fu monologhi e gag* (Turin: Einaudi, 1996), p. 101. One line in the song, *cacare è sopratutto cosa umana* (defecating is above all a human thing), has elements of Rabelais's line from *Gargantua* that laughter is above all a human thing.
2. After the Oscar and box office success of *Life Is Beautiful,* distributors targeted *Chiedo asilo* for release on videocassette on the U.S. market. The film has many of the same themes that U.S. audiences found appealing in Benigni's later film. The teacher in *Chiedo asilo,* like Guido Orefice in *Life Is Beautiful,* focuses on the idea of protecting the innocence of children by giving them an alternative key to interpret a cruel world.
3. See Cesare Zavattini, *Neorealismo ecc.* (Milan: Bompiani, 1979).
4. De Sica and Zavattini also approached the themes of the Holocaust with *I sequestrati di Altona/The Condemned of Altona* (1962) and *Il giardino dei Finzi-Contini/The Garden of the Finzi-Contini* (1971).
5. See interview with Roberto Benigni in appendix.
6. Peter Bondanella, *The Cinema of Federico Fellini* (Princeton, N.J.: Princeton University Press, 1992), pp. 327–333.
7. This undercurrent in Fellini's films is treated in more detail in Carlo Celli, "Federico Fellini's Anti-Intellectualism," *Romance Languages Annual, 8* (1997): 168–171.
8. It must be noted that the Bertoluccis were also Pasolini disciples.

# · 6 ·

# Benigni's Religious Parody on Stage

## THE LITTLE DEVIL MEETS SCHOPENHAUER

$\int$ ince the 1970s, religious satire and parody have been part of Benigni's stage performances, perhaps because of his stint in a Florentine seminary in 1966. These jabs at papal authority have occasionally landed him in hot water. For example, when Benigni hosted one night of the San Remo Music Festival in 1980, he referred to Karol Wojtyla, Pope John Paul II, as *Woitilaccio,* which translates roughly as "Lousy old Wojtyla."[1] The joke brought an indictment of defamation.[2] Renzo Arbore's film *Il pap'oc-chio/Pope in Your Eye* (1980) was criticized for disrespect to religion and never broadcast on television.[3]

For an understanding of Benigni's take on religion it is necessary to examine the treatment of such themes in his stage performances after the *Cioni* monologue. Benigni made two documentaries of his stage performances: *Tuttobenigni/Everything Benigni* (1983) and *Tuttobenigni 95/96* (1996). In these performances Benigni parodies the traditions of Christianity in a manner recalling medieval parodies and spoofs that were an example of what Michail Bakhtin has identified as the *risus paschalis,* the period during carnival in which laughter, a liberating laughter, was permitted even in churches.[4] In fact Benigni's parodies, such as *Durante Cristo/During Christ* in *Tu mi turbi/You Bother Me,* are based on the contradiction between physical reality and the details in biblical stories.

Benigni's mixture of bawdy comedy with religious themes could be seen in the Rabelaisian carnival humor tradition. Bakhtin identified the philosophical basis for what may be called a Rabelaisian or epicurean worldview, in which there is an inseparability of the life of a soul from the body that houses or is created with it.[5] Another author that Benigni has cited as a favorite also places his approach to religion in a lay, philosophical tradition. Before traveling to Rome to become an actor, Benigni read the German philosopher Arthur Schopenhauer, whose theory of the world as an expression of the will appears as a reference in *La vita è bella/Life Is Beautiful.*[6] Benigni has commented that he was attracted to the open and accessible style of Schopenhauer's writing but also by the level of tragedy in his personal life and even the philosopher's face. As always with Benigni, the physical has the last word.[7]

There are points of convergence between Benigni's comic religious monologues and Schopenhauer's obviously more serious essay, "The Christian System." Schopenhauer begins his essay with a criticism of the church's assertion that reason is useless as a guide to religious dogma. According to Schopenhauer, the church's realization that reason alone is insufficient for an understanding of faith has led to the development of allegorical interpretations of dogma, resulting in inconsistencies.[8] In his theatrical performances, Benigni lampoons precisely such allegorical inconsistencies. In the 1996 film version of his theatrical tour *Everything Benigni 95/96,* he imagines that God has come back and is surprised to discover that heaven is empty. Benigni's God confronts the administrative junta of the Christian afterlife to find out what went wrong. Benigni's impersonation of God, Moses, and Saint Peter effectively reduces whatever mystique the audience may feel for these sacred figures. Saint Peter shirks responsibility and tells God that Moses was in charge of rules for entry to heaven. But God realizes that Moses is hard of hearing.[9]

Benigni's performance parodies the contradictions in the Judeo-Christian tradition that result in God's decision to entrust his commandments and revelations to a deaf Moses. For example, instead of *verbo* (word) Moses heard *cervo* (deer). Abel's name was actually the feminine *Adele* since she was a girl; otherwise, how could Cain and Abel have procreated? The opening statement of creation, "Let there be light," was also misunderstood. Instead of *Luce* (light), God had said *alluce* (big toe), because Eve had trouble walking and needed a big toe for balance. In order to correct the confusion, God gives Moses new instructions and one final commandment that follows Saint Augustine's dictum of the supremacy of love. Benigni's God explains that a law requiring humans to act lovingly should render all other commandments superfluous. The act of living in a loving manner would eliminate sin and the need for punishment. Unfortunately Moses, still hard of hearing, understood God to say "This is the tomato sauce, eat pasta."[10] This culinary misreading of this commandment pleases Benigni's distracted God, who adds that he prefers his pasta with a bit of Parmesan cheese.

Schopenhauer wrote about inconsistencies in the biblical representation and expectations of God, who requires patience and forgiveness of every sin, but does not act according to these rules himself.[11] Benigni also exposes the flaws in God's character, protesting God's insistence on making rules that he himself does not obey. One of Benigni's routines from the late 1970s pointed out the inconsistencies in God's requirements, given God's own sinfulness. Benigni jokes that, in his opinion, if God were to die he would go to Hell. Benigni remarks that God gave Moses his laws in a state of extreme anger after the episode of Sodom and Gomorrah. Due to his anger, he was prone to mistakes and made the laws too quickly. Benigni continues that God made the seven cardinal sins (although Benigni lists only six sins, leaving out envy) without realizing that they were his sins as well:

- Pride: Benigni remarks that if God had called himself Guido and had been a little more humble, everything might have gone differently.
- Anger: Benigni asks if anyone has a hotter temper than God, who makes everyone get baptized because of the theft of an apple.
- Avarice: Benigni jokes that God promised his chosen people some land, which he has yet to give to them.
- Sloth: After an eternity of rest, God created the world in six days using only words, did nothing on the seventh day, and has not shown himself in the two thousand years since.
- Gluttony: God has insisted on the sacrifice of animals, preferably the firstborn.
- Lust: God must be lustful since the billions on Earth are all his children.[12]

Benigni's God has also been an inattentive father to his children.[13] In the 1983 *Everything Benigni* documentary, Benigni questions the Bible's insistence on the kinship between God and man. If there is such a close tie between God and man, then the oversights in creation are inexcusable. Benigni asks why God has squeezed so many people onto a relatively tiny ball and compares God's logistical skills with a man who owns a twenty-story building and makes everyone sleep in the garage.[14] Benigni continues his amazement at God's seeming negligence with respect to the most obvious conveniences of life on Earth: scientific discoveries and inventions. Benigni asks why God has not given the human race, his children, immediate access to inventions such as antibiotics and penicillin. Instead, God hid penicillin in mold and electricity in frogs. It is as if God had asked himself where he could put these things so that they never could be found.[15]

Schopenhauer points out the inconsistency in the Christian dogma with regard to man's supremacy over animals. He criticizes Christianity for having unnaturally split mankind from the animal world and anointing man as the dominant creature.[16] Benigni takes this idea one step further, commenting on Christianity's subordination of women, a topic not of interest to the chauvinist Schopenhauer. Benigni points out the absurd exclusion of women from the ceremonies and dogma of the Judeo-Christian tradition. In *Everything Benigni 95/96,* Benigni's God questions a deaf Moses and a reticent Saint Peter about the manner in which his word has been transmitted into sayings such as "Peace on Earth among men of goodwill," which ignore women. Benigni's God wonders if the framers of biblical tradition had personal problems with women.[17]

Like Schopenhauer's criticism of church dogma, the religious material in Benigni's *Everything Benigni* monologues is almost exclusively centered on the Old Testament deity. There is little irreverence for Jesus or his philosophy of love and democratic principles. Benigni does not target Jesus' mission on earth, the validity of Jesus' teaching, or even his position as the Son of God. Rather, Benigni blames the Old Testament God for incompetence, as did Schopenhauer when he identified the untenable nature of dogma as a result of the contradictions between Old and New Testaments.[18] Benigni puts the confusion between Old Testament severity and New Testament liberality into a joke about the reasoning that led God to send his son to earth in the first place. Benigni retorts that God could have asked anyone on the street and saved a lot of trouble. Then Benigni points out that Jesus, although he was supposed to be a common man, was anything but common. He multiplied various fish, walked on water, and resuscitated the dead. Benigni jokes that if God had wanted his son to have the experience of a common man, he could have had Jesus appear as an accountant from Pistoia, a town in Benigni's native Tuscany.[19]

Schopenhauer also wrote of the Last Judgment as an incongruous concept in which the punishment that God assigns can have no value or possibility to improve conditions or deter sin, since it comes at the end of existence. Schopenhauer concludes that the idea of a Last Judgment is therefore a matter of abject vengeance.[20] Benigni's religious monologues feature a spoof on the Last Judgment, which revolves around the idea of the embarrassing fallibility of God, who despite his position as Supreme Being seems hampered by typically human failings. In Benigni's parody, an impatient God, after a brief look at the pollution, portable telephones, and politicians in Italy, decides to call the Last Judgment. The result is an imagined scene of tremendous confusion. Benigni's God divides the awaiting souls not only by nationality and religion, but also by profession in a wonderful compromise of leftist and Christian ideology. In *Pope in Your Eye,* painters are put with the unemployed, electricians, and the Assyro-Babylonians; manicurists with Americans; Egyptians with tobacconists. In the 1996 version of *Everything Benigni,* Benigni even added Italian politicians to the mix.[21]

In Benigni's *Pope in Your Eye* version of the Last Judgment, there is one figure who does not accept God's final decisions, a stubborn Karl Marx whom God mistakes for cyclist Eddy Merckx or a member of the comedy troupe, the Marx Brothers. Marx insists that he should be allowed into paradise since he had followed God's instructions throughout his life by stating that all men are equal, that the rich should give money to the poor, and that the workers should work as much and eat as much as the rich. God points out that these ideas were his first and that Marx appears to be guilty of plagiarism. Marx responds that if God condemns him, he must also condemn himself. God returns to being the vengeful God of the Old Testament that Schopenhauer saw as a part of the contradictions in Christianity. God points out that Marx made the mistake of declaring that God did not exist. Therefore Marx's punishment will be to serve as God's doorman who must call out "There is no God" every time an undesired visitor calls at Heaven's gate. In this imagined dialogue Marx is not condemned because he erred in his application of Christian philosophy but because he ignored the hierarchical structure of the Judeo-Christian afterlife, which derives partly from the Old Testament and partly from medieval church dogma. Marx is correct that a New Testament Christ may not have condemned him, but the Last Judgment is part of the Old Testament, and it is the vengeful Old Testament deity who condemns him.

Benigni has never denied his Catholic roots and has even announced that he is a believer.[22] In *Everything Benigni 95/96* he expands on Pascal's argument that one might as well believe because there is no punishment for believing, whereas the penalty for not believing may be damnation.[23] Benigni reduces this cynical logic to the satisfaction to be gained in interpersonal rivalries where the prize is not paradise but having the last word in an argument with an atheist friend upon meeting again in the afterlife. Benigni has explained his seeming irreverence and certain cynicism toward Christianity in terms of his upbringing in the heavily communist, agricultural, and later semi-industrial zones of Tuscany, stating that he is the product of a conflict between the Italian Communist Party and God.[24]

But Benigni's treatment of religious themes is actually a bit more sophisticated. Despite his reputation as a simple comedian, in his treatment of religion Benigni has managed to follow specific currents in lay tradi-

tions, including the carnival physicality of Rabelais, the skepticism of
Schopenhauer, and the cynicism of Pascal.

## NOTES

1. Benigni adapted the term "Woitilaccio" from his poetic mentor Logli
   Altamante, who had referred to Marco Panella, the leader of Italy's
   Radical Party, as "Panellaccio." Andrea Cosentino, *La scena del-
   l'osceno. Alle radici della drammaturgia di Roberto Benigni* (Rome:
   Oradek, 1998), p. 60.
2. Massimo Moscati, *Benigniaccio con te la vita è bella* (Milan: BUR, 1999),
   p. 27.
3. When faced with the charges by the prefect of Aquila, Infelisi,
   Benigni turned the accusation around, claiming the film was financed
   by the Vatican. Iuseppina Manin, "Il presidente della giuria: La
   Rossellini mi parlò di lui," *Corriere della sera,* May 26, 1998.
4. Michael Bachtin, *L'opera di Rabelais e la cultura popolare riso, carnevale e
   festa nella tradizione medievale e rinascimentale,* trans. Mili Romano
   (Turin: Einaudi, 1995), p. 25.
5. Bakhtin notes how Rabelais's emphasis on physicality actually comes
   from the Padovan school of Pompanazzi who wrote of the immor-
   tality of the soul. Bachtin, *L'opera di Rabelais,* p. 398.
6. Roberto Benigni and G. Bertolucci, *E l'alluce fu monologhi e gag*
   (Turin: Einaudi, 1996), p. 86. Schopenhauer's theory of the world as
   an expression of the will appears throughout *La vita è bella.* Schopenhauer's writings on Christianity appear in his essay "The Christian
   System," trans. T. Bailey Saunders, in *Religion: A Dialogue and Other
   Essays* (Westport, Conn.: Greenwood Press, 1973), pp. 103–118.
7. See interview with Roberto Benigni in appendix.
8. Schopenhauer, "The Christian System," p. 106.
9. Roberto Benigni, *E l'alluce fu,* ed. M. Giusti (Milan: Einaudi, 1996),
   p. 138.
10. Benigni, *E l'alluce fu,* p. 150.
11. Schopenhauer, "The Christian System," p. 108.
12. Stefania Parigi, *Roberto Benigni* (Naples: Edizioni Scientifiche Italiane,
    1988), p. 79.
13. Benigni, *E l'alluce fu,* pp. 38–39.
14. Benigni, *E l'alluce fu,* p. 38.
15. Roberto Benigni and G. Bertolucci, *TuttoBenigni, Berlinguer ti voglio
    bene, Cioni Mario di Gaspare fu Giulia* (Rome: Theoria, 1992), p. 40.

16. Schopenhauer, "The Christian System," p. 112.
17. Benigni, *E l'alluce fu,* p. 137
18. Schopenhauer, "The Christian System," p. 106.
19. Benigni, *E l'alluce fu,* p. 43.
20. Schopenhauer, "The Christian System," p. 108.
21. Schopenhauer, "The Christian System," pp. 103–152.
22. Parigi, *Roberto Benigni,* p. 79.
23. Pascal's *Le pari* (the bet) argument appears in Blaise Pascal, *Pensees* (Paris: Bordas, 1966), pp. 91–94.
24. Benigni, *E l'alluce fu,* p. 83.

Benigni in *Johnny Stecchino*. Photo courtesy of the Museum of Modern Art/Film Stills Archive.

# · 7 ·

# Benigni as Director

## RELIGIOUS PARODY AND *TU MI TURBI/YOU BOTHER ME*

*A*fter the box-office disappointment of *Berlinguer ti voglio bene/Berlinguer I Love You* and a few of his apprenticeships among the directors mentioned in chapter 5, Benigni directed his first feature-length film. *Tu mi turbi/You Bother Me* (1983) is an episodic film originally conceived as a series of shorts in order to take advantage of an Italian government subsidy for short films. The first episode, *Durante Cristo/During Christ,* takes its title from the Christian calendar in which time is measured either before or after the birth of Christ—not during. In *During Christ* Benigni appears on stage, dressed as a buffoonish Alpine shepherd named Benigno who has lost his flock except for one sheep named Smarrita (Lost). While searching for his flock Benigno meets the biblical Joseph (Carlo Monni), who appears in a costume recalling Renaissance depictions of the holy family. Benigni's future wife, Nicoletta Braschi, plays Mary, in her first angelic woman role in a Benigni film. The contrast between Monni's and Braschi's saintly demeanor and garb and Benigni's bumbling clowning recalls the Pasolinian mixture between sacred and profane in films such as *La ricotta/Cream Cheese.*

The skit develops in a manner that would be a standard plot in Benigni's later films. Benigni's comic persona is put into a historical situation and the contrast between the expectations of the setting and Benigni's rereading of established material, in this case religious dogma, provide occasions for humor. Joseph asks Benigno if he would care to baby-sit for the boy Jesus, age five. Comedy results from the contrast between the aura of a figure such as Jesus and Benigni's ability to introduce physical elements of everyday existence absent in the sacred texts. Benigni and co-scriptwriter Bertolucci present the five-year-old Jesus as an angelic, if stone-faced, child. Benigni's baby-sitting shepherd is befuddled when the young Jesus floats on water in the bath (hard water) and leaves an imprint on the towel like the Shroud of Turin after drying himself. Benigni's shepherd tells the boy Jesus his daily troubles, which are parodies of stories from the New Testament. Benigno laments that he has a lazy son named Lazarus who never wants to get out of bed, a relative named Judas who is obsessed with kissing, and a friend named Battitsta (John the Baptist) who plays practical jokes by throwing buckets of water on everyone. Benigno advises the boy not to marry until he is at least thirty-three and has enjoyed his youth, and above all to stay out of religion and politics. As a bedtime story Benigno mixes the tales of the prodigal son, the casting of the first stone, and the creation tale in Genesis. When Mary and Joseph return home, Benigno admires Mary's beauty and wistfully recalls the days when he courted her. The film ends on a miraculous note when Benigno's lost sheep return.

Despite the seemingly sacrilegious content, and the fact that at one point Joseph calls Benigni "Benigno, the naughty devil," the skit emphasizes an innocence and joy in episodes of the life of Jesus that have been removed from holy texts. Benigni's target is not so much the incongruity of the traditions of the New Testament or questions of Christ's divinity, as it is the rigidity and reduction of humanity in the church's historical representation of Christ. In this context, Benigni's references to the common lower body existence contrast with the cerebral and upper-body purity of the dogmatic Christ.

In the second episode, *Angelo/Angel,* Benigni concentrates on the figure of the angelic woman in a manner that again mixes the sacred and mundane. Benigni's character appears running frantically in a city at night, looking for the guardian angel who has abandoned him because he is too boring. On the city streets every passerby except Benigni has a guardian angel following him or her. Benigni finally finds his angel in a red-light district motel room, at which point he performs a monologue of common complaints and misunderstandings in male/female relationships to the silent, winged angel, played by Olimpia Carlisi. The imagery of the angelic woman, especially after the casting of Benigni's future wife Braschi as the Virgin Mary in the film's first episode, could not be more explicit. The angel tells Benigni that she is in love with him (Jesus). Benigni rebuts that he can do something that Jesus cannot—die—and threatens to throw himself out of the window.

But as he begins to fall Benigni awakes in his bed. Friends in costume enter to thank him for throwing a masquerade party and the angel appears in what seems to be a costume with angel wings. However, the dream had been reality. Benigni as the angel's boyfriend gives masquerade parties so that she may meet people in a setting where her wings will not arouse amazement. The skit ends with more references to the struggle between the physical and spiritual, lower and upper body, which is the running theme in the film and in Benigni's comedy. Benigni copulates with the angel and then confronts her with his fears that she may leave him one day for Jesus. The angel declares that she did see him (Jesus) one day and could not keep from laughing because he was so thin.

In the third episode, *In banca/In the Bank,* Benigni puts aside religion to play an everyman who confronts the inane bureaucracy and impenetrable language of a modern consumer society. The film opens with people ascending and descending a spiral staircase like a treadmill. Benigni follows these potential buyers at the opening sale of an apartment house in which different agents (all played by Giacomo Piperno) rapidly describe each unit and are interrupted by buyers anxious to sign a contract and close a deal. Benigni does likewise and then learns from the agent that he needs money in order to buy the apartment and should go to a bank. A series of cashiers and loan officers, including a Signor Diotiaiuti (Mr. MayGod-helpyou), all played by the same actor, Piperno, send the ignorant Benigni from window to window and office to office in search of funds. Benigni's ignorance about the rules of finance eventually lands him in prison, where a guard (again played by Piperno) describes the jail cell in the same rapid sales pitch as the real estate agents from the apartment house.

The skit, in contrast to the first two in the film, seems like an homage to the verbal brilliance of comedians such as Totò or Aldo Fabrizi, whose performances revolved around plays on words and double entendres. Like Totò, Benigni plays an ignorant everyman who confronts a linguistically and culturally hostile system. For example, the loan officer asks Benigni if he has any money invested to offer as collateral. The phrase in Italian *soldi investiti* may also mean "money in clothing." Benigni, like generations of vaudevillians before him, looks inside his shirt and, finding nothing, offers an expression of bewilderment. From this skit it is evident that there are two comic formats and traditions in Benigni's directorial debut. One is the traditional vaudevillian and *commedia dell'arte* clownery, where Benigni plays a hopelessly unlucky and ignorant fool and comedy is provided by puns and double entendres. The other format, seen in the first two episodes of *You Bother Me,* reveals a Zavattinian and Pasolinian amusement at the common physical necessities of everyday life in contrast with the eternal questions of the mysteries of faith and rigidity of dogma.

In the last episode of the film, *Due militi/Two Soldiers,* Benigni appears as one of two silent guards at the Italian Tomb of the Unknown Soldier (the order is reversed to read *Ignoto milite,* Soldier Unknown) at the monument to King Victor Emmanuel II in Rome. The skit opens with a stern voice-over narration that evokes tones of Italian nationalism, explaining how the soldiers at the monument are to remain motionless and silent as a sign of respect to their fallen comrades. However, Benigni's guard is determined to annoy his companion, played by Claudio Biagli. Benigni pretends that his bayonet is a telephone. He makes fun of an ancient Roman hero whose endurance made him a nationalist icon (Attilio Regolo). He pokes fun at the Italian inventors who were lionized during the fascist period as examples of national achievement. He also reprises material from his Cioni theatrical performances, such as a monologue on the Chinese and the equation of the afterlife with the national soccer lottery. There is even a bit from his days as a magician's assistant as he pretends to be hypnotized. But rather than a farcical skit in the tradition of Totò, as in *In the Bank,* Benigni returns to the religious themes that animated the first two episodes in the film.

The other soldier, subject to Benigni's antics, defends himself by expressing his faith in God. The soldier became convinced of God's existence after challenging God to prove he existed by making it rain within ten seconds. When God performed the miracle the soldier's faith was assured. Benigni likewise challenges God to prove his existence by making it snow— a less frequent occurrence in the Roman climate—within ten seconds. There follows a bit, later reprised in Benigni's theatrical performance *Tuttobenigni 95/96/Everything Benigni 95/96,* in which the problems of the world are explained by the fact that God or his messengers are hard of hearing and the confusion of earthly existence is due to faulty communication. However, when snow starts to fall, Benigni declares his faith in a manner that attenuates the previously sacrilegious portions in the earlier episodes, such as the allusion that Benigno dated Mary in *During Christ* or Benigni's copulation with the angel and her mockery of Christ's skinniness in *Angel.*[1]

The episodic film has enjoyed a long tradition in the Italian cinema as a format that many directors in the glory days of the Italian cinema tackled at one time or another. As do *Oro de' Napoli* (1954), *Boccaccio '70* (1963), *Spirits of the Dead* (1967), or *Ro.Go.Pa.G* (1963), Benigni's *You Bother Me* has an uniting theme—the contradiction between religious dogma and the physicality of everyday existence. As with Cioni in *Berlinguer I Love You,* Benigni's personae in *You Bother Me* face off against religious traditions and beliefs with irreverence. However, unlike the *Cioni* monologue, the film ends with an acceptance of the mystery of faith. God demonstrates his existence by making it snow in Rome. With the calming landscape shots of a setting sun that open the film and the rising moon that ends it, accompanied by Paolo Conte's swing-era style songs, Benigni declares an acceptance and even fatalism of the mysteries of existence. Rather than the iconoclastic fury of the *Cioni* monologue, by his directorial debut Benigni has mellowed and his skits express joy rather than anger and protest. In *You Bother Me,* Benigni develops themes and techniques that would recur in his later work, such as the character of an angelic woman; Benigni's role as a protector and teacher of children; and the lampooning of the manner in which language is a repressive tool of dominant society.

Benigni uses the camera to emphasize his comic presence rather than as an instrument to alter or to filter reality.[2] Benigni's directing style, or lack thereof, has been a facile refuge for critics wishing to dismiss his efforts as unworthy of comparison with auteurist traditions.[3] Nevertheless, *You Bother Me* has early examples of stylistic choices that would characterize Benigni's later films. The direction is a pragmatic effort to communicate Benigni's comic persona, unaffected by cinematic artifice that could detract from performance. This cinematic pragmatism would characterize his films until Benigni sought a higher level of cinematic sophistication in such films as *Il mostro/The Monster* or *La vita è bella/Life Is Beautiful.*

## STOPPING COLUMBUS WITH TROISI: *NON CI RESTA CHE PIANGERE/NOTHING LEFT TO DO BUT CRY*

Benigni's next film, *Non ci resta che piangere/Nothing Left to Do but Cry* (1984), was codirected with Massimo Troisi, who, like Benigni, was beginning to assert himself with such films as *Ricomincio da tre* (1981) and *Scusate il ritardo* (1982). Perhaps because of Troisi's effusion of gestures and Neapolitan-tinged Italian, Benigni plays the more serious character, Saverio, a schoolteacher, while Troisi plays his friend Mario, the school janitor. In Italian schools, the janitor serves as a sort of factotum for the students and faculty.

As the film opens, Saverio is nervous and depressed because his sister, Gabriellina, has been abandoned by a U.S. (NATO) soldier after a six-year relationship. The car in which Saverio and Mario are traveling then stops at a railway crossing that never opens. In frustration, they turn around and take a country road but the car breaks down. When a thunderstorm threatens, they take refuge in a local inn. Upon awaking they discover that they have traveled back in time to the year 1492.

The time-travel plot allows an examination of the contrast between ancient and modern life and a continuation of the ex-peasant nostalgia theme in the *Cioni* monologue and in *Berlinguer I Love You*. When Saverio asks one of the locals where they are, the answer is the local town, Frittole. Saverio insists on getting an answer to his question and asks the name of the next town, but the answer is the same, Frittole. In 1492 existence was local and thus the film's characters are tied to a local reality. Yet the inhabitants of 1492 are friendly and generous, inspiring a feeling of nostalgia for peasant hospitality in an underpopulated world.

On their first morning in the past, Saverio and Mario greet a roommate who urinates out the window and is speared by a mounted soldier. Vitellozzo, the murdered man's brother, played by Carlo Monni, explains that the violence is the work of Savonarolian fundamentalists who have outlawed ostentatious clothing or any worldly display.[4] Later in the film, a Savonarolian monk appears before Mario (Troisi) and announces in the Trappist tradition that Mario must remember that he is mortal. Troisi's response, to the effect of "Yeah, I'll write it down right away," became one of his best-known lines. The Savonarolian fundamentalists have instituted an hour of darkness at noon, during which time the townspeople must go indoors and pray for salvation. The Savonarolian theme is resolved when the two time travelers write a comic letter to Savonarola asking for Vitellozzo's release from jail, in a scene inspired by *Totò, Peppino e la malafemmina/Totò, Peppino and the Femme Fatale* (1956).[5]

Savonarola, the fifteenth-century religious reformer and martyr, has a multifaceted reputation in Italy. He is respected as an intellectual and reformer but also remembered for his institution of a fundamentalist theocracy in Florence. The Vatican has yet to rehabilitate Savonarola as it did other past adversaries of the church, such as Galileo or Giordano Bruno. The Savonarolian repression in the film, with soldiers who kill Vitellozzo's brother and then carry Vitellozzo off to prison, adds a current of violence to the film. However, it would be a stretch to claim a parallel between the Savonarolian fundamentalists in 1492 and the political terrorism that headlined the front pages of Italian newspapers in the early 1980s. The references to Savonarola could be read as a barb against religious asceticism that presages Benigni's fuller treatment of such themes in *Il piccolo diavolo/The Little Devil*. For example, Saverio and Mario attend church services that are anything but spiritual and are presented as part of courtship rituals in Renaissance society. At mass the men stare longingly at the women and then follow them home.

As in his work in the Roman avant-garde theater, Benigni's use of language in the film is a mechanism for subversion. Mario makes practical use of his knowledge of the future in his courtship of a local beauty by passing off twentieth-century songs as his own compositions. He sings abbreviated versions of the Beatles' "Yesterday," the communist protest song "Avanti popolo," the Italian national anthem "L'inno di Mameli," and Domenico Modugno's "Volare." The commonplaces of mass culture are incantations for the simple souls in 1492. The contemporary subtexts of the songs are meaningless to the fifteenth-century listener as language is freed of all its limitations as a temporal and societal construct. In a scene with a similar context, as the pair try to break the spell that sent them back in time, Saverio performs a monologue that emphasizes modern technical words in the hope that the twentieth century will reappear by an act of will.[6] The words of the contemporary age lose meaning when Saverio opens the door to a preindustrial street scene.

When the two encounter Leonardo da Vinci, the film reveals Benigni's iconoclastic views about intellectuals. Benigni as Saverio unsuccessfully attempts to explain commonplaces of twentieth-century culture to Leonardo such as Marxism, Freudian psychoanalysis, and the labor union system. Benigni uses the jargon of psychoanalysis and Marxism as a comic nonsense, an adaptation of his improvisational apprenticeship and his love for word games. This rejection of the language and ideology of modernity, of the industrial codification of reality into a technocratic Babel, would become one of the constant themes in Benigni's later films. Saverio reduces the ideological and academic constructs (psychoanalysis, Marxism) of the twentieth century to a few phrases that cannot be understood by the universal genius, Leonardo da Vinci. Saverio's modern language and conception of identity and geography are meaningless in the local reality of fifteenth-century Frittole, the inhabitants of which can understand only the beauty of the melodies of Mario's twentieth-century popular music.

Given *Nothing Left to Do but Cry*'s setting in the fateful year of discovery, 1492, the main example of modernity and culprit for the changes, as might be expected, is the United States. After the disappointing meeting with da Vinci, Saverio decides to go to Palos in Spain in order to prevent Christopher Columbus from discovering America. Saverio's specialization as a schoolteacher was Columbus's voyage, and therefore he claims to know the exact dates of Columbus's departure from Spain. From this point on in the film a semiangelic woman warrior, Astrahia, follows the pair on the journey and prevents them from disturbing Columbus's itinerary.[7] Saverio's rationale for attempting to stop Columbus is that Ameri-

Benigni with Massimo Troisi in *Nothing Left to Do but Cry*. Photo courtesy of the Museum of Modern Art/Film Stills Archive.

cans have done nothing but evil, and he challenges Mario to name one good American. Mario's attempts—the Beatles, Cassius Clay, and Hemingway—are rejected by Saverio, who explains that the Beatles were English, Clay was an African whose ancestors were brought to the United States by slave-traders, and, in a comic touch, Hemingway is Cuban.[8]

Saverio's image of the United States focuses on the sins of U.S. expansionism, such as the murder of aboriginal peoples and horrific inventions such as the electric chair. Saverio's antagonistic attitude recalls the anti-American tones of the *Cioni* monologue and television programs, which might be expected, given Italian politics of the time. One of the most acrimonious debates in the waning years of the Cold War was whether Italy should allow the U.S. military and NATO to base nuclear-tipped missiles in Comiso, Sicily. However, the film ends with a personal explanation for Saverio's anti-American attitude. Saverio wants to stop Columbus so that his sister can never have an unhappy love affair with the U.S. soldier. Saverio's rejection of U.S. cultural influences and military occupation is the fruit of personal, family issues, rather than a rational, ideological choice.

After Mario promises to marry Saverio's sister, the two spot a train. But rather than a return to the twentieth century and the closed railway crossing that opened the film, the train is conducted by their friend Leonardo da Vinci, who manufactured it from a brief explanation and sketch given to him by Saverio. Leonardo's ability to understand a modern concept could be read as a metaphor for the inevitability of history and progress. In fact, all of Mario and Saverio's attempts to invent the conveniences of the future (the toilet, the traffic light) had ended in failure. The seeming lesson of this time-travel fable is that the two characters should be resigned to the confusion of whatever period they inhabit. However, the train is also a symbol of the industrial revolution that first brought changes into the peasant world of Benigni's ancestors. The disappearance of the train at the beginning of the film at the railroad crossing initiates the time travel back to the days before Europe was influenced by the United States.

The directing style, like Benigni's and Troisi's earlier efforts, emphasizes the comic presence of the actors rather than a more cinematic approach. The film is also another example of the importance of improvisation in Benigni's career. Carlo Monni, who plays Vitellozzo in the film, has recounted how the two actor/directors relied on their improvisational talents in the film to such an extent that there was little reliance on a set script.[9] With such working methods, Benigni and Troisi followed in the footsteps of classic comedians such as Totò, who preferred to approach each scene with only a general plot outline, to allow ample room for improvisation. The reason was that preparation detracts from the improvisational authenticity in performance. As mentioned, the film pays homage to Totò and De Filippo in the scene where Benigni and Troisi improvise a letter to Savonarola. The Italian public recognized the comedic authenticity of the film, and Benigni and Troisi were rewarded at the box office during a period in which the Italian national cinema was in noted decline.

## FROM BERTOLUCCI TO CERAMI

Benigni's next film as director, *The Little Devil* (1988), marks the beginning of his relationship with screenwriter Vincenzo Cerami (who has a cameo appearance in the film as a police captain) and the end of his collaboration with director Giuseppe Bertolucci. The treatment of *The Little Devil* was written by all three, Cerami, Bertolucci, and Benigni. However, the screenplay is credited only to Benigni and Cerami.

Cerami has a vast portfolio as an author, which has undoubtedly aided Benigni's development. After an initial experience as assistant director on Pasolini's *Uccellacci e uccellini/Hawks and Sparrows* and the multidirector effort, *Le streghe/The Witches* (1967), Cerami concentrated on writing rather than directing. Besides collaborations with Pasolini, Citti, and Giuseppe Bertolucci, Cerami has also worked with Ettore Scola, Francesco Comenici, Gianni Amelio, Francesco Nuti, and Mario Monicelli.[10] Cerami's credits even include a period with the Italian westerns, *Il pistolero Ave Maria* (1969) and *Il pistolero cieco/Blindman* (1971). Cerami has written a number of well-received theater pieces (*La casa del mare, Teatro Excelsior, Il Signor Novecento, Sua maestà*).

He has also written novels: *Addio Lenin* (1981), *La lepre* (1988), *L'Ipocrita* (1991), *La gente* (1993), *Fattacci,* and *Consigli a un giovane scrittore* (1996). He edited a number of works, including an anthology on Petrolini, the premier Italian comic actor of the 1930s, *Bravo/Grazie antologia petroliniana* (1992), and an anthology of Tuscan author Federico Tozzi, *Bestie* (1993). He also has a background in dialect literature, transcribing the fables of Rome and Lazio, *Fiabe di Roma e del Lazio* (1985). His collaboration with Benigni led to other noted Italian comedians, such as Antonio Albanese, seeking him out, hoping to replicate Benigni's success, although with less brilliant results thus far.

Through Cerami, Benigni reconnected with the Pasolinian influences he had encountered working under director Sergio Citti in *Il mine-strone*. Pasolini's influence on Cerami may be explained by a brief look at one of Cerami's later theatrical pieces, *Dormi che è ancora notte—apologhetto morale sul più morale dei film di Pasolini/Sleep for It Is Still Night—A Moral Apology on the Most Moral of Pasolini's Films*. In this one-act play, Cerami reprises the surviving characters from Pasolini's *Hawks and Sparrows,* thirty years after the film and without the deceased Totò. In the original film, Ninetto Diavoli played a Roman youth. A talking crow was the voice of a left-wing intellectual. A young woman, Luna, was Ninetto's love inter-est, and Totò was Ninetto's father. The film tackled themes such as the historic hunger and poverty of those in the lower classes, and their exu-berant relationship with physical urges and love, as the film shifted between a contemporary and medieval setting in which Totò and Diavoli played Franciscan monks.

In Cerami's play, an aged and wealthy Ninetto refuses to eat the crow, as he had in the film. Since he is rich, he insists on eating chicken. Luna, a prostitute, tries to interest Ninetto with a series of fetishistic displays but she finally dismisses the aged Ninetto for his materialism and inability to understand love. Ninetto has reached the material security that was the goal of Pasolini's film but as a result he is no longer interested in love or sim-ple sustenance. The crow, the voice of a left-wing ideologue, points to Ninetto's new attitudes as an explanation for the declining birthrate in Italy and the disappearance of Italy's previous identity as a peasant society.

In *Il minestrone,* the encounter with the Pasolinian school of film-making offered Benigni an exposure to a form of cinema that did not accept limits to the imagination or physical urges. Pasolini wrote of the cinema as the written language of reality. For Pasolini, oral language is natural in contrast to written language, which is a convention, a societal, and even economic creation.[11] Pasolini's films treated preindustrial and pre-Enlightenment classics such as the *Decameron, Canterbury Tales,* and *Arabian Nights,* examining the waning of indigenous culture in the face of consumerism, also a major theme in Benigni's early work. Pasolini's work with Totò was imbued with a sense of didactic fantasy, an element repeated in Benigni's films. Pasolini also experimented with the function of language with films that display a dependence on visual narrative. For example, in *La terra vista dalla luna,* Totò (Cianciacato Miao) is paired with the deaf mute Assurdina Cai, played by Silvana Mangano. The film emphasizes the power of visual narrative and even the futility or irrele-vance of verbal communication. A magical approach to plot and language is similarly apparent in Benigni and Cerami's film, *The Little Devil.*

Since Cerami has written for the stage and in prose, he is well aware of the different approaches required for each medium.[12] According to Cerami, recognition of these differences is especially important in the tone and level of language in film because of the possibilities with camera movement. Because film is so bound in verisimilitude, in the realistic power of the photographic image, the language used in film must be of a low, common sort, in order to avoid the histrionics that are required for the stage but would seem forced in film. Cerami has also emphasized the origins of the cinema in the silent era, in which the conventions that are now accepted by audiences—such as reaction shots and subjective camera—were not imprinted on the public consciousness. Cerami describes the camera's ability to mimic these human reactions and points of view as part of the "humanity" of the camera.[13] This idea of the camera's humanity and the emphasis on public reactions during the silent period by Cerami are vital clues for understanding Benigni's films, examined in chapter 6.

Benigni's cinematic style is based on the requirements of performance rather than the technical manipulation of film. Given the manner in which he came to directing, with an extensive background as an actor in theater, Benigni is somewhat of a throwback to the performer-directors of previous times. Cerami's description of his working method with Benigni reveals how Benigni's origins in the *poeti a braccio* tradition remain the foundation of his art. Cerami provides the voices of the secondary characters and then Benigni improvises the lines of the protagonist.[14] Benigni presents a persona, the same basic Cioni-like character, who relies on a series of stunts and props that are motivated by his films' different plots. Much of the staging and three-quarter and full-shot camera angles in Benigni's films could easily be transferred to and from a traditional proscenium arch.

Given the narrative roots of Benigni's performing style, it is not surprising that he has made statements about the primacy of the verbal in the cinema that are opposite from statements by Cerami.[15] This confirms that their collaboration is a synthesis of approaches. For Cerami, the cinema is a more visual medium. When Benigni was confronted with a question that pointed out the criticism of the overwhelming verbalism and the box-office disappointment of *Berlinguer I Love You,* he responded with a declaration on the centrality of verbalism in his vision of the cinema.[16] The question of the supremacy between the verbal and visual in film has a long history in Italian film criticism, with roots in the reactions of postwar film critics to the apolitical stance of Crocean aesthetics. Critics who favor the visual were more inclined to an *a priori,* irrational aesthetic than those critics who wrote of the verbal sense of linguistic certainty and rationality. Because of Benigni's abilities with improvisation and word games and Cerami's influence, his cinema clouds the two positions.

## NOTES

1. Apparently a fifth episode is also not included in the film's theatrical release. Benigni's character wins 10 million lire in a lottery, but a fortuneteller warns him that he will die that very night at midnight. Benigni runs around town desperately giving his money away and even refusing the invitations of a girl who previously had resisted his advances. When the prophecy turns out to be a hoax, Benigni goes off to find the girl and to get some of his money back. Stefania Parigi, *Roberto Benigni* (Naples: Edizioni Scientifiche Italiane, 1988), p. 144.

2. Gian Piero Brunetta, *Storia del cinema italiano* (Rome: Editori Riuniti, 1993), vol. 4, p. 568.

3. For example, see Paolo Mereghetti, *Dizionario dei film 1996* (Milan: Baldini & Castoldi, 1996), p. 805. For *Johnny Stecchino,* Mereghetti writes that despite some comic moments in the film, he would still like to see Benigni work under a real director.

4. Fra' Girolamo Savonarola (1452–1498) was a charismatic Dominican friar whose prophesies of impending doom for the Florentine republic so captured the attention of the populace that he was able to install a theocracy in the city until he was burned at the stake in 1498. The film confuses dates, as Savonarola did not take control of the government of Florence until the Medici were expelled in 1494.

5. Parigi, *Roberto Benigni,* p. 146.

6. Perhaps an early reference to the philosophy of Schopenhauer that would appear in *La vita è bella.*

7. The love triangle between this angel-warrior and Mario and Saverio, present in the book version, is cut from the film.

8. The joke about Hemingway being Cuban appears only in the book version.

9. Carlo Monni, in statements confirmed by Bertolucci, states that the two stars never wrote a formal script beyond forty-odd pages. These statements by Giuseppe Bertolucci and Monni are taken from the RAI television documentary, *Benigni da Oscar,* March 20, 1999.

10. Cerami worked with Giuseppe Bertolucci on *Oggetti smarriti* (1980) and *Segreti, segreti/Secrets, Secrets* (1985); Ettore Scola on *Il viaggio di Capitan Fracassa/Captain Fracassa's Journey* (1991); Francesco

Comenici on *Pianoforte* (1984); Francesco Nuti on *Tutta colpa del paradiso* (1985); Gianni Amelio on *I ragazzi di via Panisperna, Porte aperte/Open Doors* (1990), and *Colpire al cuore/Blow to the Heart* (1982); and Mario Monicelli on *Un borghese piccolo piccolo/A Very Little Man* (1977).

11. Pier Paolo Pasolini, *Heretical Empiricism,* trans. Ben Lawton and Kate L. Barnett (Bloomington: Indiana University Press, 1988), p. 198.
12. Vincenzo Cerami, "La scrittura creativa," in *L'officina del racconto,* ed. G. Francesio (Forlì: Nuova Compgnia editrice, 1996), p. 123. See also Vincenzo Cerami, *Consigli a un giovane scrittore* (Turin: Einaudi, 1996).
13. Cerami, "La scrittura creativa," p. 121.
14. Cerami's comments were made for the RAI television documentary, *Benigni da Oscar.*
15. Cerami, "La scrittura creativa," p. 120.
16. Parigi, *Roberto Benigni,* p. 56.

# · 8 ·

# Cioni in the City: Part 1

## IL PICCOLO DIAVOLO / THE LITTLE DEVIL

*In* the introduction to the published screenplay of *Johnny Stecchino* (1991), Roberto Benigni asks the question, "Dov'è finito Cioni Mario (Whatever happened to Cioni Mario)?"[1] Benigni's answer is a long parody of critics' tendency to find high-cultural references in popular culture. Despite Benigni's desire to joke on the subject, the answer to his question is that, as in *Il piccolo diavolo / The Little Devil,* Benigni has taken his comic alter ego, Cioni, into the urban heart of Italian society.

When Benigni played a Cioni-like cab driver in Jarmusch's *Night on Earth* in 1991, years after the theatrical monologue, it may have appeared to be an homage to Benigni's early career. However, the reappearance of a Cioni-like character is not an isolated case. Despite cosmetic changes and plot alterations, Cioni is very much alive in Benigni's later films *The Little Devil* (1988), *Johnny Stecchino* (1991), *Il mostro / The Monster* (1995), and even *La vita è bella / Life Is Beautiful.* In these films an innocent Cioni-like character confronts the problems of contemporary and historical Italy.

In *The Little Devil* Benigni plays a devil, Giuditta. Walter Matthau plays a priest, Don Maurizio, who is in the midst of a spiritual and physical crisis because of his relationship with an attractive woman, Patrizia, played by Stefania Sandrelli. In the opening sequence, Father Maurizio is stationed at the idyllic campus of the North American Pontifical College. He is on his knees in a confessional, admitting his doubts about continuing to be a priest. His confessing monsignor admits to not understanding a word of Maurizio's confession and, rather than ordering penance, suggests that Maurizio take a vacation.

This confessional sequence targets the static Catholic ceremonial and cultural tradition of Italy in the 1980s, a period in which the Roman Catholic Church suffered defeats in national referendums on abortion and divorce, and had increasing difficulty in finding priests willing to accept

77

the vow of chastity. *The Little Devil* appeared after Italian Premier Bettino Craxi's Socialist Party-led coalition introduced an element of separation of church and state into the Italian constitution, in 1984. Craxi's coalition government renegotiated the concordat between the Italian government and the papacy that was signed with Mussolini in 1929, and that had recognized the Vatican as an independent state and established Roman Catholicism as the official state religion of Italy.

After his confession, Father Maurizio performs an exorcism on an obese Neapolitan hairdresser. The procedure seems to have been successful until the lights go out and Benigni appears as Giuditta, the playful devil who had possessed the hairdresser and now, like Pinocchio, considers Father Maurizio to be his keeper. Comedic situations arise from the contrast between the physical exuberance and linguistic freedom of Giuditta and the constraints of the religious seminary. Giuditta is not of this world; he has a feral appearance, naked except for the hairdresser's fur coat. Giuditta has much in common with the earlier Cioni character since the impulses and the lessons Giuditta draws from his time on earth emphasize the supremacy of the physical. Benigni creates a childlike fascination in Giuditta's delight with intercoms, *zuppa inglese* (English trifle), blackjack at a casino, trains, cars, and police officers' uniforms. Of course Giuditta is also amazed by *quella cosa* (that thing), as he calls the reproductive organ of the female devil Nina, played by Nicoletta Braschi, whom the functionaries of the netherworld have sent to fetch him.

A urination scene recalls the scatological opening of Rabelais's *Gargantua* and Michail Bakhtin's statements about the traditional beliefs of the resuscitative power of a urine bath. In fact, after Father Maurizio gets drunk and is doused by Giuditta's urine—the before and after of an alcoholic beverage—he abandons his religious vocation.[2] Instead of trying to resolve his own spiritual crisis, perhaps the reason for Giuditta's appearance, Maurizio takes Giuditta to the city and abandons him like a dog in an impersonal cityscape of high rises and intercoms. The urban scene alludes to the city's role as a mixer of people and an impersonal place that reduces identity.

One key to Giuditta's carnival-like shattering of Father Maurizio's world is his use of language. When Giuditta is experimenting with his new incarnation as a human, one of his first expressions in language is a spoof on schooling and mathematical tables. This has a long history in popular comedy in the parodies of Latin grammars in the medieval period and Renaissance.[3] The material of high culture, learning, and seriousness is turned into nonsense, a meaningless effusion for Giuditta's verbal delight. Benigni's Giuditta is completely ignorant of the social barriers and class relationships that language is designed to enforce. The devil repeats the phrases of everyday life at inopportune moments as language is liberated from the constrictions of societal decorum. Benigni plays on the Pirandellian theme of the impossibility of communication by the manner in which Giuditta alters the meaning of words.

Benigni's humor in *The Little Devil* is not based on double entendres or puns but on a rejection of the codes of language and society. Benigni's devil does not play to a straight man in the manner of Totò or Groucho Marx with the sort of play on words that he employed in Jarmusch's *Down by Law*—"I ham a good egg." Rather, Giuditta is a straight man to the ridiculousness of the conventions of language in which language has lost all meaning. Examples include Giuditta's use of the phrases heard on the street that he repeats in inappropriate situations. When Giuditta plays at the blackjack table, his repetition of the words *carta* (card) and *nove* (nine) are a delightful expression of the manner in which social, class, and sexual barriers are subverted in a carnival-like and lower bodily effusion of nonsense.

The folly of the societal constraints of language, the Pirandellian impossibility of communication, is best demonstrated in an exchange between Giuditta and another devil, posing as an intellectual: the German scholar Cusatelli, who has a background in the supposed rationality of northern European culture. Giuditta approaches Cusatelli for advice on how to approach Nina, and Cusatelli responds with a monologue on the progression in relationships from infatuation to marriage and divorce. Giuditta completely alters this monologue when he encounters Nina. In the scene, Benigni employs a theatrical setup where the character speaking is watching the approach of another character, who is out of earshot. The second character enters the scene and completes the sentence of the first character.[4] After Giuditta rehearses the script given to him by Cusatelli, Nina enters the scene and completes Giuditta's sentence when he asks her whether they should take a walk. Giuditta then inverts Cusatelli's description of courtship and eventual divorce. Cusatelli's opening anecdote about Schiller becomes Giuditta's conclusion.

The film's playful confusion of meaning extends to signs, icons, and physical gestures. Giuditta throws a bottle of wine at a table of prelates, instead of handing it to them politely. When Nina kisses a stranger in order to provoke the reaction of his companion, Giuditta mimics her actions but kisses a man instead. This confusion of societal signs is devastating for Father Maurizio, whose doubts about his calling began when the attractive Patrizia did not recognize him as a priest. Once the societal

signal of the priestly collar is removed, Maurizio is vulnerable to the physical impulses personified by Giuditta. Benigni's film reduces the authority
of class intellectuals by reducing Father Maurizio to his physical impulses.
The film's lampoon of societal manners and commonplaces subverts the
certainties of dominant cultural standards. There is also a citation of Totò,
such as the scene on the train in which Giuditta takes the ticket and clothes
of a wealthier passenger (Giacomo Piperno).

One example of the manner in which Benigni criticizes society's
signs and conventions is his treatment of fashion. By his very physical
presence Benigni challenges classical and commercial notions of beauty.
In *Berlinguer ti voglio bene/Berlinguer I Love You,* Cioni wears the oversized suit and pants of the "country bumpkin come to town" on festival day. In *The Little Devil,* Giuditta goes through Maurizio's closet until
he finds the Benigni signature outfit, a loose and shiny dark suit with a
white shirt, an outfit easily transferable in any context of the modern
period. In fact, Benigni wears the same outfit, the heir of Chaplin's
baggy tramp suit, almost as a uniform in all of his later films except *Life
Is Beautiful.* Vincenzo Cerami, Benigni's screenwriter beginning with
*The Little Devil,* has noted that all great comedians (Chaplin, Laurel and
Hardy) tend to dress formally. Formal attire allows the comedian to provoke comic contrast as well as reassure the spectators' position in society. The comedian, as an incompetent outsider, cannot gain entry to
society and remits the spectators' fears of exclusion from community.
The uniformity of Benigni's costumes also points to the universality of
comic expression and the affectation inherent in fashion culture, which
Benigni has referred to with typical hyperbole and insight as "the sister
of death."[5] The scene of Giuditta opening a closet of nearly identical
suits is repeated in his films that follow *The Little Devil,* with the exception of *Life Is Beautiful,* where the universal gray suit of a deportee has
a more tragic connotation.

References to the fashion industry also appear in *The Little Devil*
when Giuditta and Maurizio happen upon a fashion show interrupted
by a windstorm. Giuditta appropriates the language and gestures of the
event when he substitutes for Father Maurizio in the celebration of mass
and transforms the religious service into a fashion show. This transformation recalls the medieval and Renaissance traditions of student and
carnival parodies of mass.[6] The source of humor is the manner in which
a situation may belong to two simultaneously independent events and
may be interpreted two ways.[7] The equation between mass and mundane spectacle also has an element of social criticism that returns to the

theme of Catholic culture. Giuditta's posing as priest elaborates a sequence in Fellini's *Roma* (1972), in which bejeweled monsignors and other high prelates parade the latest religious ceremonial garb. Father Maurizio's parishioners parade before the altar like models in the tradition of antimasses. The confusion of signs of behavior and language points to a surrealistic subtext in Benigni's film. The confusion is accompanied by an emphasis on chance and causality that would have appealed to a surrealist vision of the absurdity of existence. For example, when an actual gambling table appears in the film, Giuditta's ability to ignore the rules of the game results in his financial and sexual conquest of Nina.

The spoof on fashion and societal conventions extends to Nina's exhibitionism. Displays or expressions of sexual vitality have a long history in Italian film. Such motifs existed in Mario Camerini's romantic comedies of the 1930s, in the neorealist period, and in the *commedia all'italiana* in the 1950s and 1960s with the *maggiorata fisica* (buxom lady) displays of actresses such as Sophia Loren and Silvana Mangano. A recurring plot theme in such female displays was the potential for physical exuberance to overturn societal barriers, a theme also central to the *novellistica* and *commedia dell'arte* traditions. In *The Little Devil,* Nina's displays could be discussed in terms of psychoanalytic theory, especially recalling the oedipal theme in *Berlinguer I Love You.* However, Nina does not display a traditionally fetishistic body part such as the leg, foot, or breast. Rather, the emphasis is on the female reproductive organ, a part that rarely receives visual attention in the cinema and has been studied mainly as a lack or absence in contrast to the male's reproductive organ. Nina's organ is not perceived by Giuditta as an absence that would evoke a standard reading of castration anxiety. Instead, her part inspires propulsion to physical action that Giuditta, as an ignorant devil, cannot understand. Before Nina and Giuditta consummate their relationship, Benigni sets the stage with a male dancer who performs a tango with a female puppet. The implication is of male control over the female image and societal domination of men over women. After the dancer completes his performance, couples dance in mimicry of his actions. However, the societal roles are reversed with Giuditta and Nina. After their copulation, Nina enters Giuditta's body in the manner that Giuditta had entered the Neapolitan hairdresser. Nina controls Giuditta's physical being, as evidenced in the scene of his final greeting of Father Maurizio.

Comic tales with mischievous but harmless devils have appeared in Italian literature over the centuries, such as Machiavelli's *Belfagor.* Bakhtin wrote of the medieval tradition in which playful devils appear in order to reverse low and high culture.[8] There have also been Italian film treatments of comic devils in Rossellini's *La macchina ammazzacattivi/The Machine That Kills Bad People* (1952) and *Totò al giro d'Italia/Totò at the Tour of Italy* (1948), or Pasolini's *I racconti di Canterbury/The Canterbury Tales* (1972). In such films the possessed character or the devil is often an innocent, misguided, and naive creature. Benigni's comedy is very much in this tradition. However, unlike most devil stories, this film does not reaffirm Catholic ideology with a final moral. It is an epicurean fable in which the priest is taken out of his ascetic world and confronted by the joyful confusion of the physicality expressed by Benigni's devil. In the last scene, Father Maurizio is no longer identifiable as a priest. Benigni's character thus maintains his role as a teacher in the film, by showing Father Maurizio how to reconnect with his physical self.

## NOTES

1. Roberto Benigni and V. Cerami, *Johnny Stecchino* (Rome: Theoria, 1991), p. 9.
2. Michael Bachtin, *L'opera di Rabelais e la cultura popolare riso, carnevale e festa nella tradizione medievale e rinascimentale,* trans. Mili Romano (Turin: Einaudi, 1995), p. 163.
3. Bachtin, *L'opera di Rabelais,* p. 25.
4. This theatrical setup is repeated extensively in *Life Is Beautiful* in Guido's courtship of Dora.
5. Massimo Moscati, *Benigniaccio con te la vita è bella* (Milan: BUR, 1999), p. 46.
6. Bachtin, *L'opera di Rabelais,* p. 85.
7. Bergson defined this sort of setup as a reciprocal interference of series. Henri Bergson, *Laughter* (New York: Doubleday, 1956), p. 123.
8. Bachtin, *L'opera di Rabelais,* p. 48.

# · 9 ·

# Cioni in the City: Part 2

## JOHNNY STECCHINO

$\mathscr{B}$enigni's film *Johnny Stecchino* (1991) was timely, released at a time when Italians were ready for some comic relief on the subject of the mafia. In the early 1990s, the Italian police had made significant inroads against the Sicilian mafia for the first time since Cesare Mori's brutal efforts in the 1930s. The police captured several famous bosses, including Totò Riina. The police were aided by the climate of political uncertainty among Italian political parties following the fall of the Berlin Wall and the adoption of a system of state-protected witnesses, *pentiti,* who testified in exchange for immunity from prosecution.

The plot of *Johnny Stecchino* revolves around an angelic but diabolical woman who creates a double identity for Benigni's character. Benigni's wife, Nicoletta Braschi, plays Maria, who notices Dante's physical resemblance to her husband, Johnny Stecchino, a mafia boss in hiding. Maria brings Dante to Sicily in order to stage Johnny's death and have Dante play the part of the corpse at Johnny's funeral, thus allowing Johnny to assume Dante's identity. As with Nina in *Il piccolo diavolo/The Little Devil,* who ends up being the real devil in the film, Maria plays a double game with both Johnny and Dante, whom Agata, the lawyer (Paolo Bonacelli), and other Maria collaborators refer to as *il fesso* (the fool).

Through the commonplace of mistaken identity central to classical comedy, Dante, the innocent if mischievous bus driver, enters the double-dealing upper echelons of Italian political power. Dante's unknowing impersonation of the mafia boss is a negation of society's codes and power structures. Dante meets government ministers and is paraded at the Palermo opera house before the flower of Sicilian society. In Benigni's parallel between Dante and Johnny Stecchino, small-time criminality and lack of civic standards among the Italian people explain the larger picture of corruption and organized criminality. What in northern Italy are innocuous infringements of civic virtue are sources of cultural disintegration in southern Italy, where a sense of civic responsibility has either decayed or never been firmly entrenched.[1] Dr. Randazzo, the insurance investigator who catches Dante's fraud, represents the austerity and serious commitment to law and order that is stereotypical of northern Italy. In Sicily, the state representatives are far less rigorous in their observance of legality.

After Dante steals a banana, Judge Cattaratta advises him not to collaborate with the police. Dante, misinterpreting this advice, returns to the police station and finds the reporting officer eating the stolen banana in a parody of the *pentito* (penitent) witness protection program. The final statement on the mafia and the southern Italian culture is anything but conciliatory. In one of the last scenes, Dante leads a grotesque chorus of mafia hit men in the same barnyard song sung by handicapped students at the beginning of the film. The inference is that the mafia is an organization for the mentally retarded.

The film also presents a criticism of Italian government and religious officials. At the party sequence at the end of the film, Dante subverts the social etiquette of the table of power where all the functionaries of the political and religious establishment have come to dine: a cocaine-sniffing minister who is involved with the mafia; the police; and a cardinal. Benigni's Dante releases a Rabelaisian vitality into the static acceptance of criminality. He lifts up the skirt of the minister's wife and attempts to feed the cardinal the illegal drugs that are the source of underworld profits and political power.

The religious themes that were so prevalent in Benigni's earlier films are absent from *Johnny Stecchino*. However, themes concerning U.S. influence are still extant, although somewhat subdued when compared to *Non ci resta che piangere/Nothing Left to Do but Cry*. When Dante enters the Grand Hotel unknowingly masquerading as the mafia boss Johnny Stecchino, he passes the inspection of the doorman/guard by pretending to speak American English with Maria. Also, the real mafia boss in the film, like his namesake from the Billy Wilder film *Some Like It Hot* (1959), is not the traditional Sicilian family head whose roots are in rural culture. Johnny is an international gangster who brags about the time he spent in New York. The character is an oblique reference to the changes in traditional culture seen in Benigni's early work. But Maria and Johnny's mafia enemy, Cozzamara, reaffirms ancient mafia codes. Johnny admits to Maria that he accidentally killed Cozzamara's wife. It is due to this transgression of patriarchal codes that Maria decides to betray Johnny.

*Johnny Stecchino* opens with the same cityscape from *The Little Devil* that also returns in *Il mostro / The Monster*. In *Johnny Stecchino*, a Boccaccio-like gang no longer surrounds Cioni as in *Berlinguer ti voglio bene / Berlinguer I Love You*. However, the roots of the Benigni/Cioni persona are still evident. Dante, the protagonist, is reticent to speak to women without being overly polite. He is not fully integrated into Italian society, taking Cioni's sense of alienation to an urban setting. The old theme of Cioni's oedipal trajectory is transferred to Johnny Stecchino, who identifies his wife, Maria, with his mother. Johnny's fastidious abhorrence of dirt and aversion to kissing is directly opposed to the orally fixated nature of Maria, who sucks cake frosting from Dante's finger and wipes dirt on her dresses.

Benigni again casts himself as a teacher and guardian to youth, happy in his job as a bus driver for learning-disabled students with whom he improvises a barnyard song on the calls of different animals at the zoo. Dante also teaches Maria a children's word game in which one player places his hands over the ears of the other person, speaks, and asks the other person to guess what he said. The result is a nonsensical interpretation of language as the social function, and communicative aspects of language are rendered meaningless, a theme repeated from *The Little Devil*.

A further play on language is in the Grand Hotel scene in which Dante pretends to speak English, a gag first seen in *Clair de femme* (1979) when Benigni plays a bartender who speaks a mixture of French and Italian. However, the language games in *Johnny Stecchino* are not as surrealistic as in *The Little Devil*. *Johnny Stecchino* is a return to a more traditional form of comedy based on double entendre and linguistic wordplay rather than the complete rejection of language, as in *The Little Devil*. Cerami has identified the basic structure of such routines as a format known as *la vacca e la moglie* (the cow and the wife). One speaker is speaking about his wife but the listener thinks he is talking about a cow, or worse, a prostitute. Benigni employs this setup in *Johnny Stecchino* in the double meanings of the insurance fraud routine and the banana theft.

*Johnny Stecchino* has metacinematic moments in which Benigni not only ascribes to a self-referential aspect of his comic persona but also to the comic traditions of cinema. Besides the title citation from Billy Wilder's *Some Like It Hot* (1959), there are gags that recall the character doubling in the silent films of Charlie Chaplin and Buster Keaton, as well as sequences that owe a debt to the Marx Brothers *A Night at the Opera* (1935). There is a notable lessening of the racier or semiobscene material, particularly when compared to *Berlinguer I Love You*.

The film also marks the first occasion in which Benigni makes a conscious parody of an established genre. Johnny is a gangster antihero whose working-class roots clash with the immense wealth that he has accumulated or stolen as a mafia boss. True to genre, Johnny's death at the end of the film affirms middle class morality. But *Johnny Stecchino* reverses the expectation of genre with a continuation of the female domination from *The Little Devil.* In the last scenes Maria walks away from Johnny's ambush to the admiring gaze of the mafia hit men, the *picciotti,* recalling the revenge-seeking mafia molls of previous Italian films such as *Sessomatto (La vendetta)* (1975) or *A ciascuno il suo* (1967).

Johnny Stecchino was a tremendous box-office success in Italy and was even distributed in the United States. However, in terms of a directing style Benigni was still tied to the performance-dominated model displayed since *Tu mi turbi.* It would not be until his next film, *The Monster,* that Benigni would present his running themes of ex-peasant alienation in a manner where the camera becomes an interpreter of a social reality that complements his comedic body rather than merely records it.

## NOTE

1. For an Anglo-American perspective on the southern Italian question, see Robert Putnam, *Making Democracy Work: Civic Traditions in Modern Italy* (Princeton, N.J.: Princeton University Press, 1997).

# · *10* ·

# Cioni in the City: Part 3

## IL MOSTRO/THE MONSTER

*T*he third film in the Cioni-in-the-city trilogy, *Il mostro/The Monster* (1994), repeats the successful angelic/adversarial woman and switch-of-identity formula. Instead of being used as the double for a mafia boss, the Benigni character, Loris, is mistaken for a serial killer, and the genre spoofed is the psycho/thriller film. Once more, Benigni's film received unexpected publicity. The film's title led many in Italy to think of the serial killer near Florence whose crimes have remained unsolved since the late 1960s. *Mostro* in Italian means "monster" but may also refer to a serial killer. A suspect from the Tuscan countryside, later acquitted, was captured and tried while the film was in theaters. Although an unintended coincidence, like the anti-Catholic message in *Il piccolo diavolo/The Little Devil* or the mafia spoof in *Johnny Stecchino,* the connection proved to be a boon for publicizing the film.

In *The Monster* the impersonal world of media culture and high capitalism is juxtaposed with Benigni's character, the nonconformist Loris. The film opens as a helicopter descends to the murder scene of the serial killer's latest victim, in what seems like an homage to the opening of Fellini's *La dolce vita* (1960). Loris lives in an apartment building near the murder site. Like *Johnny Stecchino* and part of *The Little Devil, The Monster* is set in the outskirts of the postindustrial Italian metropolis in the midst of brutally impersonal and dysfunctional, Gropius-style apartment buildings. Beginning with the film's opening sequence, *The Monster* alternates between settings in the personal space of Loris's apartment and the impersonal space of the public.

The urban setting has a political subtext through Benigni's concurrent jokes about Silvio Berlusconi, the Italian real estate and media magnate who made his fortune developing high rises on the outskirts of Milan. In 1994 Berlusconi's right-wing political party Forza Italia led the Pole of

Liberty coalition in a defeat of the ex-communist Olive Branch Coalition of the PDS (Partito Democratico della Sinistra). Benigni supported the PDS to the point of hugging and straddling members of the PDS leadership in public. The condominium's president in *The Monster,* who tries to evict Loris, has been widely identified with Berlusconi. The president may be the brunt of Loris's antics, but Benigni's clown character is not a member of the collectivity. The other tenants do not second his opposition to the president's rule. At a condominium meeting, Loris makes a speech that targets the impersonality of bureaucratic language and proposes himself as condominium president—a scene cut from the U.S. print. But angry tenants chase him off the stage into a basketball hoop, and he leaves the meeting muttering "*Vaffanculo la maggioranza* (To hell with the majority)," an echo of Alberto Sordi's imprecation against the working class in Fellini's *I vitelloni* (1953). The scene also recalls Benigni's rallies in the late 1970s in which he spoofed political meetings.[1]

Loris, like Dante in *Johnny Stecchino,* is an outsider who maintains his individuality by living against the norms of consumer society. He avoids paying for anything, including food and rent, and gets service at a bar by pantomiming the actions of paying customers. In another reference to Berlusconi, Loris steals food, foiling the security system of a gigantic supermarket by placing antishoplifting censors on unsuspecting customers. Besides his interests in the media and real estate, Berlusconi also owned a large supermarket chain in Italy, the Standa. As part of the modern cityscape, the supermarket has replaced the traditional family shop in *Johnny Stecchino,* where Dante stole bananas. However, Loris is not respectful to traditional proprietors. He sends a telegram announcing his death to a family-owned jewelry store, to which he owes money.

Benigni continues the challenge to language seen in *The Little Devil* and *Johnny Stecchino,* but in *The Monster* the target is urban consumer society. The rejection of meaning in *The Monster* extends to the objects that the protagonist adapts to his existence outside the economy. In a scene similar to ones in *Johnny Stecchino,* in which Dante cannot drive a bus in forward and thinks that a car cigarette lighter is disposable, Loris plays with a television remote control by pretending it is a cellular telephone. He places the antitheft sensors at a supermarket on other customers and workers in order to subvert the alarm system. In *Johnny Stecchino,* the misinterpretation of the meaning of an object, such as the banana, or a gesture, such as the minister's limp, confused Dante into misreading the signs of hermetic mafia culture. In *The Monster,* Loris's adversary is the object-driven consumer society of the urban north and the panoptic police state that falsely accuses him because of his reaction to and trouble with common objects such as chainsaws, mannequins, pickaxes, butcher knives, and screwdrivers. Loris's Keatonesque accidents become the signs of presumed guilt. Loris's trouble with objects could be interpreted in terms of carnival imagery as assertion of the unity between objects and the earth, the universal body that grows and recreates itself.[2] But the number of references to a consumer culture point to a more contemporary meaning for the hostility toward inanimate objects.

The themes of fashion and the commercialization of the human image from *The Little Devil* reappear in *The Monster*. Loris's job is to transport store-window mannequins. The fashion show from *The Little Devil* is repeated in the numerous outfits worn by the undercover police officer Jessica, played by Nicoletta Braschi: zippered leather jacket, schoolteacher suit, snakelike dress, lingerie, maid outfit, red and gold evening gowns, and, finally, a Little Red Riding Hood outfit. The antifashion theme is continued with a brief shot of Loris's closet full of identical dark gray suits, Benigni's comedian's uniform.

The conflict between the Benigni persona and consumer society is also played out in the use of language. Loris takes Chinese lessons in hopes of finding employment with a Chinese multinational corporation, a repetition of the language confusion gags that appear in nearly every Benigni film. In *The Monster,* Benigni portrays Chinese as an impenetrable language. Loris's lesson with his Chinese teacher, in which he recites an absurd version of the multiplication table in Chinese, recalls a scene from *The Little Devil,* in which Maurizio asks Giuditta if he has ever been to school. Loris's attempts to learn Chinese could be read as a reference to the incapacity of Italians of Benigni's generation to learn foreign languages. Loris's explanation for his failure—that the first question in his Chinese entry exam, "How are you?" must have been in dialect—seems like a reference to the peasant culture of his upbringing. However, for contemporary Italy the skit is relevant not for the Chinese tongue but for English, the language actually required for entry into the business world. In any event, Benigni's clown persona confronts a consumer society that requires a linguistic rejection of the Italian indigenous culture. The villain of the film turns out to be an Italian who earns a livelihood from immersion in foreign culture, the Chinese professor, the purveyor of the foreign tongue.

Benigni's lampoon of the verbal codes of consumer society is best expressed when Loris's employer, Pascucci, advises him to counteract the sexual provocation by Jessica, the undercover policewoman, by reciting economic figures and exchange rates. Loris's robotlike recitation of the jargon of the neoliberal economy becomes a verbal cold shower. For Cerami, the creation of capitalistic wealth explains the decline in physical urges and the subsequent decline in Italian national nativity. In Cerami's theatrical homage to Pasolini's *Dorme che è ancora notte* discussed previously, Ninetto is not interested in Luna's displays because of his absorption in materialism. In *The Monster,* Loris denies sexual provocation through a forced repetition of the jargon of the exchange economy. Incidentally, the conversation between Pascucci and Loris takes place on a modernist public sculpture inappropriate for human interaction.

Jessica's provocations, a repetition of Nina's displays in *The Little Devil,* are performed by order of Paride Tacconi, the police psychologist. As in the earlier film, Nicoletta Braschi assumes a role as an enemy agent, ready to entice a feminized Cioni character. If the female protagonist in these films aims to entrap the Cioni character, she is never the agent of her own destiny but always the representative of a greater power: the diabolic netherworld in *The Little Devil,* the mafia in *Johnny Stecchino,* and the panoptic police state in *The Monster.* Despite this subservience to a greater system, the female characters have ultimate power over the Benigni-Cioni persona. When Giuditta and Nina both inhabit Giuditta's body in *The Little Devil,* it is Nina who is in physical control. In *Johnny Stecchino,* Maria decides to betray her mafia-boss husband and abandons Dante to enjoy her life as a free, rich, and beautiful woman, in the words of Johnny's rival, Cozzamara. In *The Monster,* Jessica is armed with a gun and is ready to kill Loris should he make a sexual advance. In the first half of *La vita è bella/Life Is Beautiful,* the woman again has the power. Dora is rich, beautiful, and engaged to the most powerful and rising fascist in town.

In *The Monster,* with Braschi's fashion show of outfits to entice Loris, as in classical cinema the woman is paraded as the man watches and decides on action. However, if the female is the object of attention, in Benigni's films the female characters also observe the Benigni-trickster persona as he subverts dominant society. The Benigni persona attracts the female protagonist as a subverting agent living in contrast to society. The surveillance camera depicting Loris as a serial killer is projected for an audience exclusively of policewomen. The Benigni persona does not necessarily provoke a sexual gaze but what may be called subversion voyeurism, inciting the iconoclastic desire to rebel in the female characters. Jessica eventually abandons the positivistic line of her police psychologist superior, Tacconi.

Loris's role as a subverting agent is expressed in the police surveillance film within a film, where Benigni toys with the idea of the photographic image as an objective record. The all-knowing spectators in the theater are first presented with a version of events that Benigni, as director, poses as the truth. A series of accidents cause Loris's spastic, physical reactions. A cigarette butt falls into Loris's pants and a jeweler chases him to collect a debt. Benigni's version for spectators is staged with a camera style dominated by three-quarter shots, a standard format for comic vignettes. The performance basis and visual narratives borrow heavily from Keaton and Chaplin. The bar scene adopts gags from Chaplin's *The Gold Rush,* and Loris's avoidance of the jeweler bill collector recalls Keaton's chase sequences.

These establishing sequences are followed by a police surveillance film of the same time period for an audience of policewomen, narrated by the police psychologist, Tacconi. The surveillance film begins with landscape shots. The camera then zooms in to identify Loris's deviant behavior. The screening room technician edits the film for narration by Tacconi. In this film within a film, a feminized Loris is the object of attention of female spectators. Loris's feminization is further proven by the film's reversal of sexual roles from the psycho/thriller and horror genre. Loris's decision not to act on the physical impulses caused by Jessica's provocations actually saves his life. In the last conversation between Jessica and Loris, Jessica reveals that had he made a sexual advance, she may have shot him. Like the "good girl" in a psycho/thriller film, Loris survives because he controlled his sexual impulses.

A constant in the Benigni films since *Berlinguer ti voglio bene/ Berlinguer I Love You* is a theme of violence toward women. In *Johnny Stecchino,* Johnny callously recounts how he accidentally murdered the wife of his rival, Cozzamara. *The Monster* revolves around a serial killer whose victims are disemboweled women. In the opening scene a reverse zoom reveals a murdered woman lying in an elevator; the elevator door repeatedly opens and closes on her foot, separating it, visually, from the rest of her body. It is not difficult to find castration anxiety in Benigni's films as a continuation of the oedipal theme from *Berlinguer I Love You.* That film focused on the oedipal triangle formed by Bozzone, Mammina, and Cioni, with displays of violence against women, such as the theater lobby posters. In psychoanalytical theory, female fetishism is a reaction to the fear of castration, in which the subject seeks a male physical identity in the female to deny difference and act out the desire for reunification with the mother. Benigni turns this theory around in his film within a film. A female audience masquerading as males, complete with phallic props (guns), observes Loris's film image. They are forced to watch a film in which his double image, created by police editing, seems to castrate himself. Actually, Loris is smacking his groin in an attempt to extinguish a cigarette that has fallen into his pants.

The irony in a psychological interpretation of Benigni's films is that such readings are mercilessly lampooned in *The Monster* in the absurd positivism of the police psychologist, Tacconi, who extrapolates fables and insists on dressing Jessica like Little Red Riding Hood. For Tacconi, police work should be reduced to a psychological experiment that is a sort of peep show he titles "niente tregua per Loris (no break for Loris), un bombardamento osceno (an obscene bombardment)." The psychoanalytic references reinforce the theme of Benigni's criticism of the intellectual class. Central to Tacconi's approach is the adaptation of fairy tales and fables to explain urban deviancy. Tacconi even cites an article, "I fantasmi e le favole nello stupro modern dai 'Tre porcellini' al mostro di Rostov (Ghosts and Fables in Modern Rape from the Three Little Pigs to the Monster of Rostov)," by Andersen. Historically, fables were stories with origins in the oral traditions of the peasantry, adapted by the middle and upper classes to impart a preventive lesson to the inexperienced and to inculcate a sense of justice and reward for personal initiative. But in the consumer society of *The Monster,* fables become the model that class intellectuals, such as Tacconi, use to identify sociopathic behavior.

The role of the intellectual is further lampooned in the character of the Chinese professor. He has the skills needed to gain entry into the exchange economy, and yet consumer satisfaction is of no use to him. He prefers to objectify things (women's body parts) that are not exchangeable goods. The professor's guilt also reverses the structure of the psycho/thriller genre, where the plot often centers on the brute force and bestial behavior of a working-class villain who threatens the procreative future by murdering middle-class women. In *The Monster,* the victims' class status is reversed. The first victim is identified as a nurse, a member of the working class.

The direction in Benigni's earlier films emphasized his comic body in a manner similar to the style of television comedy skits. In *The Monster,* Benigni's directing style strives to re-create the style of the silent comedy. There is a preference for a static camera and a notable reduction in the number of close-ups in *Johnny Stecchino. The Monster* develops as a series of proscenium arches with the opening scene of the nymphomaniac, the parking garage, the condominium meeting, supermarket, and police screening room. Other debts to classic comedians include the homage to Totò in the telephone dance and Keaton in the final chase sequences. Another influence on film style, cinematically and thematically, is from cartoons. A cartoon by Franco Mattichio accompanies the opening credits and two cameos of Tex Avery cartoons are featured. These U.S. cartoons of the 1940s were rebroadcast in Italy in the early 1990s as a companion to the *Blob* television blooper program that preceded the RAI 3 evening news program.

Benigni experiments in *The Monster* with the possibility of an altered reality, offered by the manipulation of the photographic image. In the police surveillance film Benigni presents two views of the same series of events when Loris leaves home, goes to a bar, and runs to escape a bill collector. One sequence is presented to the cinema audience, and the other is filmed for an audience of policewomen. Each action in the two short films evokes a different response. Thus Benigni reveals the power of the point of view and the possibility of different interpretations of the objective reality. Benigni's double version of reality in *The Monster* is also a comment on the idea that the spectators' privileged position is a metaphor for the rational calculations of a consumer to make a purchase. Benigni's film points out flaws in the idea of spectator omniscience by confronting his audience with the reality of the illusion inherent in the photographic image.

The surveillance film ends with a freeze-frame of a satisfied Loris, who is relieved that his private parts are not aflame. Yet the policewomen read the same image as a sadomasochistic glare. Reality is distorted and enlarged in order to convey the message desired by the police/intellectual system voiced by Tacconi. An earlier example is the police composite photograph of Loris's face, taken from his chainsaw victim. Loris's face seems fatter because of the technique of pasting together a series of otherwise unrelated photographs. Similarly, the police surveillance footage is a version of reality that is altered to serve the panoptic system. Benigni's dual film effectively separates the levels of ideology present in the film between that of the police surveillance view of Loris and the cinema spectators' view of him as a harmless clown. Paradoxically, the police surveillance film must be recognized as more realistic because of its handheld naturalism.

Before the final chase scene, Loris's television-transmitted image as serial killer becomes a joke in which his image has replaced reality.[3] The television broadcast of Loris's police-composite photograph unleashes mass hysteria, and a crowd forms in front of Loris's apartment building awaiting news of the alleged serial killer's arrest. The impulse of a crowd observing an accident is a well-documented phenomenon in which the mixture of identification and separation from the object of horror attracts viewers. The true victim of the police/intellectual/media complex is this mob that chases Loris. Benigni's treatment of the mob mentality may be another fable reference (Chicken Little) as Loris takes the crowd on a Keaton-and-Chaplin-inspired chase, finally eluding them. Loris climbs up the scaffolding of the high-rise apartment building and jumps down a construction site garbage chute, becoming an object of refuse. After Loris's escape, his pursuers remain motionless on the scaffolding, looking at the camera in a shot that encompasses the entire edifice. The role of the privileged spectator is reversed and a parallel forms between the mob manipulated into thinking that Loris is guilty and the theater spectators expecting the guilt of the police or the condominium president. Hints in the plot lead spectators to believe that the serial killer will be one of Jessica's police superiors in what would have been a comic version of the political commentary of Petri's *Indagine su un cittadino al di sopra di ogni sospetto* (1970). The police investigators react with trembling excitement to any news regarding the serial killer and Jessica feels the power of their gaze when she buttons up her blouse in the commissioner's office.

The film's ending evokes Fritz Lang's *M* (1931), when the serial killer is given away by a tune he whistles. In *The Monster*, the guilt of the Chinese professor is revealed by the jingle of a Chinese charm doll. As in *M*, the identification of guilt is turned back to the spectators for their participation in the system. Benigni even includes a brief scene of a patient being led away in a straitjacket at Tacconi's clinic, as in Lang's *Dr. Marbuse* (1922) in which the psychologist is the criminal.

However, the parallel between Nazi Germany and the brief reign of Berlusconi in Italy is a bit stretched. The ex-communists in the PDS (Partito Democratico della Sinistra) did gain political advantages from the *Tangentopoli* political corruption scandals and ensuing prosecutions of the mid-1990s that focused on Berlusconi's cronies in the Italian Socialist Party, and on ex-premier Bettino Craxi in particular. In the film, Loris continually accuses the condominium president of embezzlement. When the mob gathers at the apartment building to arrest the serial killer, Loris is convinced that the culprit is the president.[4] Ironically, the accused serial killer who dominated Italian headlines when *The Monster* was released was the product of the naturalistic cruelty of Tuscan peasantry that was alluded to in Benigni's first film, *Berlinguer I Love You*—far removed from Benigni's imagined Berlusconian consumer surveillance state.

The film ends on quite a conservative note and with an homage to Chaplin's *Modern Times*.[5] In a recurring gag, Loris tries to sneak past the condominium doorman by walking in a squat. An elderly gentleman, played by Massimo Girotti, a screen star since the 1930s, observes Loris. The Girotti character's polite greetings and questions about family life to Loris and Jessica make him a representative of traditional Italy. He asks the squatting couple, "A quando un figlio (When can we expect a child)?" Until the gentleman's question, children in *The Monster* had been negative. One of Loris's neighbors, a young girl with an American name, Sue Ellen, even tosses a dead cat into his apartment. Yet Benigni's character still plays the role of a teacher; but his pupil is Jessica, the policewoman played by Braschi. Loris's lesson for Jessica is not about reconnection with the natural world, as in *Chiedo asilo,* or the joys of physicality, as in *The Little Devil.* Loris's intellectual function is to train the policewoman Jessica how to live in opposition to consumer society.

## NOTES

1. *Il comizio* (1978) is a short film that captures one of Benigni's spoof political rallies in Tuscany with Carlo Monni.
2. Michael Bachtin, *L'opera di Rabelais e la cultura popolare riso, carnevale e festa nella tradizione medievale e rinascimentale,* trans. Mili Romano (Turin: Einaudi, 1995), p. 46.
3. Jean Baudrillard, *Simulations,* trans. P. Foss, P. Patton, and P. Beitchman, (New York: Semiotext(e), 1983).
4. Before the release of *The Monster,* screenwriter Vincenzo Cerami had edited a collection of theatrical works by the 1930s comedian Ettore Petrolini, whose *Nerone* piece has been identified as a lampoon of Mussolini. (Ettore Petrolini, *Bravo! Grazie! Antologia petroliniana,* ed. Vincenzo Cerami [Rome: Theoria, 1992].) The spirit of Petrolini's nonsensical use of language in works such as *Fortunello* may be seen in Benigni attacks on the condominium manager identifiable with Berlusconi in *The Monster.*
5. Vito Zagarrio, *Cinema italiano anni novanta* (Venice: Marsilio Editori, 1998), p. 18.

# La vita è bella/Life Is Beautiful

*La vita è bella/Life Is Beautiful,*[1] cowritten with Vincenzo Cerami, is one of the most internationally successful non-English language films in cinema history. The film triumphed at the Cannes Film Festival and at the Academy Awards, where it was recognized as Best Foreign Film. Benigni also took home the Oscar for best actor, achieving a recognition for the Italian cinema unseen since Sophia Loren won similar recognition for her starring role in Vittorio de Sica's *Two Women* (1960).[2] This success catapulted Benigni onto the international stage, making him a name sought after in Hollywood. However, the film stirred a great deal of controversy, particularly over the delicate question of the suitability of using comedy to depict the Holocaust by Nazi Germany.

In Benigni's previous films the contrast between Benigni's jocular or giullaresque approach and the underlying terror of such subjects as the mafia or serial killers provided occasions for comedy. Like Benigni's previous protagonists—Dante, Loris, and Giuditta—Guido in *Life Is Beautiful* subverts societal order with a carnival-like suspension of the rules, a reversal of power relationships.[3] For example, when Guido replaces the school inspector at Dora's school, he sticks the tricolor sash between his legs and performs a mock striptease before teachers and students who had expected a speech endorsing racism. As in his earlier films, Benigni uses the lower body in order to ridicule the pomp and affectation of the cerebral, official upper body in an expression of Rabelaisian vitality and rebellion.

With the Holocaust, however, Benigni tackled a subject whose aura of historical defeat and pessimistic resignation to evil was much more profound than the topics he had chosen before. The simple Rabelaisian contrast between lower and upper body, between unofficial and official society, would not seem to be enough to deconstruct a subject of such inherent horror and collective guilt as the Holocaust. After the Holocaust, critics wondered about the possible effects of the event on the human soul and artistic expression. Critics have doubted anything would be able to explain Auschwitz in a manner suitable for rational comprehension.[4] Some also voiced concerns that lyric poetry would be impossible after Auschwitz. The difficulty in representing the event is that it breaks down the commonplaces of genre. The camps were ruthlessly efficient at eliminating any act of nobility needed for tragedy. Similarly, the sense of societal affirmation in classical comedy, which ends in marriage and promise of procreation, is not applicable to the event.[5] The most evocative accounts, such as the memoirs of Primo Levi, communicate a sense of detachment perhaps needed to approach the subject without complete despair.

At first glance Benigni's Tuscan clown persona seems out of place in such a context. When the subject of *Life Is Beautiful* became public knowledge, there was apprehension, due to Benigni's reputation, that he might not approach the subject with appropriate sobriety and respect. Benigni has commented on this prejudice as a sort of artistic bigotry against comedians.[6] Benigni insists that it is natural for him as a comedian to approach tragic subjects, although he has recognized the difficulty in switching from comic to more serious theme, due to what he admits is his inherently comical physical presence.[7] The idea of a comedian or comedy director attempting a film involving Nazi Germany is not new. Other films often mentioned in comparison to *Life Is Beautiful* include Lubitsch's film with Jack Benny, *To Be or Not to Be* (1942), Mel Brooks's *The Producers* (1968), Chaplin's *The Great Dictator* (1940), and Jerry Lewis's never released *The Day the Clown Cried* (1972), in which Lewis plays a clown, Helmut Drook, who performs for children destined for the gas chambers. Given the potential pitfalls of the subject, the story line of *Life Is Beautiful* was kept under tight secrecy until the film was released.

Benigni's film was partly inspired by the experiences of his father, Luigi, who spent time at a Nazi work camp during the war. Luigi Benigni was drafted into the Italian army that occupied Albania. He was forced into a camp after the Italian monarchy switched sides on September 8, 1943, following the Allied invasion of Sicily. Benigni has claimed that conditions in his father's camp were comparable to those in the death camps, with the important difference that there were no gas chambers. Benigni also recalls that his father never retold the story of his internment in a way that would frighten or depress his children. This respect and protection of innocence made a profound impact on Benigni, who sought to repeat his father's approach to the subject.

This memory of Luigi Benigni's stories led Benigni and Cerami to construct the film as a fable.[8] Benigni made extensive use of common-places of fables in his previous films with a stylistic debt to the fabulous current in the Italian cinema in works of Zavattini, with whom Benigni had an extended apprenticeship. *Il piccolo diavolo/The Little Devil* is a devil tale. *Non ci resta che piangere/Nothing Left to Do but Cry* is a time-travel tale. *Johnny Stecchino* could be interpreted as a mafia fable. In *Il mostro/The Monster,* the intellectual elite of psychiatrists and police officers misuse fables and fairy tales to explain sociopathic behavior. In *Life Is Beautiful,* Benigni returns to the fable as a defense against the sociopathology of Nazi-fascism. The opening scenes with Giosué's adult voice introducing the film as a fable add an element of omniscience that conditions the specta-tor's interpretation of the film. The spectator is led to believe that there will be a happy ending due to the comforting knowledge that a narrator, later identified as Giosué, will survive.

The reconstruction of the camp as a brick rather than as wooden-frame complex adds to the fable setting. Benigni has stated that the camp was constructed to represent the concentration camps, not just the lagers of World War II.[9] However, there is an Italian source for the stage set of which Benigni was aware: the Risiera at San Sabba in Trieste, one of three concentration camps in Italy. It is a former factory building made of brick that resembles the complex in *Life Is Beautiful.* However, San Sabba did not have gas chambers and the barracks were small cells that packed eight prisoners at a time. It was used mainly for detainment and interrogation rather than extermination, a task assigned to camps further north.[10] Thus the barracks in *Life Is Beautiful* are a hybrid between the San Sabba factory setting and more familiar Auschwitz-like images, such as the multiple lay-ers of boards for bedding and the single train track under a clock tower where the deportees arrive for selection.

The fable approach is evident in the plot structure of the film. Guido assumes the role of regenerating prince in the first half of the film, when he substitutes for the king of Italy in a parade. Nicoletta Braschi, again, plays an angelic woman; Guido calls her *Principessa* (Princess). She lands on Guido's lap as a gift from heaven, willing to abandon wealth and fam-ily for an ideal love story. Braschi plays up the character's childishness and rebelliousness.[11] But as with other elements in the film, Braschi's charac-ter exists on a higher level than in Benigni's previous films, as indicated by her decision to follow her husband and son to the camp.

In fables the normal rules of society and even physical reality are sus-pended with the introduction of fantasy elements, such as magic or sor-cery. Because of the suspension of normality, events between characters in a fable take place on a plane outside of historical time.[12] The key to a protagonist's success in a fable is the ability not only to act effectively, but also to use language to trick the ogre with a strategic lie that serves as an edifying lesson. One example is Gretel's lie to the blind witch in "Hansel and Gretel" that the oven is not working so that she may push the witch inside.

The Nazi deportations and extermination camps were a negation of the laws of civilized behavior, a reality based on violence and horror that was skewed to the extent that a sense of disbelief was one of the first reactions of newly arrived inmates. Benigni's plot setup, in which the father retells the rules of the camp to his son as a game, makes use of this historical reaction of disbelief. As in a fable, the protagonist adapts to the hostile rules of his enemies by re-creating them for his own benefit. The difference from a standard fable structure is that in *Life Is Beautiful,* Guido as protagonist does not lie only to the villains. He also lies to his son, his heir, in order to preserve not only his son's life but also his mental stability.

Nietzsche, in words that seem to anticipate the spell that Hitler and Mussolini cast over their countries, wrote that it is vital for the deceiver to believe in the sincerity of his own deception.[13] The theme of deception, or self-deception, in the film makes allusions to those who suffered the consequences of Nazi dictates. Benigni has commented that the boy Giosué is much more aware of the reality around him than his father Guido may believe. Benigni has pointed to the scene in which the grandmother visits Guido's stationery shop shortly before their deportation. The boy knows who the grandmother is, although they have never been introduced.

Guido spends the entire film, like a contemporary audience that may be unfamiliar with the historical facts, not wanting to believe the worst about humanity and insisting on protecting his son from the terrible knowledge of the camps. In the first half of the film Guido objects to his uncle's initial warnings about the vandals who ransacked his house and later painted his horse green. Guido then subverts and rejects the ideology that led to the Holocaust by impersonating the government minister who was expected to give a talk on racist anthropology at Dora's school. Guido's parody and comic striptease are in the best tradition of lower bodily humor. He jumps on the table and makes the Nazi/fascist ideology risible to the audience of Italian schoolchildren in a *saltimbanco* (mountebank) performance that alludes to the possibility to fool or charm the masses. At the camp, Giosué questions his father's "rules of the game" but eventually has the wisdom to accept the illusion.

Benigni, as a director attempting to portray the horrors to which

German civilization sank under the Nazis, insists on the playful aspects of life, echoing Nietzsche's identification of a similarity between the jocular impulses of artists and children in *The Birth of Tragedy*. For Nietzsche nihilism lays in attempts to find order and reason in a reality devoid of such attributes. Benigni's insistence on play and his own role as an artist capable of creating and sustaining the illusion presented in *Life Is Beautiful* could be interpreted in this philosophical vein.

The film's theme of denial of reality also reveals the possibility of a continuing influence from Zavattini and Pasolini. These icons of the Italian cinema made dramas that approached the subject of the atrocities resulting from fascism with plots premised on such a denial. Zavattini wrote the screenplay for De Sica's film *The Condemned of Altona* (1963), based on Sartre's play of the same title. The film recounts the tale of a German ex-officer who hides in his attic, unable to accept the fact that the war has ended because his conscience will not allow him to return to normal life. De Sica and Zavattini's *The Garden of the Finzi-Contini*, based on the Bassani novel, depicts a wealthy Jewish family in Ferrara who cling to the comfort of their aristocratic existence behind the walls of their estate until they are deported. Pasolini's *Salò 100 Days of Sodom* (1975) is a hermetic world of torture and perversion set in the puppet state created by the Nazi-fascists in northern Italy in the waning years of the war. In these films the insistence on not accepting, or in the case of Pasolini's *Salò* of perpetuating, an abhorrent reality is a parable for the manner in which the war and the Holocaust lowered the threshold of human behavior. When Guido re-creates the camp as a game by mistranslating the Nazi guard's instructions, Benigni takes up these themes in a manner suited for his comic persona.

## HOMAGE TO CHAPLIN

Benigni's film is rich in references to the mixture of genre seen in Charlie Chaplin's films *The Great Dictator* (1940) and *Monsieur Verdoux* (1947), in which Chaplin condemned Nazi-fascism. Before the introduction of sound, silent film stars were universally popular because they were translatable into all languages. With *Life Is Beautiful*, Benigni harks back to the universal appeal, the anti-Babel, of silent film. For example, in *The Great Dictator* (1940), Chaplin delivered a screaming parody of the sharp cadences of the German tongue into wilting microphones. With Chaplin's *Modern Times* (1936), spectators finally heard Chaplin's voice in a nonsense language song that mimicked all languages and yet was none, dependent on

Chaplin's pantomime for meaning. In *Life Is Beautiful,* Benigni makes frequent reference to communication difficulties due to language differences. The Nazi guard's orders are first mistranslated by Guido and then translated correctly by Bartolomeo. In the camp dining room, Guido must teach German children to say "thank-you" (*grazie*) in Italian in order to disguise the potentially fatal sign of linguistic difference carried by his son, Giosué.

Benigni also relies on cinematic techniques reminiscent of the silent era in which physical props and visual signs are as important for communication as the verbal. Like the flower and Chaplin's facial expressions in *City Lights* (1931), Benigni's films are replete with running jokes in which a physical prop is the means of communication. Like the banana and hand tremor in *Johnny Stecchino,* there is the exchange of hats with the upholsterer, the smashed eggs on the head of the prefect, and the alternate rules for Giosué's benefit in the camp in *Life Is Beautiful.*

With the references to the silent comic era, Benigni has claimed that he carefully avoided images that could carry a strictly comic connotation, such as a sidecar.[14] Despite Benigni's statements, the second half of the film retains comedic elements. In one scene, Guido struggles to carry an anvil, a cartoon commonplace. In an opening joke Bartolomeo is injured and must receive *punti* (stitches), which Giosué interprets according to Guido's explanation of the camp's point system. In Italian, *punti* also means "points." Finally, in the final chase sequence Guido dresses as a woman and improvises a Keatonesque escape, hanging upside down to avoid a searchlight. Thus even with a subject as horrible as the Holocaust Benigni relies on the Rabelaisian contrast between grotesque lower body vitality and the static upper body of official culture.

In his use of traditionally comic motifs such as anvil carrying and cross-dressing Benigni had to tread a very fine line between effectively deconstructing the power of Nazi imagery with his Rabelaisian method, and offending spectators by seeming to laugh at or within the tragedy of the Holocaust. For Benigni's approach to have any hope of working he had to emphasize the cold, official, and cerebral aspects of Nazi-fascist culture, such as the numbing bureaucracy or the seeming efficiency of the gas chambers, rather than the lower body, animalistic violence and cruelty of the Nazis. The first half of the film, with its emphasis on the oppressive bureaucracy of the fascist state and the satire of the minister's speech to Dora's school, provides the setup for a contrast between Nazi-fascism as official culture and Benigni as a desecrating Rabelaisian clown.

Benigni's physical presence also recalls death and serves to exorcise the audience's fear of mortality and suffering. Like great Italian comedians of

previous generations, such as Totò and Petrolini, Benigni has a physiog-
nomy that announces death, and his liveliness and joyfulness provide a
contrast to this first impression. In fact, all of Benigni's films are permeated
with the shadow of death. Numerous references are made to death by cancer in *Berlinguer ti voglio bene/Berlinguer I Love You,* assassination in *Johnny
Stecchino,* serial killing in *The Monster,* and the Holocaust in *Life Is Beautiful.* In medieval carnival tradition, laughter signaled a victory over all that
is serious, official, authoritarian, and violent.[15] Laughter at popular festivals
was evoked in order to overcome the fear of the beyond and all things
sacred and powerful, including death. Thus the carnival conception of the
world may liberate human consciousness and provide a victory over fear.[16]
Michail Bakhtin wrote of the union between laughter and death in the carnival tradition, with death as a necessary moment in the continuity of life.
In *Pantagruel,* Gargantua's wife dies giving birth to his son, and Gargantua
does not know whether to rejoice or to cry.[17] Benigni's film offers a similar dilemma. Guido's death coincides with the defeat of Nazism and the
survival of his son.

Benigni's film also makes numerous references to previous films that
attempted to mix comic elements under the shadow of a serious historical context. Besides Chaplin, the most evident debt in this respect is to
Fellini and his comic/melancholic memories of life in prewar Italy in
*Amarcord,* where life under fascism is reflected in the pranks and day-to-
day activities of a group of juveniles. *Life Is Beautiful*'s Grand Hotel scene,
designed and filmed by Fellini's cinematographer and set designer Danilo
Donati Tonino Delli Colli, recalls similar sequences in *Amarcord.* The
foggy scene in which Guido and Giosué approach a pile of clearly fake
cadavers recalls a similar sequence in which the grandfather in *Amarcord* is
frightened by a horse in a foggy mist.

## TACKLING A FASCIST PAST WITH
## CHILDHOOD INNOCENCE

Benigni's film, like Fellini's, mixes historical recollections of fascism with
slapstick and lower body humor. In Fellini's film the mitigating factor for
the use of humor in such a setting was innocence. Benigni has stated that
besides the influence of his father's war recollections, the story of *Life Is
Beautiful* was born from the idea of being alone in a concentration camp
with a five-year-old child. Benigni insisted that it would be normal to try
to keep horror from the eyes of a child, even making reference to the lie
that Abraham told while taking his son to be sacrificed in Genesis. Benigni

has also referred to the scene in the bookstore where Giosué sees his grandmother and says good-bye to her in a normal fashion. The child's innocence rises above the squabbles that may have resulted from his grandmother's disapproval of his parents' marriage. It is through this emphasis on innocence, a paradoxical concept given the process of the Holocaust, that rendered such concepts meaningless, by which Benigni seeks to justify the indirect recursion to comic imagery.

By contrasting the violence and evil of the Shoah with the innocence of a child, Benigni and Cerami hark back to the greatest films in the Italian canon. Vittorio De Sica and Cesare Zavattini depicted the injustices and contradictions of Reconstruction Rome though the eyes of Bruno, the son of the poster hanger, in *Ladri di bicidette/The Bicycle Thief* (1948). Roberto Rossellini and Sergio Amidei, in *Roma città aperta/Rome Open City* (1945), presented the brutality of the Nazi occupation of Rome through the eyes of children in an apartment complex who witness the murder of Pina and the execution of Don Pietro. Benigni's film and his costar, child actor Giorgio Cantarini, are very much in the tradition of the neorealist dependence on the reactions of children. The perspectives of Benigni's approach may have a sociological explanation in an Italy whose birthrate has declined rapidly since the industrial boom of the early 1960s, and where traditional agricultural society has been transformed by the influence of a consumer economy. The neorealist emphasis on children in the late 1940s came at a time when children dominated the West demographically. The contemporary audience of *Life Is Beautiful* identifies with a father who is protective of his son in a period in Italian demographic history when children are comparatively rare. In fact, Guido's recreation of the world to preserve Giosué's innocence has been criticized as a metaphor for the manner in which children have become the rulers of consumer society.[18]

Benigni emphasizes the controlling eye of the child in a scene in which Giosué, hidden in a utility box, observes Guido as he is taken away for execution. The camera shows Giosué's reduced field of vision in a sort of rectangular camera obscura.[19] Once Guido realizes that he is within the field of vision of his son, he performs a comic goose step with a broad smile for the benefit of his chuckling son. The nature of film as a medium allows an audience to feel a sense of control of the images being projected. The spectator, due to his privileged position in the screening room, feels that he dominates the world the film portrays due to the laws of perspective, which derive from the camera obscura, from which the camera descends.[20] When Giosué is in the camera–obscura-like box, he accepts his father's version of reality, laughing as Guido is taken away.

Perhaps due to a plot that emphasizes a child's reactions, Benigni has been criticized for patronizing the spectator in the same manner that Guido patronizes Giosué.[21] Benigni's choice of the ogre (Nazi-fascism) and the period of World War II could be seen as a search for ideological certainty, putting Benigni's film in the category of works that use the Holocaust to simplify the lines between good and evil.[22] However, the recursion to a setting in the years immediately preceding and following World War II is part of a long trend in the Italian cinema.[23] Since neorealism the Italian cinema has cultivated the concept of the nation-state as the projection of individual themes and essence of a collective based on the historical memory of the defeat of Nazi-fascism.[24] Just as the western genre has come to represent the essence of U.S. nation building, Italian films such as *Rome Open City,* set in the period surrounding fascism, represent the essence of the Italian political and ideological collective consciousness of the postwar Italian republic.[25]

In the early 1960s many films reexamined Italy's fascist past, a period which had been ignored, perhaps for generational reasons.[26] Films such as *La ragazza di Bube* (1963), *Le quattro giornate di Napoli* (1962), *L'oro di Roma* (1961), and *Il generale Della Rovere* (1959) reemphasized the values of collectivism and political cooperation against Nazi-fascism. In these films the myth of the Resistance was a defining moment in the creation of the postwar Italian republic. It was also a time of high prestige for the communist movement, which suffered periodic defections after the Soviet Union actions in Hungary, Czechoslovakia, and Poland.

By the mid-1970s, films about the fascist period had become less heroic, reflecting the generational decline in the postwar political culture founded on the memory of the Resistance. There were detailed examinations of how fascist culture and mentality turned characters into servile hypocrites. Examples include Bertolucci's *Il conformista/The Conformist* (1970), *Strategia del ragno/Spider Stratagem* (1972), and *1900* (1976); Wertmuller's *Pasqualino Settebellezze/Seven Beauties* (1975), *Film d'amore e anarchia/Love and Anarchy* (1973), and *Fatto di sangue* (1978); Pasolini's *Salo'* (1975); the Tavianis' *La notte di San Lorenzo/The Night of the Shooting Stars* (1982); Comenici's *Il prefetto di ferro* (1977); Visconti's *La caduta degli dei/The Damned* (1969); De Sica's *Giardino dei Finzi-Contini/The Garden of Finzi-Contini* (1970); Fellini's *Amarcord* (1974), *Roma* (1972), and *Intervista* (1987); and Scola's *Una giornata particolare/A Special Day* (1977).

Benigni's adherence to the nostalgia mode with *Life Is Beautiful* could be seen as his adhesion to a hegemonic position in which the nostalgia film presents a strategy of containment, of retention of the political tropes that created the postwar Italian republic. Due to Benigni's close relationship to the progressive political parties in Italy, the film did receive criticism for expressing the new centrism of the Italian left.[27] However, the protagonist Guido is not a political activist and there is no mention of the Italian Resistance against the Nazi-fascists, a movement so important to the political mythology of the postwar Italian republic. Given the anti-American tones of Benigni's earlier films, such as *Nothing Left to Do but Cry*, the ending of *Life Is Beautiful* with the arrival of a U.S. tank presents an ideological shift for Benigni that reflects changes in a postcommunist world. The limitation of a U.S. presence to a smiling GI who gives Guido a ride to his mother may also have reassured U.S. audiences regarding Allied inactivity in stopping the Holocaust.

The prevalence of fascist-era settings could be criticized as a format only able to re-create a past in terms of style.[28] Benigni himself has explained the appeal of the World War II-era film as the manifestation of a cultural identity crisis, even the result of a colonial subordination to the United States, a theme developed in more detail in Benigni's earlier films. The stylistic elements of the nostalgia film set between the 1930s and 1950s reaffirm Italian cultural identity and solve the iconographic challenge of expressing an Italian cultural uniqueness separate from the postwar consumer culture.[29] As demonstrated by the warm reception for such films as *Life Is Beautiful* and *Il postino/The Postman*, Italian films that are successful abroad rely on the folkloric, racial, and cultural stereotypes of the pre- and immediate postwar period.[30]

However, unlike some nostalgically themed Italian films such as Salvatores's *Mediterraneo*, *Life Is Beautiful* does not gloss over the responsibility of the Italian fascist regime that permitted and aided Nazi crimes. The first half of the film is set in 1939, a time of imperial aspirations following Mussolini's victory in Ethiopia, celebrated at the engagement party for Rudolfo and Dora.[31] The film confronts Italian audiences with the image of Italy as an arrogant and aggressive nation, not the country defeated and torn by the civil war that followed the Allied invasion of 1943. *Life Is Beautiful* has specific references to the regime's 1938 *leggi razziali* (racial statutes), by which Jews were prohibited from entering certain professions, intermarriage, owning more than a limited amount of property, and attending public schools. Benigni brilliantly parodies these laws in Guido's explanation for Giosué of the signs prohibiting Jews and dogs from entering stores and again in Guido's comic subversion of the minister's speech on racism at Dora's school.

In the film, Italian war guilt is attenuated by the implicit comparison with German culpability. Benigni's film is far subtler in its recreation of the mood of historical events than has been credited. For example, at Dora and Rudolfo's banquet the schoolteacher lauds the intelligence of the Reich's schoolchildren by citing a math problem in which the object lesson is the economic savings gained from euthanatizing the handicapped. Besides revealing the social Darwinist cruelty and barbarism of Nazism, her anecdote alludes to the Nazi euthanasia program of the late 1930s, an important step leading to the death camps.

Benigni did not rely on caricatures of "the evil German" but merely decided to use German actors. Rather than focusing on stereotypical German efficiency and the modern industrial techniques used to execute Nazi crimes, the film examines the progressive dehumanization that led to the death camps. Benigni's film portrays the pervasiveness of fascist and racist ideology in everyday life. The fascist regime's intrusiveness progresses from the prefect Rodolfo's refusal to issue Guido a business permit to his eventual deportation. The theme of the abuse of power appeared in earlier Benigni films. In *The Monster,* police investigators and a psychologist invade Loris's life in order to frame him as a serial killer. In *Johnny Stecchino,* the government minister is a cocaine-sniffing business colleague of the mafia boss in hiding. In *Life Is Beautiful,* there is a jump from arrogant government service to the idea that an elite of functionaries can appropriate the right to eliminate entire populations due to an insane ideology. With his Rabelaisian effusion of lower body humor Benigni in his teacher/clown role in *Life Is Beautiful* criticizes the pompous and respectable representatives of the repressive system. Guido's rival, the fascist Rodolfo, who ends up with egg on his face, is a city bureaucrat tied to the interests of the government.

Benigni's appearance at Dora and Rudolfo's banquet reveals another aspect to his clown persona. The equation of Benigni's physical appearance with death and suffering extends to scenes having to do with food or eating. Given his thin appearance, Benigni's clown persona is never identified with the enjoyment of food but rather in the disruption of the banquet of high society. Giuditta interrupts the dinner among Father Maurizio's colleagues and the parents of his seminary charges in *The Little Devil.* In *Johnny Stecchino,* Dante disrupts the dinner table of high society. His banana grenade causes a panic in the Palermo opera house and his introduction at the party at the table of the minister and cardinal is a complete subversion of societal protocol. In *The Monster,* Jessica invites Pascucci and his wife to dinner, during which Pascucci's wife panics because she believes Loris is the serial killer. In the first half of *Life Is Beautiful* Guido destroys Rudolfo and Dora's engagement banquet. In the second half of the film the references to abundance are contrasted by the scarcity of food, and Benigni's presence recalls the starving *zanni* of the *commedia dell'arte*.

## INTELLECTUALS AND RIDDLES

The film's treatment and criticism of the status quo is most effective when it turns to an example of a German intellectual to explain the Nazis' destruction of less barbaric traditions of German civilization. Benigni and Cerami give the failed German intellectual in their film the same last name as one of the greatest exponents of the German Enlightenment, Dr. Gotthold Ephraim Lessing (1729–1781).[32] Lessing, a guest at the Grand Hotel, appreciates Guido's company and quick wit. He is an entirely cerebral character disinterested in eating in the first half of the film and unconcerned with the suffering of the deportees in the second.[33] The two play word games and solve riddles together. Lessing speaks Italian and is even reluctant to leave Italy. The Lessing character is in the tradition of nineteenth-century German Romantics, such as Goethe, who made Italy a second home. Lessing reappears in the second half of the film as the camp doctor, a figure with a horrible aura given the record of war criminals such as Rudolf Mengele. Due to Lessing's previous friendship with Guido, there is the expectation that he will be a "good German," who might reject the insanity of the Nazi system.

The riddles from the first half of the film are quite beautiful, even poetic.[34] The final riddle that Lessing asks Guido to solve seems like a metaphor for the cowardice and failure of the better angels of German civilization to resist the Nazis. Lessing asks Guido to name something that is fat, ugly, yellow, and walks about defecating.[35] Lessing claims that the expected answer "duck" is incorrect. The solution to the riddle is something that is "fat, ugly, and yellow," which could be a physical color, perhaps blond. The answer to the riddle seems to be the German people or German intellectuals like Lessing. These fat (rich), ugly, yellow people march about like ducks or geese with the Nazi army parade step, producing infantile excrement. However, Benigni has explained the riddle as "nonsense" that appears at a point of great tension in the plot since Guido expects a more rational response from Lessing. Lessing's retreat into nonsense is a blow for Guido and emphasizes the great tragedy and utter irrationality of the Holocaust. The emphasis on Lessing points out how many Germans reacted to the *Shoah* by retreating into their personal microcosms.[36]

In the first half of *Life Is Beautiful*, Guido's word puzzles and riddles with Lessing provide a reference point for the role of language to create meaning. The hostility of official language that Guido encounters is depicted in his unsuccessful application for a store permit, the sign prohibiting Jews from entering a store, the list of names for the train to the camp, even the graffiti on the horse: *achtung cavallo ebreo* (Attention Jewish horse). Once in the camp Guido uses language to attempt to save his son, not only on a physical level but also on a mental level. As mentioned above, Guido teaches the German children in the officer's quarters to say *grazie* (thank-you), thereby canceling the potentially fatal sign of linguistic difference carried by his son. In a scene of noted implausibility, Guido infiltrates the space of official language in order to greet Dora over the camp public address system and he later sends a love message to her by playing their song, Offenbach's *Barcarolle,* over the dining room phonograph. In the camp Guido creates a reverse world, a mirror image where everything is play instead of horror and Giosué is eventually freed from both language systems (Nazi and Guido). Thus, the film reveals the manner in which ideology as expressed as language may create a paradoxical world of reverse meaning. In fact, the paradox of the film is that Guido's reexplanation of the camp rules and his rebuttal of Giosué's questions about gas chambers and crematoria are much more rational than historic reality.

The film has other references to German intellectuals of the previous century, emphasizing the idea of Nazism as a defeat of the noble traditions of German culture, in particular the traditions of the Enlightenment. Benigni's film could be interpreted as an artistic representation of the idea that the barbarity of Auschwitz rendered obsolete the scientific optimism that grew out of the Enlightenment. In *Life Is Beautiful,* Guido is a fan of the philosophy of Arthur Schopenhauer (1788–1860), an opponent of Hegelian idealism who had a great influence on Wagner and Nietzsche. In his best known work, *The World As Will and Idea,* Schopenhauer wrote that the world that makes up the object of our consciousness is based on the reality of our own will, which Schopenhauer thought was essentially evil. Guido, at Ferruccio's instigation, makes a joke of Schopenhauer's philosophy by preventing Ferruccio from sleeping by repeating the phrase, "Wake up." Guido repeats the trick at a performance of the fourth act of the opera *The Tales of Hoffmann,* by German-born composer Jacques Offenbach (1819–1880) in order to capture Dora's attention. The passing reference to Ernst Hoffmann (1776–1822) could even be read as a reference to Kracauer's explanation of the spell cast over the German people by the Nazis as similar to the plot of Hoffmann's tale *The Sandman.*[37]

The intellectual characters aligned with the hegemonic system in *Life Is Beautiful* (the teacher, Lessing, even the bureaucrat Rodolfo) are portrayed as dangerous fools. This is a thematic carryover from Benigni's earlier films where the representatives of official culture, such as the priest in *The Little Devil* or the cardinal and government minister in *Johnny Stecchino* were the targets of his lower body rebellion and grotesque satire. However, in *Life Is Beautiful* there is a positive intellectual figure. Guido's uncle Eliseo, who runs a restaurant, is not tied to any dominant social class and, like Guido, is an assimilated Jew.

When Guido and Ferruccio arrive at his house, Uncle Eliseo shows them artifacts of Italian culture and history, rather than of Jewish origin. One item is a bed slept in by Garibaldi, the national hero who unified Italy in the 1860s. There is also a biography on Petrarch by Lorenzo Paolino and a bicycle that Uncle Eliseo refers to by the more Italianate, D'Annunzian term *velocipede*. In the years surrounding World War II, cycling was one of Italy's most popular national sports. These hints at Uncle Eliseo's assimilation point to the special identity of Italian Jews who, more than other Jewish communities in Europe, were willing to identify themselves with the nationality of the country in which they lived.[38] An Italian audience may recognize Guido's last name, Orefice, as Jewish but there is otherwise no identification of Guido or Uncle Eliseo as Jewish until the Grand Hotel party sequence, when Uncle Eliseo's horse Robin Hood appears painted green with the graffiti "cavallo ebreo (Jewish horse)." Guido's assimilation is evident in his decision to marry a non-Jew. Also, he is not involved in the practices or worship that identify the more orthodox forms of Judaism.

Uncle Eliseo first appears after being beaten by fascist thugs who violated his home. Their intrusion is dismissed as juvenile vandalism rather than a specific attack on his Jewishness. The uncle defines the vandals as "barbarians," a term that was used to describe people who were foreign to civilized (Greek) culture and that was later used to describe the Germanic tribes who destabilized the Roman Empire. In the film, its use is a description of opponents of the uncle's rational culture. Benigni emphasized this early abuse of the uncle as a key point in the development of the *Shoah*. In fact, the background music that is heard while the youths ransack Uncle Eliseo's house is heard again when the deportees go through the camp's selection process in the second half of the film.

As the film's wise man, Uncle Eliseo voices the points Benigni and Cerami wish to make about God and free will. While admonishing Guido that a waiter should not behave like a sycophant, Uncle Eliseo insists that, like God, a waiter must maintain his dignity. Uncle Eliseo explains that God is the first servant. God serves man but he is not man's servant. According to Uncle Eliseo's interpretation, God's place is not to do everything for man, but to aid man in the struggle to behave according to God's instructions. Therefore, the crimes by the film's Nazi-fascist villains are the result of their individual choices of behavior and should not be attributed to God's negligence. The statement is a quick synthesis of the differences in philosophical and religious traditions between free will and determinism, and points to a Catholic undertone in the film. Catholicism considers the world as a receptacle of evil in which salvation is achieved through the repentance of sin and the excuse of free will.

The Catholic undertone is confirmed by elements in the film's plotline. A holy family hides their child from an infanticidal regime. Guido lives on in the son saved by his sacrifice. Incidentally, the age of Giosué (Giosué is Italian for Jesus) in the film, five years, is the same as the boy Jesus for whom Benigno, the shepherd, baby-sits in *Tu mi turbi/You Bother Me*. There are also thematic similarities between the two films. An innocent child plays straight man to Benigni's reexplanations of a sacred event or period. In each film, Benigni introduces a level of humanity into a topic such as Christ's boyhood or the Holocaust, which retains such a forbidding aura due to its sacred nature.

The Catholic undercurrent could be interpreted as failure on the part of the authors to sufficiently imbue the characters with a sense of Jewishness. However, Benigni's relationship to religious themes is rooted firmly in the lay traditions of his theatrical parodies, examined in chapters 6 and 7. The key to the Catholic subtext to the film is not in any expression of religious insensitivity but in a rejection of the social Darwinism that was at the heart of Nazi ideology. The source of the mentality that led to the camps is depicted during the Grand Hotel engagement party, when the Italian schoolteacher recounts the anecdote about the skill of German children in mathematics. The teacher expresses the violence of the crude, Darwinian Nazi rationale that eliminating unhealthy students would save the state the money needed to sustain them.

## FABLE VERSUS REALISM

Besides questions of the incompatibility of comedy and the Holocaust, most criticism of *Life Is Beautiful* focused on the film's lack of historical realism and viewers' inability to achieve a suspension of disbelief. Daniel

Vogelmann, an Italian Jew who lost family members at Auschwitz, wrote that attenuating the horror of the *Shoah* might mislead new generations into regarding the film as factual. Vogelmann cited gaps in the story, such as the seeming ease of the train trip to the camps and the omission of the fact that after the Italian monarchy switched sides in the war, many Italian Jews looked desperately for a way to escape.[39] In the United States, film critic David Denby led the protest by panning the film as "unconvincing" and "self-congratulatory," and accused Benigni of perpetrating a Holocaust denial.[40] A cartoon of a despairing concentration camp prisoner holding an Oscar statuette accompanied Denby's review in *The New Yorker*. It was drawn by Art Spiegelman, the author of the Holocaust comic book series *Maus*. Spiegelman's depiction was surprising because the anthropomorphism of his *Maus* series, like Benigni's film, made the subject of the Holocaust more approachable.

Benigni's screenwriter, Vincenzo Cerami, warned of the capability of contemporary film to remove all barriers of representation as a factor in reducing a film's expressive quality. Material that was previously deemed obscene and required evocation due to moralistic sensibilities or technical limitations can now be readily depicted. The decision to limit realistic displays and story lines in *Life Is Beautiful* was a conscious effort to avoid what Cerami has called the sense of "hyper-reality" in contemporary cinema that has led to a lessening of its poetic power.[41]

In previous films, Benigni introduced elements of the grotesque and even the horrible, such as the severed hand at the serial killer's table in *The Monster*. But in *Life Is Beautiful*, the tragedy of the Shoah is already so enormous that Benigni felt no need to expand on it. In *Life Is Beautiful*, he reduces the comic grotesque imagery that had characterized his previous films. The film consciously attenuates the historical reality of the Nazi deportation and murder of European Jews and other victims. Elements of horror were carefully avoided to retain the aura of a fable as a means to reach the large numbers of children expected to see the film. For example, in one scene a pile of cadavers is clearly fake, and Guido is murdered off camera. Following a suggestion from Auschwitz survivor Schlomo Venezia, who worked in the gas chambers as a *Sonderkommando* (a prisoner charged with removing bodies from the gas chambers) and was a consultant on the film, the camera cuts away from the undressing scene in the antechamber to the gas chambers. Instead of depicting the humiliation and suffering of the Nazi's victims, the film shows Guido's uncle performing a paradoxical gesture of politeness to a female Nazi guard and reacting with resignation to her hostility.

Benigni has defended himself against charges relating to the film's suspension of disbelief by citing Proust and Poe, who felt that a story should never provide all the details but should allow room for the reader's or spectator's imagination.[42] Benigni's approach is to allude to the sense of events while maintaining the dignity of the victims. A reduction of graphic horror is the style adopted by some of the most effective films on the *Shoah,* such as *Ambulans* (1961) by Janusz Morgenstern and *The Passenger* (1961) by Andrzej Munk.[43] Given the reaction of a public increasingly numb to depictions of violence and murder, Benigni's more subtle approach was well advised. The central problem of representing the *Shoah* is that the level of horror required for a realistic depiction would be so graphic that it would actually prevent a wider public from gaining a sense of solidarity and political consciousness.[44] Ultimately, the reality criticism fails because Benigni's goal was not to provide a realistic depiction of the horrors of the Holocaust. Rather, his film reveals the hypocrisy of those who perpetrated and allowed a repressive system, in contrast to the love among members of Guido's family.

Benigni prepared for potential criticism by inviting Marcello Pezzetti of the Centro di Documentazione Ebraica Contemporanea (Contemporary Jewish Documentation Center) of Milan to serve as historical consultant for the film. The aim was to gain not only the approval of the Italian Jewish community but also its expertise.[45] Benigni asked for Pezzetti's assistance after Ruggiero Gabbai's documentary *Memoria* (1997) was broadcast on Italian television. In the documentary, Pezzetti interviews Italian Auschwitz survivors, including some Roman Jews, who tell stories and sing songs in a startling expression of the instinct for survival. Primo Levi, in his memoir, *Survival at Auschwitz,* also mentions the behavior of Roman Jews in the camps. In the Auschwitz infirmary Levi met Piero Sonnino, a Roman Jew who is one of the rare people for whom Levi cites both a first and last name, indicating the extent to which Sonnino was able to retain and transmit a sense of his identity.[46] The retention of hope and a sense of identity was fundamentally important for any chance at surviving the camps. In *Memoria,* Romeo Salmoni, a Roman Jew, states that once a prisoner lost the desire to live, death soon followed.[47] Viktor Frankl has written of the existence of humor among the deportees as a "weapon in the fight for self-preservation."[48]

Through Pezzetti's aid Benigni was able to contact Auschwitz survivors who had been deported to the camp as adults, as well as survivors who had been interned as children. Pezzetti showed Benigni specific documentation on the *Shoah,* including a photo album produced by the

Benigni with Schlomo Venezia and Marcello Pezzetti on set of *Life Is Beautiful*.
Photo courtesy of Centro di Documentazione Ebraica Contemporanea.

Nazis, *The Auschwitz Album, Lili Jacob's Album,* a startling document because it includes photographs prepared by the Nazis as part of reports for their superiors on the camps' management.[49] The Nazis chose photographs that conveyed an aura of efficiency. Thus, instead of the images of postliberation destruction and starvation, the photos have an eerie quality of normality in which the deportees are walking, or standing in line, unaware that they are headed for the gas chambers and crematoria. This understated approach is used in films such as Morgenstern's *Ambulans* (1961) by Janusz and Munk's *The Passenger* (1961), where horror is evoked rather than depicted.

Pezzetti, who refused to be paid for his services, realized the enormous professional risk involved in aiding an actor with Benigni's comic reputation on such a delicate project. The danger was that the film could spark a Holocaust comedy genre in the manner that Liliana Cavani's *Portiere di notte/Night Porter* (1974) spawned an entire genre of Nazi pornography films.[50] Pezzetti was also well aware of the disappointing history of Italian films depicting the Shoah. Since the Holocaust is unlikely to deliver visual pleasure, films on the subject have been infrequent, as demonstrated by the small number of U.S. productions. In fact, 80 percent of films on the Shoah have been produced in Europe, and U.S. production is only half of French production.[51] Italy in particular was almost without films on the Holocaust until Gillo Pontecorvo's *Kapò* (1959) and a sequence of Jews praying before an execution in Roberto Rossellini's *Il Generale della Rovere* (1959). The first Italian film on the subject, *L'ebreo errante/The Wandering Jew* (1947), portrays the myth of the wandering Jew who expiates his sins in the Nazi camps; despite intentions, the film has anti-Semitic overtones. Later Italian films on the Holocaust were not any more convincing. Again, despite intentions, Gillo Pontecorvo's *Kapò* has glaring historical and plot inconsistencies, most notably the final love story between the Russian prisoner and the deportee turned *kapò* (camp trustee). Pontecorvo's film, unlike Benigni's, was criticized for showing too many scenes of suffering deportees, to the point of being accused of "pornography."[52]

Later Italian films presented more visually pleasing portrayals of the deportations, such as Vittorio de Sica's bourgeois Holocaust drama, *The Garden of Finzi-Continis,* which won an Oscar for Best Foreign Film. In this film, the spectator feels sympathy for the attractive and noble deportee, as played by Dominique Sanda. If Benigni's film has roots in Italian cinematic depictions of the Holocaust, it is in Lina Wertmuller's *Seven Beauties,* which was nominated for Best Foreign Film and which focuses on survival and a crude joy for life. The film opens with a depiction of barbaric executions of Jews by Nazis, in which the characters are forced to consider their own culpability as Italians, Germany's allies in the war.

Wertmuller, like Benigni, was criticized for profaning the Holocaust in the scenes of Pasqualino's copulation with the camp commandant, the fatalistic acceptance of events, and the insistence on procreation as a means to assure survival.

As Benigni's historical consultant on the film, Pezzetti was well aware that 98 percent of the deported children were killed immediately upon arrival at the camps and that the Benigni-Cerami plot in which a parent saves a child in such a setting would have been historically untenable. Yet Pezzetti claims that there were cases of children found alive when the death camps were liberated, including about fifty at Auschwitz, to which the majority of Italian Jews were deported. After the film was released, stories appeared from survivors whose testimonies seem almost as unlikely as the plot of Benigni's film.[53] Also, Pezzetti has explained that most films on the *Shoah* are portrayals of exceptions. Examples include Agnieszka Holland's *Europa, Europa* (1991), the story of Salomon Perel, the only Jew to join the Hitler Youth. There is also Stephen Spielberg's film *Schindler's List* (1993), about an German industrialist who saved Jews, and Jack Gold's *Escape from Sobibor* (1987), about the only documented revolt and escape from a death camp.[54]

A more realistic portrayal of the Holocaust would, of course, have to be compared to the documentaries from the Allied armies and the hidden camera interviews of the death camp personnel in Claude Lanzmann's documentary *Shoah* (1985) or Resnais's compelling *Nuit et brouillard* (1955). Even a television miniseries of Herman Wouk's novel, *The Winds of War,* has a riveting episode depicting the building of a death camp, presented from the amoral perspective of the camp commandant whose family regarded the whole affair as a means to gain a generalship. To compare Benigni's films to these more realistic dramas and documentaries is inapt. They are not the same genre of film. Benigni's film, particularly the North American print, is presented as a fable. Benigni's reduction of elements of horror was a conscious decision, seconded by Pezzetti, to respect the dignity of the suffering camp victims. There was a realization that no form of realism, no matter how graphic, can adequately communicate the sense of unreality in the camps. Thus, the encounter with Pezzetti's documentation center was fundamental to developing an approach to the subject, which limited realism to the reproduction of uniforms and suggestions from survivors about the manner in which deportees behaved in the camps. For example Shlomo Venezia, the survivor of the *Sonderkommando,* prisoners charged with removing bodies from the gas chambers, suggested the subdued and somber mannerisms of prisoners entering chambers expecting a shower, which is what he remembers.

Of course, Benigni and Pezzetti did have some disagreements. For example, because of the historical implausibility, Pezzetti did not think the boy Giosué should survive. Benigni felt that the death of his character, Guido, was enough to imbue the film with a sense of tragedy, especially since Benigni, who had always been a comic actor, had never died in a film before. Perhaps due to such disagreements, Pezzetti has remarked that Benigni was primarily interested in the story based on the power of love of a family.[55] Given this reaction from Benigni's own historical adviser, one is tempted to accept Vogelmann's criticism that the film might give a false impression of the evil of the Holocaust, particularly to an audience ignorant of the event's history. However, Pezzetti has ultimately defended the attenuation of horror in the film by remarking that Benigni never laughs at the *Shoah* but rather portrays laughter as a survival instinct within the *Shoah*. Also, the very idea of realism in the *Shoah* is paradoxical since no level of technical artifice could adequately portray such evil. Benigni and Cerami therefore decided to rely on the evocative power of the spectator's imagination to avoid the "hyper-reality" of the contemporary cinema.

After receiving a prize at the 1997 Cannes Film Festival, Benigni appeared with European intellectual George Steiner on the French television program *Bouillon de culture,* a forum for intellectuals to discuss new publications and trends. Also present were Emile Shoufani, a Catholic priest who runs a school in Palestine, and Gottfried Wagner, the great-grandson of the composer Richard Wagner, who had written a book about the anti-Semitism in his famous family. On the program, as in many interviews, Benigni anticipated much of the criticism of the film by citing Primo Levi's statement that the first reaction to the reality of the camps was disbelief. Steiner then explained the history of Jewish persecution as revenge for the Jewish faith's invention of the idea of the conscience. According to Steiner, for this advance in human moral philosophy, the Jews have earned periodic explosions of scorn from humankind who are unable to behave properly.[56] Steiner concluded that despite the temptation to be fatalistic about humanity's future, especially given the horrors of the Holocaust, he insists on retaining a sense of hope, as in the Greek myth of Pandora's box.

Benigni responded by stating that his explanation for Guido's actions in the film is not intellectual or philosophical, but physical, insisting on the importance of the film's final chase scene. After successfully protecting Giosué from death and from the terrible knowledge of the events in the camp, Guido risks his life to search for his wife. Guido's rationale is not emotional or familial, but physical, driven by a desire to make love with her. This emphasis on the physical, animal joy of existence at the most tragic moment of the film is a return to the physical first seen in the *Cioni* monologue. Despite the historical setting, Benigni's character still retains the mentality of the peasant physicality that drove Cioni in *Berlinguer I Love You.*

With this recursion to the Cioni-like physicality represented by Guido's search for Dora, Benigni portrays a protagonist who is indelibly tied to the instinctual, naturalistic impulses of life. In the semihappy ending where Giosué and Dora are reunited by a smiling U.S. soldier, the film, like Wertmuller's *Seven Beauties,* insists on the continuation, the regeneration, of life despite tragedy and suffering. Benigni's return to the physical simplicity imbues the film with lower bodily themes as a vehicle of pathos, a constant in Benigni's work from the days of the *Cioni* monologue.

## NOTES

1. Two other Italian films go by the same title: *La vita è bella* (1943), directed by Carlo Ludovico Bragaglia, and *La vita è bella* (1979), an Italian Russian coproduction directed by Grigory Tchrouchai and starring Giancarlo Giannini and Ornella Muti.

2. The triumph established Benigni as a national hero. Upon his return to Italy the residents of his hometown erected a statue in his honor.

3. See Michail Bakhtin, *Rabelais and His World* (Cambridge, Mass.: MIT Press, 1971).

4. Jean François Lyotard, *The Postmodern Condition,* trans. Geoff Bennington and Brian Massumi (Minneapolis: University of Minnesota Press, 1984), p. 6.

5. Colin McCabe, "*Life Is Beautiful* (review)," *Sight & Sound* 9(2) (February 1999): 46.

6. Francois Gorin and Vincent Remy, "La comique peut rendre compte de l'horror," *Telerama,* May 27, 1998.

7. Roberto Benigni and V. Cerami, *La vita è bella* (Turin: Einaudi, 1997), p. viii; Roberto Benigni, *E l'alluce fu,* ed. M. Giusti (Milan: Einaudi, 1996), p. 81.

8. See interview with Roberto Benigni in appendix.

9. Benigni and Cerami, *La vita è bella,* p. ix.

10. Elio Apih, *Mostra storica della Risiera di San Sabba* (Trieste: Comune di Trieste, 1989).

11. It is interesting to note the similarities between the plot structure of *Life Is Beautiful* and the film that received favorable attention at the previous year's Oscar competition, *Titanic* (1997). Both films feature a disgruntled wealthy princess character engaged to an unsympathetic representative of her class. In each film, the heroine is swept off her feet by a rebel character. In the second half of each film, history steps in and the rebel character sacrifices himself for the heroine's survival.

12. Max Picard, *The World of Silence* (Chicago: Gateway, 1952), pp. 145–149.

13. "The point of honesty in deception. . . . For men will believe something is true, it is evident that others believe it firmly." Friedrich Nietzsche, *Human all too Human,* trans. M. Faber and S. Lehmann (Lincoln: University of Nebraska Press, 1996), p. 51.

14. See interview with Roberto Benigni in Appendix.

15. Michael Bachtin, *L'opera di Rabelais e la cultura popolare riso, carnevale e festa nella tradizione medievale e rinascimentale,* trans. Mili Romano (Turin: Einaudi, 1995), p. 102.

16. Bachtin, *L'opera di Rabelais,* p. 58.

17. Bachtin, *L'opera di Rabelais,* p. 448.

18. Charles Tesson, "L'enfance de la mémoire a propos de 'La Vie est Belle,' " *Cahiers du Cinema,* 529 (November 1998): 46–48.

19. Tesson, "L'enfance de la mémoire."

20. J. L. Baudry, *L'effet cinéma* (Paris: Albatros, 1978).

21. Slavoj Zizek, "Camp Comedy 4" *Sight & Sound* 10(2) (April 2000): 28.

22. See Alain Kinkielkraut, *Une voix vient de l'autre rive* (Paris: Gallimard, 1999).

23. Studies have been made of nostalgia films and their relationship to a larger cultural and historical context for the French cinema. See Naomi Greene, *Landscapes of Loss: The National Past in Postwar French Cinema* (Princeton, N.J.: Princeton University Press, 1999).

24. Jean Michel Frondon, *La projection nationale: cinema et nation* (Paris: O. Jacob, 1998). See also Elio Girlanda, "Il cinema delle nazioni," in *Gillo Pontecorvo. La dittatura della verità* (Assisi: ANNCI, 1998).

25. See Gary Wills, *John Wayne's America* (New York: Simon & Schuster, 1993).

26. Mauro Manicotti, *La resistenza nel cinema italiano 1945/1995* (Turin: Istituto Storico della Resistenza in Liguria, 1995), p. 322.
27. Alfonso Bernardinelli reviewed the film in "Benigni, la nuova estetica di sinistra ha fatto splash (Benigni's new left-wing aesthetics makes a splash)," *Corriere della Sera* (Janauary 7, 1997). Negative reviews in Italy include Giuliano Ferrara's review in "Olocausto Show," *Panorama,* January 22, 1998, p. 30; Goffredo Fofi, "La vita è una furbata," *Panorama,* January 15, 1998.
28. Fredric Jameson, "Postmodernism or the Cultural Logic of Late Capitalism," *The New Left Review,* 146 (1984): 53–92.
29. See interview with Roberto Benigni in appendix.
30. See Paola Casella, *Hollywood Italian gli italiani nell'America di celluloide* (Milan: Baldini & Castoldi, 1998).
31. Benigni would continue his criticism of the arrogance and cruelty of fascist imperialism indirectly in *Asterix* (1999), in which he plays Deterious, a villainous Roman officer occupying Gaul during the period of Italian history (the Roman Empire) idealized by the fascist regime.
32. Gotthold Ephraim Lessing (1729–1781) was one of the prime figures of the German Enlightenment. He treated themes that are seen in *Life Is Beautiful,* such as the sacrifice for love in *Minna von Barnheim* (1763) and the idiocy of religious intolerance in *Nathan the Wise* (1779), based loosely on the Boccaccio story on the legend of the three rings, the common origins of Christianity, Judaism, and Islam. Lessing was also a theorist of the stage and wrote in his *Hamburg Collection* (1767–1769) on the idea of bourgeois tragedy as a derivation of classical tragedy in which the process of history is a manifestation of divine will, projected for human edification. Lessing also defended the role of such comic figures as Harlequin in the theater from critics who sought to separate serious and comic theater.
33. Marcia Landy, *Italian Film* (Cambridge: Cambridge University Press, 2000), p. 120.
34. The sources of some of Benigni's riddles are quite ancient. For example, Lessing's riddle about silence has a Greek source in enigma 22 in *The Greek Anthology,* "Speak not and thou shalt speak my name." See P. A. Paton, *The Greek Anthology,* vol. 5 (Cambridge, Mass.: Harvard University Press, 1953), p. 37.
35. Benigni and Cerami, *La vita è bella,* p. 172.
36. Marcello Pezzetti, Benigni's historical consultant on the film, remarked, "I am reminded of the diary of a German physician at

Auschwitz, Kramer, who had been an anatomy professor and was sent to perform pathology experiments at Auschwitz. He was a truly horrible figure who left us a diary in which, for example, in the afternoon he writes, 'Today I saw Hell, I saw what happened in the gas chambers,' and he describes this terrible scene and then immediately after he writes, 'Tonight the food wasn't very good, there aren't enough vegetables here.' Both events are described with the same pathos, comparing the deaths with the food. For me this is Lessing, a man without sensibility. . . . He becomes a slave of the riddle, of something that is not part of the reality of the moment. He is abstracted from reality, as many Germans abstracted themselves from events during and after the war." Carlo Celli, "Interview with Marcello Pezzetti," *Critical Inquiry*. Autumn 2000, 156.

37. Film historian Siegfred Kracauer has interpreted German film history, from the Hoffmann-like film *The Cabinet of Dr. Caligari* (1920) to the films of Goebbel's propaganda machine, as a metaphor for the rise of Hitlerism. See Siegfried Kracauer, *From Caligari to Hitler* (Princeton, N.J.: Princeton University Press, 1966).

38. Unpublished interview with Marcello Pezzetti. Celli, "Interview with Marcello Pezzetti," 154.

39. Daniel Vogelmann, "*La vita è bella* (review)," *Il tirreno,* December 18, 1997, p. 1.

40. David Denby, "In the Eye of the Beholder," *The New Yorker* (March 15, 1999): 96–99.

41. Vincenzo Cerami, *Consigli a un giovane autore* (Turin: Einaudi, 1996), p. 15.

42. Giovanna Grassi, "Benigni: Moretti ha già vinto l'ulivo d'oro," *Corriere della sera,* May 18, 1998, p. 1. The title refers to attempts by Giuliano Ferrara, former culture minister of the Berlusconi government, in the journal *Il foglio* to incite a controversy between Benigni and Moretti, who at the time was seen as more of the establishment director, for attempting to depict themes of contemporary Italian society.

43. Marcello Pezzetti, "Considerazioni sulla rappresentazione della Shoa ad opera del cinema," in *Storia e memoria della deportazione* (Milan: Giuntina, 1996); Marcello Pezzetti, "Rappresentare la Shoah, trasmettere la memoria," in *Il racconto della catastrofe. Il cinema di fronte ad Auschwitz* (Verona: Cierre, 1998).

44. Statements to this effect were made by Ishayahu Nir, a professor of communications at Jerusalem University, on a television program in

which Benigni, Marcello Pezzetti, and Cerami also appeared as part
of a panel discussion. Gad Lerner, *Pinocchio,* RAI 2, February 9, 1999.

45. See Carlo Celli, "Interview with Marcello Pezzetti," *Critical Inquiry,*
27 (Autumn 2000): 149–157.

46. In the Auschwitz infirmary Sonnino was able to pass himself off as a
victim of dysentery by the risky operation of switching chamber pots
with a true sufferer of the disease before inspection, thereby proving
his status. Despite the pluck shown by Sonnino, the incident also
stands out as an example of the dehumanizing horror of the camps
in Levi's book. Primo Levi, *Survival in Auschwitz* (New York:
Macmillan, 1958), p. 48.

47. Despite Salmoni's seeming good humor, some of the most devastating moments in *Memoria* are his descriptions.

48. Viktor Frankl, *Man's Search for Meaning* (New York: Washington
Square, 1984), p. 63.

49. See Serge Klarsfeld, *The Auschwitz Album, Lili Jacob's Album* (New
York: The Beate Klarsfeld Foundation, 1980).

50. Benigni's film is part of a current in Holocaust films featuring chil-
dren as protagonists. Examples include Roberto Faenza's *Roberto che
visse nella balena/Jona Who Lived in the Whale* (1993), Alexander
Rosler's *Mendel* (1997), Soren Kragh-Jacobsen's *The Island on Bird
Street* (1997) based on a story by Uri Orlev, Jon Blair's documentary
*Anne Frank Remembered* (1995), and an animated version of *Anne
Frank's Diary* (1999) by Julian Wolff. The experiences of the chil-
dren murdered by the Nazis are also the focus of the Museum of the
Holocaust in Los Angeles.

51. Vanina Pezzetti, unpublished thesis, DAMS, 1998, p. 13.

52. See J. Rivette, "De l'abjection," *Les cahiers du cinema,* 120 (1961).

53. Joseph Schleifstein was four years old when Buchenwald was liberated by U.S. troops in 1945. He had been successfully hidden by his
father in a story similar to that of Guido and Giosué, except that
Buchenwald was not a death camp. Pezzetti put Benigni into contact
with two sisters living in Belgium, Anna and Tatianna Bucci-Perlov,
who as four- and six-year-olds survived without undergoing experiments, despite being separated from their mother. Benigni contacted
the Bucci-Perlov sisters to thank them for coming forward with their
story.

54. Unpublished interview with Marcello Pezzetti.

55. McCabe, *"Life Is Beautiful"* (review), p. 46.

56. Portions of Steiner's statements are allowed to in his novel *The Portage
to San Cristobal of A.H.* (New York: Simon & Schuster, 1981).

# Afterword

*I*n his seminal history of the Italian cinema, Gian Piero Brunetta noted how Roberto Benigni combines a high level of cultural sophistication while maintaining popular appeal.[1] As a contemporary *giullare,* Benigni has the remarkable ability to shift cultural register and provoke laughter and a sense of the joy of life in any subject, no matter how sacred or traditionally off limits.

Benigni's directing career began with a spoof on Christ's boyhood and continued in this vein in his approach to subjects such as the mafia, serial killers, and even the unlikely subject of the Holocaust. Benigni's forays into so-called high culture are not readily apparent in his film performances, due to the nature of the medium and Benigni's desire to model his film performances and directing style after the great comedians of the past. It is interesting to note that in a period of increasing linguistic and cultural homogenization, the Italian public has gravitated toward popular comedians such as Benigni, whose roots are in Tuscan language and humor. It is premature to identify a new cultural paradigm, a *nuova toscanità,* removed from the high culture usually associated with Tuscan literature. However, one of the great strengths of Tuscan authors in the canon is an ability to transmit the authentic forms and earthy themes of the Tuscan dialect and rural culture to a national audience.

As director and even coproducer of his films, Benigni has put himself into a position to control the angles, camera movement, and editing that portray his image, all of which is evident in the more ambitious directing style of his last two films. In Benigni's films, as in the work of other great comedians, the same basic character reappears with changes in the stunts and props as suggested by the plot. Benigni's self-referential character progresses from the infantile Giuditta, to media victim Loris, to the heroic Guido. This recalls how Chaplin was able to evolve from a self-referential parody of his own characterizations into a more sophisticated comedy that treated weighty issues as in *The Great Dictator* (1940) or *Monsieur Verdoux* (1947). In the urban Cioni films and finally in *La vita è bella/Life Is Beautiful,* Benigni has arrived at the same level of sophistication with his treatment of weighty themes.

Perhaps because Benigni's films are not quickly identifiable with the historic categories of the Italian national cinema, critics who were unsure where to place his work often dismissed his directorial abilities. However, Benigni has worked with directors in a number of traditions of the Italian cinema. He made films in the current of the political cinema with the themes of social solidarity and alienation in Ferreri's *Chiedo asilo* and Citti's *Il minestrone*. The political subtexts and long-take style in the urban sequences of *Il mostro / The Monster* are very much in this school of filmmaking. Benigni also worked in the cabaret tradition revived by Renzo Arbore that recalled the *commedia all'italiana* period, when films featuring cameos by recognized stars were a staple of Italian film production. The stage performance of Guido impersonating the minister at Dora's school in *Life Is Beautiful* is very much in this style. Benigni also enjoyed an apprenticeship with Cesare Zavattini and learned as Zavattini expounded on how to write a screenplay and how to incorporate dialogue and music.[2] Benigni's films have echoes of the magic realism in films by De Sica/Zavattini, such as *Miracle at Milan* and *Il giudizio universale*. Benigni's *Il piccolo diavolo / The Little Devil* and *Life Is Beautiful* both make ample use of the commonplaces of fables, much like the films of De Sica/Zavattini and Pasolini. Benigni also owes a debt to the anticonsumer themes and cinematic formalism he encountered on Fellini's *La voce della luna*. Benigni's later use of Fellini's set designer and cinematographer on *Life Is Beautiful* confirms his debt to the often dreamlike quality of Fellini's films, *Amarcord* in particular.

Given his experience with Fellini and the magical side of Zavattini, it is no surprise that Benigni admits that he has never been a complete follower of the realist school of filmmaking. Benigni has stated that he feels his films have an element of a new style that combines all of the previous traditions mentioned above. When his films appear it is difficult for critics not to attempt to define them according to one of the traditions in the Italian cinema, whether that be from Fellini, neorealism, Pasolini, or others. Benigni's films actually owe a debt to all of these traditions.[3] In fact, Benigni's films are very much in the tradition of collaborative efforts in Italian film. Benigni/Cerami and Bertolucci, like De Sica/Zavattini, Rossellini/Amidei, Pontecorvo/Solinas, and Fellini/Flaiano, to mention only a few, are part of a method of filmmaking that has combined theatrical and literary talents. Because of Benigni's adhesion to this collaborative elite, his films confirm continuity in Italian film that surpasses the traditional categories identified with Italian national cinema.

The question of how Benigni will further adapt his Tuscan clown to an international audience is, of course, open. After the worldwide success of *Life Is Beautiful*, Benigni has stated his desire to find a lighter subject for his next film, something in which his comedic talents could shine. His first attempt at a post-*Life Is Beautiful* project was to be a film from the life of Saint Francis, a subject for which he had been approached previously by director Michelangelo Antonioni. Cerami wrote the lyrics for a musical on Saint Francis that approached the life of the saint from the perspective of a young boy, a narrative tool to render the life of such an august figure more accessible. However, Benigni eventually felt unable to adapt the material to a character he could play.[4] The danger for Benigni's future projects is that they could distance him from the improvisational brilliance of his cultural origins. For example, since the box-office success of *Life Is Beautiful*, Benigni has been approached by U.S. producers to play roles of Italian immigrants, which he has thus far refused.

Benigni's latest statements regarding future projects have revolved around plans to do a film version of *Pinocchio,* to be coauthored with Cerami. Thus the homage that Benigni paid to Fellini in *Life Is Beautiful* in the use of Fellini's set designer and cinematographer would continue. Fellini's last project was to be a film version of *Pinocchio,* starring Benigni. The choice of *Pinocchio* coming some three years after the completion of *Life Is Beautiful* would seem to satisfy all of Benigni's requirements. The tale is internationally renowned and has the sort of mass appeal that would attract a worldwide audience. Collodi's fable is set in the rustic and poor Tuscany of Benigni's upbringing. In its original form, as a series of stories in the *Giornale dei bambini* in 1881, it was not only a children's story but also an acute and biting criticism of nineteenth-century Italian society. As such, Benigni could approach the subject with a combination of comic and tragic elements that was so effective in his last film. Benigni could also increase the level of grotesque imagery from earlier films that was perhaps attenuated in *Life Is Beautiful* in deference to the subject matter. Thus, audiences used to the sweetened fable presented by Disney as an animated feature in 1940 may be exposed to the rich variety of characters in the original and plot details such as Pinocchio's killing of the talking cricket.

Like the Etruscan clowns who warded off evil spirits from ancient ceremonies, Benigni has tackled the most evil topics in the modern world: serial killers, the mafia, and the Holocaust. Benigni has already proven himself as an artist who has been able to treat the most daunting and tragic themes of the contemporary world. With a topic such as *Pinocchio,* Benigni will have a chance to remove himself from the historical woes of the contemporary world and allow his eye for invention free rein.

## NOTES

1. Gian Piero Brunetta, *Storia del cinema italiano,* vol. 4 (Rome: Editori Riuniti, 1993), p. 168.
2. Zavattini was also an influence on Cerami. In his advice to a young screenwriter, Cerami reproduces the Zavattini script for *Umberto D.* that employs a tri-partition of the page to indicate visual, verbal, and musical elements. Vincenzo Cerami, *Consigli a un giovane scrittore,* (Turin: Einaudi, 1996), p. 106
3. See interview with Roberto Benigni in appendix.
4. Benigni says: "I would very much like to tell you all about my next film but I have not been able to find the right light for Saint Francis which is a film that I have been trying to make for ten years. Every year I try again. Three days ago I went to visit the Cathedral in Assisi with the Franciscan friars but I but I still have not been able to get into the role. I even tried with Antonioni and Fellini who told me that he would have preferred to do Pinocchio before Saint Francis. So now I am trying to find something in between, something light that would allow me to think about things without fear. I hope that the sky above will help me to do something. Anyway, this is a great moment of satisfaction and enjoyment and so I would like to find something light and exciting that would allow me to do something very funny and comical after [*Life Is Beautiful*]."

# Appendix

*Conducted by Carlo Celli*

*Let's start with Misericordia, where you were born, in the Tuscan countryside.*

In those years rural Italy, in fact all Italy, was not that well off economically. But I remember that period as one of great happiness. At the Oscars I joked about it, saying, "I would like to thank my parents for the greatest gift—poverty," poverty almost in a Franciscan sense. I recall the poverty of those years as richness because the entire world was waiting to be discovered. The wealth of poverty is to be able to recognize the fantastic side to everything in life. In my early childhood I remember a sense of extraordinary wonder about everything I experienced. The strongest emotions are connected to when I saw people laugh. I felt that that was my path, the most genuine thing in my life. I followed that calling without second-guessing it. Then there were the elements of fantasy from my parents and my grandparents' storytelling in front of the hearth. We also slept in the same room, which was like something out of Fellini. When I was six we emigrated from Arezzo [Misericordia] to Prato [Vergaio], a distance of only about 150 kilometers, but for a six-year-old child it was like going to another planet. We moved from a rural to an industrial city, where the dialect was different. Changes between dialects are more difficult than between languages because you felt as if you belonged, but not quite. We did not have a house ready for us since my father had just found a job. So we slept in a horse stable. I remember the horses' muzzles; apart from the stench there was this great warmth. The place was a small suburb of Prato [and] was called *via fra i campi* [street between the fields] it did not even have a real name. The things that influenced me the most were the stories and the sense of fantasy they generated. In those days we did not have any other source of entertainment.

*At Prato you came into contact with the Tuscan improvising poets, the* poeti a braccio.

My father was enamored of the *poeti a braccio* because of the mystery of improvisation. He couldn't believe that they could really improvise in verse. In those days these old men would perform at country festivals. The youngest among them was about eighty years old. When I was about eleven or twelve, my father put me on stage to find out if it was really true, that one could learn to improvise. He tried to get these poets to teach me their ways. I went along with it but I would get the rhymes wrong because I did not have a very strong vocabulary. After two or three years I started to improvise, adding things that were more modern, like using curse words in order to get the attention of the crowd, the sort of infantile thing that kids do. I remember when I was about fourteen or fifteen I took a poem by Leopardi and put curse words in it for effect; it's the sort of thing that kids do in order to get attention. So my father, in order to understand this mystery of improvisation, started me on the hendecasyllable, Dante, and these poets, who called themselves the *Bernescanti,* taking their name from the poet Berni.

*Your father had you read Berni?*

No, the only poet that my father knows is Dante. He also liked Petrarch, because he is the poet from our city, Arezzo, along with Guido d'Arezzo. Then there is the painter Piero della Francesca whose *Madonna del parto* has a face that looks so much like my mother, truly wonderful. But anyway, he only knew Petrarch and Dante. You know that Petrarch was jealous of Dante's popularity. Petrarch said, "I leave Dante to the tavern keepers and the marketplace." But Petrarch never makes a mistake in the hendecasyllable. He always put the accent on the fourth-sixth, fourth-seventh and fourth-eighth syllables, never making a mistake. His technique is spectacular in terms of its refinement. In fact, his style dominated European literature all the way until the sixteenth century. But he was terrified of Dante's popularity because Dante is a bit overbearing, always so pissed off, mad at everybody, then he suffers and curses everybody, but these are such heights that one has to enjoy them.

*The idea that you can improvise verses makes a tremendous impression in the U.S. where such popular traditions have waned.*

The tradition in Tuscany is particularly strong and elaborate. In Tuscany and upper Lazio, the ancient region of Etruria, there remains a complex tradition of alternating rhyme schemes of the octet as used by Ariosto and Berni. These rhyming couplets are tremendously hard to grasp, among the most difficult in the world. I always tell poets to begin from the octet because if one can master the octet then everything else comes easily. From the point of view of the structure of poetry the octet can drive you mad with its difficulty. It is no accident that Tasso ended up in an asylum, even Ariosto went a little mad. Many of the singers of the octet I knew like Altamante, Landinello were a bit touched. Idillio, the greatest of them all, died insane. You enter into a world, a labyrinth like something out of Borges. When I composed octets the musicality of it remains with you day and night. You can't rid yourself of it. It makes your head explode, like an impossible challenge. The rhymes are alternating and closed, but in the improvised octet they never close. The first hendecasyllable of the next verse repeats the last verse of the previous octet. So the rhymes are alternating, linked, and coupled all at the same time. It is the most difficult form in existence. But the octets are really wonderful because they come from the most ancient traditions of poetry that are epic, and the verses must be shouted out loud. Poetry was born as a yell, declaimed; in fact, Borges said that a poem that cannot be read aloud is not a good poem. When you hear Ariosto or Dante out loud the effect is a thousand times more powerful. You understand the embryonic guts, the mud of poetry that is something that has to be called out. The octets were yelled in the town squares and poetry is born of this sense of the epic that also leads to an understanding of storytelling because the octet is part of the epic. It is characters, in time, with a sense of a story.

*Do you still perform any of these improvisations?*

Well, it may seem strange to you but the only person with whom I have these poetry contests is Umberto Eco. We get together a couple of times a year among friends to have contests of octets on improvised topics that last all night. He is really something because he does not come out of the tradition. But he is very competitive and likes to be challenged. He is incredible in linguistic games but he enjoys challenging me in something where I am better prepared than he is. Guccini, the singer, songwriter, is someone else who can improvise. Every once in a while I get together with him as well. Because Romanelli is dead, and Altamante and the others are a little crazy. Even Landinello is not well anymore; every once in a while I call him. He is an old Pisan who sings off-key, but marvelously. Then there is Guerci from Vinci who has a face that looks like something out of Masaccio and a physique like a peasant—short and stout, big and hairy. When he sings he has a voice like a soprano. At our first encounter I closed my opening octet by saying,

> *Tu vien da Vinci da quei colli verdi* (you come from the green hills of Vinci)
> *tu vien da Vinci ma con me tu perdi* (you come from Vinci [you win] but with me you lose)

The rhyme with *verdi* (green) and *perdi* (you lose) is extremely difficult. It is called an "aggressive entry" and is usually not done. When he responded it was really something. He went,

> *Attento il mio Benigni tu ti smerdi* (watch out Benigni because with me you'll stop)"

Since he was the better between us, he accepted the challenge right away with something more vulgar, which is something that he usually never does. *Smerdi* is really dialectal, although it sounds as if he invented it, a neologism, on the spot. The word can mean "to fill up with shit" but also "to stop cold." But since there are so few rhymes that end with *erdi* he had to come up with something. After *smerdi* he had to repeat *verdi* (green) and *perdi* (you lose) because there are so few words that fit the *erdi* rhyme scheme. Anyway, my father introduced me to these octet competitions and I developed a passion for it. For a fourteen- or fifteen-year-old kid it was very exciting to be in front of a crowd and these festivals only took place in the summer. I would spend the entire period before summer preparing the last two closing lines of the octet because the last couplet is open and can be prepared beforehand.

*Speaking of traditions, what about the fescennini? You have been compared to these ancient Etruscan clowns.*

The *fescennini* are wonderful. They are celebrations that are sort of improvised and goliardic. The clowns are like something out of the ancient Orphic rites, from a time before Greek tragedy. They were born out of exorcisms and there is a carnival-like freedom about them, which is a bit frightening. They were held at night with a bonfire and the masks all around. Every once in a while they still do it in Tuscany. I have a friend in Castagneto Carducci, Carducci's town, who calls me every so often to invite me; he'll call to say, "Hey there is a *fescennino*." They get an open truck and there are bonfires at night to celebrate a wedding or a birthday. But these things are no longer common; even the singers of octets can't be found anymore. I went once with some octet singers to a university but when these things are removed from their place of origin they lose their vitality. They are beautiful in the squares and the threshing floors of the old farms.

*Have these poetic interests and traditions entered your films?*

In *Berlinguer ti voglio bene* there is a brief sequence of an old man from my town who sings a few octets, but it's hard to put those things in film. It would become a documentary.

*I understand that you had a brief stint as a Jesuit seminarian in Florence.*
When I arrived as a boy in this new town, Prato, I was extremely shy like all immigrants and I had trouble. I was quiet because I spoke a different dialect. I wore a little beanie that was common in Misericordia but was thought of as funny in Prato. I dressed, talked, and behaved differently. When I went to school the religion teacher, a priest, saw that I was quiet and studious, always raising my hand to answer in class. One day he came up to me and asked, "Do you feel something, my son?" This big red-faced priest hovering over me. I said, "Yes," so he went to my family and said that this boy probably has the calling. I agreed but I was not really that convinced.

*Can we trace any of your religious satires in* Tuttobenigni *to this experience with the Jesuits?*
I was with the Jesuits for a very short time, a month or so. I don't remember much except that we slept in these dormitories with medieval writings on the walls. I was actually afraid because I was all by myself. My mother let me go but she wasn't that convinced either. Since we did not have much money with three women in the house, my mother let me go. Then I went home because of the flood in November of 1966. I had to go home by foot because Florence was full of water and everyone was leaving. As for the monologues, I liked doing this God who is a little bit angry and incompetent, and they are quite popular. There is nothing more popular than talking about God and the Bible and the creation of the world.

*What about music?*
Well I should say that even though I am Italian and Tuscan, unlike other Italians and Tuscans my parents and family couldn't stand opera, they thought it was ridiculous and always made fun of it. I suppose I inherited their attitude. My relationship with music is something sort of like in Homer where Ullyses is attracted by the songs of the sirens. So I had no music education beyond the basic, ancient attraction to music. Then I discovered Rossini who along with Strauss I think is a marvel. Then I worked with [Claudio] Abbado the orchestra conductor and we did *Peter and the Wolf*. Abbado was also interested in Rossini to the point that he re-introduced Rossini in Vienna and in Germany, where Rossini had been considered a minor composer. So we did *Peter and the Wolf* with the Vienna Philharmonic, the great orchestra, and he even asked me to do some Rossini, even sing in an opera, which would have been curious. But

I still have this former reticence towards opera from my family. Then I started to play the guitar in the sixties. My mother did not have the money to send me to study but there was a friend of mine in town who took lessons and even had an electric guitar. He would return from his lesson and repeat what he learned for me. That is how I learned. He even gave me a guitar later. Then with my guitar I tried to get into the Celentano Clan in Milan when I was fifteen. I sold my watch, which gave me the exact amount for my fare to Milan, but they would not let me in, so I returned home.

*Then you became interested in the theater.*

I met Donato Sannini and Carlo Monni, who were involved in the theater and said they were going to Rome, so I went with them. Before that Monni and I toured the region [Tuscany] to put on fake political meetings, like storytellers. There is even a film of one that was completely improvised. But there has been such a tremendous change from the Italy of those days that it seems like the Middle Ages. The traditions were still strong. Pasolini described how they are disappearing due to the homogenization of culture. But what I remember is the sense of fantasy and the wonder of life, which was so amazing.

*It was in Rome that you did the monologue* Cioni Mario di Gaspare fu Giulia.

When *Cioni Mario* came out I was attacked because of the strong language. At Caserta and Pisa I actually had to escape because they came after me, all because of the strong language.

*Was it because of the references to Berlinguer?*

No, it was the language itself that represented the subproletariat of those times. The ones who protested above all were women; feminists in particular found it offensive. The year it came out, 1975–76, was the year of feminism in Italy. They did not understand the idea of the separation between character and actor. My character was desperate because he had no luck with women. In the monologue there is a terrible and frightening invective against women. Dacia Maraini came to see the show in Rome and enjoyed it very much. She said it was the first time that a male had done a feminist performance. She wrote a long piece on it. Then I went to perform the monologue in a town in Romagna before an audience composed entirely of women. They attacked me and broke one of my ribs, sent me to the hospital. At the time I was a devil for women. So I had Maraini's piece copied and put on a placard at the show for the women, because I couldn't perform if they attacked me. At Leghorn when I performed the invective against women someone threw a full can of beer at me, hitting me on the shoulder. Since I knew that the tent was full I jumped down and escaped under a hail of beer cans. They chased me all the way to the station and I jumped on the first train out of town.

*But when you first did the monologue in Rome wasn't it a success?*

Oh yes. The monologue was performed at the avant-garde theater in Rome, the Albericchino, and it was a hit. In those days nobody was doing monologues because there was the Roman school of the avant-garde. People like Perlini, Vasilicò, and Carmelo Bene were doing experimental theater. It was very unconventional but still quite beautiful, really an extraordinary moment, a wonderful school that attracted me. The idea of returning to narrative and doing a monologue was the exact opposite of what had been happening there, almost like a challenge although this was not done consciously. I told Giuseppe Bertolucci that I wanted to do Dostoyevsky's *Memories of the Underground* but he said it was too refined for me. Since every night I would tell stories, sexual stories about my hometown; we decided to do this monologue and everything took off from there. The Albericco Theater sold out. It was one of the strongest emotional experiences of my life. There were long lines every night. We started doing it four, even five times a day. With success came attention and it even stirred some aggression. I received some very harsh criticism, especially from the right because there is the bit with Almirante [neofascist leader] in the monologue. I had to be escorted from place to place. The same thing happened with *La vita è bella*. At the premiere at the Cinema Cavour we received threats; the neofascists who handed out fliers and tried to prevent people from entering.

*Could we think of the* Cioni Mario *monologue as a combination of Dostoyevsky and Rabelais set in rural Tuscany?*

That's right. *Memories of the Underground* and *Gargantua* put together. In fact, Albericchino Bertolucci, the poet, told me to read Rabelais the first time. Rabelais is really one of the creators of French literature. I was astounded that in the sixteenth century someone could write something with such liberty.

*So the opening of the* Cioni Mario *monologue with the father on the commode is like the beginning of Rabelais.*

That's right, and then there is the *Inno del corpo sciolto* (*The Hymn to the Loose Bowel Movement*). There is a sonnet at the beginning of Rabelais where he says that defecating is the most human thing in the world. So I wrote this little song that is still very popular among children; they all know it by heart.

*How about the film version of the monologue,* Berlinguer ti voglio bene? *With director [Giuseppe] Bertolucci you introduced more characters but retained the strong language.*
The language was extremely graphic. People left the theater when they saw it. The language in the film is still very, very strong.

*But the language seems archaic, almost out of place in a medium like film.*
The problem with the film is that one could not really translate the theatrical work to the screen. I love the film and think it is beautiful. Giuseppe was really wonderful and did a great job. But it was too strong. During the tracking shot in which I curse after the supposed death of my mother, people left the theater. The scene is accompanied by a soundtrack of frogs and toads which crescendos, Bertolucci's idea, to the point that it becomes unbearable. Then there are also other very strong themes like the character of the mother, played by Alida Valli.

*There is also a strong presence of death in the film, all the references to cancer. What did Cioni's little sister die of in the film?*
From cancer. Oh, in *Berlinguer ti voglio bene* there is death everywhere. But it was too strong; it was so rural, scary.

*Then there are references to the [Communist] Party in one scene you are on a barrel and the soundtrack is of protest songs.*
That is also a very crude thing but it was not against the party. It was the subproletariat, because Cioni is sort of fablelike. We thought it would be appropriate to accompany this fablelike story with these very powerful worker protest songs so that one felt the contradiction. That was also very powerful.

*After your success with the* Cioni *monologue you appeared in a number of films but you also spent some time with Cesare Zavattini.*
Zavattini was amazing. I worked for a whole year with Zavattini. I would go to his house at ten in the morning and this is something that I have said very few times because we ended up not doing the film together. I went to his house from morning to evening for an entire year. We ate together every day. He taught me so much. I really owe him a great deal

and must thank him. He would do the screenplay and the music and the actors all at the same time, jumping on the table, and he was about eighty years old when we were working together. He told me that I just had to watch and then after six months of observing him I could participate too. So I didn't open my mouth for six months. He taught me how to write a treatment, how to write a screenplay. Then there is Zavattini's style, neorealism. He was such a great dreamer. It is not true that he was so serious. *Miracle in Milan* is a film of such poetry, it is truly marvelous. I will never stop thanking him.

*Would you aspire to be an heir to his style in his fablelike films with De Sica:* Miracle in Milan *or* Il giudizio universale?
    I would very much like to have something of Zavattini in what I do. He was a great intellectual and a creator of a new style. Something can be Zavattinian just like something can be Fellinian. We must be grateful to these people who gave us so much. They taught us how to see and to understand what we have in front of us. They are people that we must always thank and the fact that I was able to meet a few of them was a great gift for me.

*It was in the first years in Rome that you also went to some film revivals and clubs.*
    Well there I saw everything by Chaplin at a small film club in Via Garibaldi and I discovered other films that are often shown in those circles. I remember Dreyer in particular, which are dramas but also comedies, because I was interested in trying to look at Dreyer from a comedic standpoint. Dreyer really fascinated me, along with Chaplin.

*Later you did a film with Massimo Troisi,* Nothing Left to Do but Cry/Non ci resta che piangere. *In an interview Carlo Monni said that it was completely improvised and that there was very little by the way of a script.*
    Yes, well, that was joyful madness. Troisi and I had only recently met so the film was done almost instinctively, based on the extreme joy of our friendship. We became such good friends, so quickly, it was healthy but dangerous because it was so strong. Each one felt that since the other was there that we could rely on one another. So we did this film as if it were a game, without any sense at all. Kids still love that film, which is something that I would never have expected. It was a great gift, the result of the happiness that we felt just being together. And the whole thing was completely improvised. In the morning we would go to the cinematographer, [Giuseppe] Rotunno, a great artist. We did not know what to tell him about what we were going

to do. This went on from August to December. Then we reshot the entire thing. We did a first version that was completely incomprehensible. It seemed like the work of madmen, based entirely on fun and joy. We tried to stop the film's release and write something but we could never come up with anything beyond the idea of just going to shoot and improvising speeches on who invented shampoo, the letter to Savonarola, the meeting with Leonardo da Vinci. That was also completely improvised. [Troisi] always gave me the part of the intellectual. I spoke to Leonardo about Freud and Marx and he spoke about *scopa* [a card game]. We drove the construction crew and the set designers mad because they needed to have some ideas about what the town from the fifteenth century should look like, but we did not know what to tell them. The sets were done by chance without any sense at all. That film is ugly and beautiful. It has this spirit of joy and light of friendship. When I saw the film again it frightened me because it has that tremendous light of our friendship.

*What about the idea for* The Little Devil/Il piccolo diavolo?
   That film is very much like *Pinocchio*. It begins with me speaking inside a woman like Pinocchio begins speaking inside a piece of wood. Then I come out asking all these questions. Walter Matthau in the film is like Geppetto, my favorite Geppetto. I escape and then I call him daddy. It is very much like *Pinocchio*. I enjoyed the absolute freedom that the part gave me. He [Giuditta] is a child, like a newborn baby. Then I always refer to the female part, to "that thing there," as the origin of the world. In fact, in *Il piccolo diavolo* there is a citation of Rabelais of the female organ as the origin of the world. In *Gargantua* and *Pantangruel* there is a devil who leaves the world because a woman shows him her thing. He is so frightened that he departs. I wanted to put a citation of Rabelais at the beginning but it was taken out later. The seeming confusion in the film is deceiving because it was constructed very, very carefully, based on three or four basic ideas. Then it has a style that did not resemble anything else in Italy. It was not like the *commedia dell'arte,* the *commedia all'italiana,* neo-realism, or historical films, anything.

*Is there any sense of a debt to Pasolini in the film with its mixture of a fable, inno-
cence? You had made a film with a Pasolini disciple, Sergio Citti [Il minestrone].
Cerami was a Pasolini disciple and this was your first film in which he was screenwriter.*
   There probably is something of Pasolini in there since Cerami was a Pasolini disciple. My characters, my poor, pure characters may have some-

thing of Pasolini in them. But Pasolini had a style that was so personal and identifiable, strong like a bulwark. He also made all of those films with Totò *Al di la delle nuvole, Uccelacci uccellini*. But that is more from Cerami, the Pasolinian side. Donati and Delli Colli also worked with Pasolini. I once asked them who was the person that they were most attached to, Fellini or Pasolini. They both responded that Pasolini influenced them the most from a personal and artistic standpoint.

*How did the idea for* Johnny Stecchino *come about?*

Cerami had written a story about a mafioso who finds a double to take his place but it was for television and it was tragic. There is such strong tradition of stories with character switches in Plautus or the doubles in Stevenson that it is a little dangerous to try to measure oneself with the classics. But I liked the idea because a comedian's material always has a tragic base. Also, for an actor it is always enticing to play a double role, a bit narcissistic but fun. Then there is the fact the entire film is based on a joke about a banana, the same gag. This fascinated me to no end because it seemed impossible to organize a film on a single gag. A whole film about a banana being stolen and the character who doesn't realize about the banana. That is actually what the film was most criticized for, that it is a banana joke from beginning to end. But it is a marvelous nonsense that was quite difficult to write, although we had a joyful, wonderful time making the film. There is always the doubt of having done something completely crazy, some marvelous nonsense. It was recently rebroadcast on Italian television and still received the highest share after all of these years. I thought that it was a bit slow in terms of the directing, because I was still learning. There is also an enormous amount of work that goes into having the gags come off well. The counterpoints, the construction of the gags are the things that I love the most, even though they are difficult, like in *La vita è bella* it is the thing that I love most.

*The final scene of* Johnny Stecchino, *when Lillo snorts cocaine because Dante tells him it is a cure for diabetes, was cut from the American print.*

They told me that the film would never be released in the States with a scene of a kid with Down's syndrome who mistakenly sniffs cocaine. In Italy it did not cause any controversy so it may be a matter of a cultural differences. It was practically my first film experience in the States, where *Il piccolo diavolo* did not get released for bureaucratic reasons that I have never understood. They wanted to cut *Johnny Stecchino* as if it were a film for nuns. I thought they were kidding. I wasn't the producer of the film and so I tried to make sure that the cut was done well, but I suffered a bit over that one.

*How about the idea for* The Monster/Il mostro?
I work with Vincenzo Cerami for the ideas for the films. With *Il mostro* I had just made *Johnny Stecchino,* which at the time was the biggest success ever in Italy. I do not know how to thank the Italian public for the great favor they have shown me. Then I was called by Blake Edwards to do the *Son of the Pink Panther.* When I heard the name Blake Edwards I wanted to work with him. I would do it again. The idea for *Il mostro* came about because I like to do things in the present, although there is absolutely no reference to the monster of Florence. It was the point of arrival of the films that I had done previously—*Il piccolo diavolo* and *Johnny Stecchino.* I am always very interested in the repetitions, the metonyms created from a narrative point of view. The gags were all so strong because they are all about sex, just like in *Il piccolo diavolo.* In *Il mostro* there was the idea of playing with the way that people read each other. It is a film about prejudices, the way that Nazism was based on prejudices. All one has to do is change a point of view by a millimeter and everything, all reality changes. The most pure being suddenly can become the most horrible. I also liked the fact that the protagonist was not a complete innocent. He is like Pinocchio. He steals and lives by his wits, and is even a bit nasty, quite a modern character. There are also some dark passages in *Il mostro.* It becomes quite dramatic at the end, especially in the final chase scenes. Also the gags are not really part of the comedy genre. In fact I directed it as if it were a horror film. It is a film that I am quite attached to, although it is difficult to speak in that way of one's own films.

*The play on the different points of view of the main character is very sophisticated. There also seem to be many references to the films of Fritz Lang like* M, Dr. Marbuse.
I have seen *M* many times and there are bits taken from Lang's films like the music that reveals the identity of the killer. The film also has scenes taken from other films, a sort of film-buff game. Like the number on my uniform in *La vita è bella* is the same as Chaplin's [*The Great Dictator*]. In *Il mostro* there is a scene taken from Kubrick's *The Shining.* When the protagonist played by Nicholson loses his mind he is at the typewriter typing "The quick red fox jumped over the lazy brown dog" over and over again. When my character goes into the house of the real monster,

there is a clue that he is the killer. I had that phrase from *The Shining* written on the blackboard fifty times in Chinese.

*There has been a steady increase in your abilities as a director from your first to last film.*
I was always interested in the cinema, not technically, but as a manner of storytelling. In film the technical aspects are ever changing so it is not easy to keep up. Like everything, even Dante, it is simple but not easy.

*If we compare* Johnny Stecchino *and* Il mostro, *for example, there seems to be a reduction of close-ups.*
I realized that the face of a comedian is so powerful that it has to be dealt out carefully. Even in Chaplin close-ups are rare because the face of the comedian is almost blasphemous or pornographic, you can sense the power in it. Chaplin once said that the three-quarter shot was better for comedy. He gave a practical explanation but the deeper reason is that the face of the comedian is frightening and might even scare the spectators. It is like a flavor that is too strong, like putting only red pepper in a dish. There is something in the face of the comedian, something in the soul, like a little fire that lights up. When I saw my own close-ups I began to think that the close-up of the comedian is something that should be guarded, like an energy that can be consumed too quickly. There is a similar relationship to camera movements in comedy films, which are also rare. It takes a great effort to understand the right moment to use them.

*There are some close-ups in* La vita è bella *with Nicoletta Braschi that convey powerful emotions, such as when she looks about the window at the ashes rising from the crematoria.*
The close-ups in my films are always wide, never too tight. There was a trend to do tight close-ups recently, but I feel that a sense of space should be allowed to flow in the shot. Even in *La vita è bella* there are no tight shots. If anything I reserve them for the female image. In *Tu mi turbi* there is one close-up of Nicoletta Braschi [as the Madonna]. She is always seen in close-up, even when viewed from behind. There is a quick close-up and a cut so that the Madonna appears and disappears, like an apparition. Then Nicoletta and I are like that even in my memory, like Mickey and Minnie Mouse, always together. It is an image I cannot live without. I could not go forward without her even as an image. She has been so wonderful in these roles from playing the Virgin Mary [in *Tu mi turbi*], a devil [in *Il piccolo diavolo*], and a killer [in *Johnny Stecchino*].

*On* La vita è bella *you had technicians who (Donati, Delli Colli) who had been part of Fellini's troupe. Were you also thinking of Fellini's films like* Amarcord *and the contrast between innocence and fascism?*

I thought of the buffoonery of the representation of fascism in *Amarcord,* but I did not want to repeat it because I preferred for it to be absent. It is like the poets say [in English], "Absence makes sharper presence." There is also an absence of a realistic vision of the concentration camps in the second half of the film. There is the same absence of fascism in the first half although it is nonetheless quite markedly present. There is always going to be a homage to Fellini in everything that I do. With Delli Colli and Donati the presence of Fellini is always felt. They were there when I made *La voce della luna* with Fellini. I would like there always to be a spark of Fellini in my films.

*In* La vita è bella *is the child aware of what is going on around him?*

I put a scene in the film, which might even have been cut, but I wanted to keep it to emphasize a sense of ambiguity. Objectively the child should not be aware, but he actually does know what is happening. He knows because I made it evident, although everyone can read the film as they please. In the first part of the film Giosué is in the bookstore when the grandmother enters. The child says that he does not know his grandmother, and has never seen her since she no longer wanted to have anything to do with her daughter after the marriage to Guido. When the grandmother leaves, the child says, "You forgot your change, Grandmother." I put that scene in on purpose because it may seem that he is not aware, but actually he is. The child is playing with his grandmother. In the memory of the third person who narrates the story the child probably knows. I put this scene in order to show that the child knows more than we might think, like all children, who are so amazing. Who can tell how they actually see the rain or the barking of a dog? So in my opinion he knows, but he still goes though all of the stops on the journey.

*The film features a number of names from Florentine history—Ferruccio, Guicciardini.*

Ferruccio's last name is Papini, another figure in Italian literature.

*The Guicciardini character was cut from the U.S. version.*

Guicciardini was in the screenplay from the very beginning but when they suggested that it be cut for the American print, I agreed since I had already thought about cutting it, although it is in the Italian version. Even though I think that that screenplay was so complete and so many elements depend upon one another that nothing should have been cut so when they proposed this cut I figured that it could be put back later. Guicciardini was there to show the sense of joy in the two friends, Guido and Ferruccio, and to create a setup for the hat joke, because one is not enough and four is too many. The number three is needed for the metonymy, the repetition of a gag. So now the second setup has been cut.

*In* La vita è bella *the protagonist plays games with language which reminds me of scenes in earlier films like Giuditta's comic version of multiplication tables in* Il piccolo diavolo *or the Chinese lessons in* Il mostro.

That is because all of my characters are little bit like Pinocchio, a chain leading to *Pinocchio,* which is what I would like to do now.

*What type of* Pinocchio *do you have in mind?*

I want to do Collodi, the original version. There have been other Italian versions. Comencini did a fantastic version in eight episodes for Italian television but he used a real boy. But I am an adult so it will be different. I am almost afraid to look at Comencini's version because I might end up copying it so it is better to forget about it; fortunately he did it for television so there is no competition. *Pinocchio* is such a powerful piece. It is so full of meaning that if I were to limit it to one interpretation or one style I would be leaving too much out.

*Didn't Collodi have some political interpretations in mind? Politically he was a Mazzinian.*

But like all masterpieces it sort of got away from him. He did not even want to write it. Any one of us can write a masterpiece except in the moment when we set down to try to do so. *Pinocchio,* the story took off on Collodi, you can tell that he was unable to control it. He wrote it to pay his gambling debts. *Pinocchio* is actually a bit frightening. Fellini wanted to do it as a nightmare. He had in his mind a nineteenth-century Italy that was like a nightmare. I think that the most important things in *Pinocchio* are freedom and fantasy. I just saw a version recently with Martin Landau which is quite scary. They took some liberties with the story but the power of *Pinocchio* is hard to define. It was certainly an involuntary masterpiece.

*In* Pinocchio *there are choices to be made in the story. For example, will Pinocchio kill the cricket as in the original?*

That is a question that I have asked myself many times because *Pinocchio* starts out violently. Pinocchio has a great heart but he starts out violently. It is actually a very violent book. Disney erased all of the violence from the story, even if technically his version is a masterpiece. I just saw it again recently but Pinocchio is not there. There is no poverty, repression, violence, the torturing of Pinocchio. The interesting thing about Pinocchio is that once he becomes a good boy, he turns into a sort of perfect employee. Another great European writer, Kafka, wrote the *Metamorphosis,* which in my opinion is like a sequel to *Pinocchio.* The employee in Kafka's story becomes an insect. It is like Pinocchio transformed again, the next part of *Pinocchio.* Because at the end it is very sad to see the lifeless puppet and the real boy who becomes this perfect employee. It makes you cry, no, no you have killed him, killed him. So as for the cricket, yes, I think I will kill him because that is the way Collodi wrote it. The decisions about the characters will be part of the joy, the fun of making the film. Collodi was not a writer who learned the technical aspects of his craft the way that one learns to play chess or bridge. He learned for the pleasure of it. He didn't even really review what he had written so that there are mistakes in it, which is part of its charm. As for the characters, for example, there is not a great relationship between Pinocchio and Geppetto. Geppetto disappears almost right from the beginning. As soon as he makes Pinocchio he thinks, "Oh my gosh, what have I done, look at all of the trouble this one is going to cause me." Then Pinocchio runs away and Geppetto only finds him again in the boat at the very end. Pinocchio owes everything to his father only because he is his father. It is like the blackmail of life. He is your father and you owe everything to him even though there was little between them.

*Doesn't Geppetto sell his coat to get the books for Pinocchio?*

He sells the coat in order to buy the spelling book but Pinocchio had been born just twelve hours before. He lives with Geppetto for twelve hours and then he goes off. When he finds him again in the belly of the whale there is a big scene. He cries, "Oh father, father," and the whole story seems to be about his father. But they only lived together for twelve hours. He is the father and that is enough.

*Your performances of Dante in the States made an enormous impression on those fortunate to hear you. One of your recitations and commentaries of canto 5 was broadcast on the RAI television program* Babele *in 1993.*

Oh yes. Well there I was being a bit of a rascal. But when I made my first film in America with Jarmusch, *Down by Law,* I recited Whitman, who is another poet that I know some pieces by heart in English even if it was in a raving sort of English. But Whitman is also a bit Dantean, perhaps more biblical than Dantean, but he is certainly sort of an American Dante in my recollection. I had learned Whitman without even really knowing any English. When I recited Whitman, Jarmusch was very taken by it and wanted to put it in the film *Down by Law*. For Italians, knowing some Dante isn't unusual, everyone knows Dante. When I was growing up, my relatives knew some verses of Dante. Even my mother, who was illiterate, knew a couple of verses by Dante and she would point him out to me as a model for his memory or because he could tell a story; she would say "See that Dante Alighieri, he did well because he studied." So Dante was always the example for all kids my age in Tuscany. Dante even scared us a bit. He was a part of our childhood.

*Speaking about an author such as Dante brings up the question of your feelings about divisions between high and low culture.*

Dante is actually the one who gives an answer to this question. Dante wrote in Italian in a period when all writing was done in Latin as the exclusive language of intellectuals. These boring intellectuals wanted to keep Latin as the only language for poetry until the 1400s. But Dante made poetry and narrative multilingual. So there is the first reading one can do of Dante, which is the popular reading, even for the uneducated like my mother who knows a few lines and some sayings by Dante. But then there is the second, third, fourth, and fifth reading of Dante. But everyone recited Dante out loud because like Homer we shouldn't forget that poetry was born as song, recited, even yelled by the evening fireplace. They used to tell it to us when we were kids to scare us. I had a relative named Tuccio who went around during the war with a copy of the *Divine Comedy* in one pocket and his gun in the other. They were two great weapons. Besides, Dante is a popular figure. In Tuscany the anecdotes about Dante are about his love for women or about sex. So I did that introduction [for the RAI program] at a popular level about how Dante made love all of the time because in many towns there are stories about Dante's girlfriends.

Then in the Italian language 97 percent of the words we use come from Dante, the same words unchanged for seven hundred years with the same meaning. This is why Dante is such a miracle and every time that I read the *Divine Comedy* or some verses from Dante I feel that they are of such a scandalous beauty. But I am always attracted to that first reading that is always tied to the story itself. Whenever I finish I notice how incredible and even scandalous it is that it has remained unsurpassed. In two thousand years of Christian poetry nobody has been able to do a better description of the Madonna in Paradise or the damned in Hell. There is such an orgy of sensations of the baseness of the body and all of the carnal elements as well as the sublime. He is the syntagma, the living symbol of contradiction because he is like the Madonna, humble and sublime. He is a miracle, truly a great gift, this Dante. Maybe because of that I have never really considered it that carefully. When I was young I went to learn how to improvise with the singing poets in the Tuscan tradition that my father loved so much. He would always say, "The greatest of them all is Dante Alighieri and you have to become good at it just like he was," as if someone could become as good as Dante. But for musicality the terzine is infinite and so every time that I read some verses like "he lifted his mouth from the savage meal,"[1] it is like the beginning of a great musical score when a cello starts to play the first notes of a famous tune. The first verses of every canto are like notes of great music, which could be like a *Stabat mater* by Verdi or Rossini. So actually it is like knowing the words to songs. Dante is truly a great gift.

*Your performance of Dante at UCLA went over very well.*

When I did Ulysses and Paolo and Francesca at UCLA it was wonderful, spectacular. There were all of these American schoolkids who had come by bus. It was very special. They even asked me to give some lessons on Dante. Another wonderful experience was in Florence at Piazza Belvedere in front of 20,000 people. It made one cry, it was really moving. When you do something that you truly enjoy, the spirit of it comes across, although I was still being a bit of a rascal. I just did something on Dante that will come out soon, on television. I met with students at the Normale di Pisa, the University of Bologna, the University of Padua, and the University of Rome. They knew about my love for Dante and asked me to do a canto. So I jumped up on the table and improvised a brief introduction and then recited a canto. They always ask for something out of *Inferno,* but at Bologna for the first time I did something from *Paradiso,* and it was a little difficult.

*Which part of* Paradiso *did you perform, when Dante meets [his ancestor] Cacciaguida?*

No, I did the last one, the thirty-third, the canto to the Virgin Mary, which is difficult but it is the most beautiful poetry of all Catholic poetry of all time. It is of a scandalous beauty, when I did I became emotional. I had never done it [*Paradiso*] in public so it did not go that well except for the fact that I felt the emotion of the canto. Dante in that canto does not betray us because one must imagine the real Dante with the stench of his clothes heavy with sweat and saliva, hanging on his wrists, in front of the Madonna and God. Just think about this man from the 1200s with his dirty and stinking clothes who has come from Purgatory and Hell having made this trip for us, always believing in it. We have to believe in it too. He tells us what God looks like in a language of the future of his invention. Dante does not let us down. He tells us that we will see God and he shows us. It is not as if Dante says, "I saw him but because of the light I do not remember what he looked like." No, Dante describes him in minute detail. That is amazing and it is not something that one can understand at the first reading but only upon reading and rereading. It makes one emotional. At Bologna my explanation of *Paradiso* was also a bit rascally. Then at Pisa I did Conte Ugolino. They asked me to do that canto because the tower [of the Muda] is right there where the events occurred at Piazza dei Cavallieri. It made an impression on me to do it right there and that was also a great emotion. I made the mistake of lowering my voice; one has to remain more detached in order to continue. But it came off well because one could feel that there was a true passion among the spectators. I would like to do something a bit more structured on Dante and after *Pinocchio* that may be my next project.

*There are some projects that you ended up not doing, a Ferreri film based on a story by Levi, an Olmi film on a story by Chesterton,* Pinocchio *by Fellini, and an Antonioni version of Saint Francis.*

These things weren't done because we eventually decided not to do them. If Fellini had not passed away we may have done his *Pinocchio.* With Olmi we decided that we couldn't do the Chesterton piece. Olmi is a marvelous director, very Catholic. I felt that I would not be able to perform it they way he wanted. There is a little bit of Chesterton in *La vita è bella,* in the love story. With Antonioni we never got beyond a couple of letters, whenever I see him now we joke about it. Before I had decided on doing *Pinocchio* I also was thinking of doing a version of Saint Francis, there is a little bit of Pinocchio, the joy, the torment in Francis as well.

*With Ferreri you met Primo Levi.*

It was sort of a trick of destiny. If anyone had ever told me, a comedian, that I would make a film about the concentration camps I never would have believed them.

*His book* [Survival at Auschwitz] *is one of the most important works of the past century.*

Levi's book unites the story of the death camps with chemistry, the manipulation of basic materials in science, because Levi was a chemist. They are the two metaphors for the century, the extermination camps and the manipulation of prime materials. I met Levi because of Marco Ferreri, with whom I did *Seeking Asylum,* another film with children. Ferreri wanted to do a film on Levi's book *The Monkey Wrench,* a story about a worker and engineering. The meeting with Primo Levi was at Marco Ferreri's house in the Ghetto in Rome. Levi was like a dignified gentleman, he had a small goatee, and his face was so small, gentile, dreamy, almost lost. He sat on a chair, hands folded and hardly said anything. He was honored that Ferreri was going to make a film out of one of his other books, where the subject was not the Holocaust. His life had been so obviously marked by that experience. So he had a great sense of liberation and he seemed truly pleased that we were going to do a film on this book. Unfortunately, nothing ever came of the film project. I was a bit nervous meeting him because I come from the generation that read his books in school and it gave me very strong emotion to meet him.

*Abroad the Italian cinema is known and remembered for various movements like neorealism, the* commedia all'italiana *with Sophia Loren, or the political films by Pontevcorvo.*

When my films came out here in Italy, like *Il piccolo diavolo, Johnny Stecchino, Il mostro,* I read some of the criticisms of the films and I understood that they were not able to insert them into a style or tradition of the Italian cinema. To a certain extent I did not mind because they did not say, "Oh here is the *commedia dell'arte,*" or "Here is something that is like Zavattini, Pasolini, or Fellini." They did not understand that my films are in the tradition of all of them instead of a single defining characteristic. I was quite pleased by this idea that there was something new, a new style here. I have never really been taken by realistic films, not even neorealist films. I have always been far from neorealism even if I like the films. But it is not my favorite genre. In fact, when neorealism is not well done it was really terrible and many Italian filmmakers who were fanatics of that genre were ruined by neorealism. It is a genre of film that I have never espoused, just like the *commedia all'italiana,* which was a great period that produced many marvelous and unique things. Then there were outsiders like Fellini and Antonioni who one could not call a neorealist. So I am not sure what exactly in what school or style I belong.

I feel that cinema should separate itself, it should fly. Neorealism left a deep imprint with Zavattini who theorized it and who created some absolute masterpieces. But in a certain manner it is as if it was not able to take off. There is the example of Fellini who was not a neorealist and Rossellini who was like our Homer, the discoverer of Italian cinema. They tried to stop Fellini from working in the studio where he would make the magic and the dream of the cinema, truly re-create everything from zero, to take a voice from a face, to reinvent everything. That is truly the soul of cinema, not taking from reality. This is something that has even frightened me a bit. There we were in the dream factory and they closed the doors. But the sun and dreams are the things that console us so it was like closing the doors on dreams. Yet at the same time when they were successful there was this marvelous contradiction with dream and reality together, as in the films by De Sica or Visconti for which perhaps one should make a separate category. Then after the school of the *commedia dell'arte,* the *commedia all'italiana,* the Italian cinema has suffered a decline. We still are not sure if it has stopped tumbling down. But we hope that we are at the end of this abyss and that some extraordinary things will appear.

*Some Italian directors now make films directly in English.*

The English language is marvelous because it is an extraordinarily infantile language. There is no middle ground in English; it is full of ono-matopoetics. It really has a sound at a very primary level. Like an infantile language, it is beautiful for poets and so attractive that you can become enchanted by it. They really do speak like children. At the same time I don't have any roots in the English language and the best way for me to do a film in English is to do it in Italian. When Gandhi or the Dalai Lama were asked what is the best way to be a good Buddhist in Italy he said the best Buddhist in Italy is a good Christian, and he is right. A film will do well if it is a good film, no matter the language. In fact the greatest Italian films were done in dialect and then were successful in America.

*Many recent Italian films popular in the States depict an Italy of the past from the 1930s or '40s.*

This is true and it is something that I have asked myself at times. Perhaps because they are aware of the great Italian cinema of that time. They know that Italy and want it depicted over and over again. Films set in contemporary times are more difficult because one cannot recognize or know just what it is. Therefore there is this sense of loss. It is even quite difficult in terms of the sets or the colors, the dialogue, and above all the costumes are difficult to make understandable. I love making contemporary films about Italy because I recognize this loss of style which is a style in itself. Like the outskirts of cities which are becoming identical all over the world, the gray, red. There are colors that I see which are very strong and quite vulgar, like the color of chicken thighs, the colors of the gates, the buildings of the Roman outskirts. I believe that it is something that is difficult to do well. One could easily sink into banality or into provocation rather than the simplicity that should be the objective. There is such a fine line between banality and simplicity, it is very difficult to handle.

*In* Il mostro, *for example, you depict some contemporary settings.*

Yes, and also in *Johnny Stecchino* and *Il piccolo diavolo*. I tried to find this language of uniformity in the outskirts that are the same in Bangkok or Ohio. They are so identical and therefore extremely difficult to express.

*What about politics? You have always been identified with progressive politics.*

I have always belonged to a world where there was a tradition where the left represented equality and the right was identified with order. That is how I have lived my sense of the left and yet it is not as if I have ever been active in politics. We could say that I have swum in the river of the people that I loved the most and they were all on the political left. I do not know if it was by chance but I was surrounded by all of these marvelous glances. In them I never saw the dream of the leftist utopia but the satisfaction of being surrounded by beautiful thoughts which always came from that direction, whether from my generation or my mother and father. However, comedians in particular are notorious for being great reactionaries because the comedian originates from the clown who was always close to power, close to the king. Only at a certain point he cannot resist and that is why buffoons were often killed, because they got too close to the king. Since the clown cannot resist joking, the king has him killed. The clown can't help himself. This is the great medieval tradition of the buffoon who wants to be close to power, even Shakespeare's clowns. Because of this the more reactionary the state, the more power a comedian has.

*How about your interest in the German philosopher Arthur Schopenhauer.*

He was the first philosopher that I had anything to do with. Many years ago in my hometown, almost by accident, a friend gave me a book of his, *World As the Representation of Will*. Schopenhauer amazed me because like Plato, Spinoza, or Descartes and *The Discourse on Methodology*, Schopenhauer can be approached at the first reading. They are philosophers that can be read almost like a novel. Then there are others who are impossible to understand although that does not mean that they are any less extraordinary than Schopenhauer. But Schopenhauer along with Plato has an open style that is so approachable. But more than the writing I was struck by his biography and by his face. Because of the contradictions, I found him to be a great clown. He was the greatest pessimist of his century, with Byron and Leopardi. He was like Groucho Marx, who got mad about everything and criticized everything in his diaries. He surrounds himself with so much tragedy that it becomes like a form of clowning. Schopenhauer is great when he writes about the art of conversation, the art of reasoning, all of these essays and pamphlets that he wrote against Hegel and German philosophy. There are pearls of comedy and humor but of a tragic humor because his life was one of the most tragic and pessimistic. His vision of the world is like a gothic cathedral during an earthquake. It is truly frightening, but at the same time I was taken by his life and his face and the things he says and the words he uses. There is also his love for animals or for Buddhism and pantheism. He was also scared, terrified of women, which makes him sort of like Giacomo Leopardi, another great pessimist who was terrified of women. Schopenhauer had the same terror of women that truly ripped him apart.

*With your educational background your interest in so many subjects, Dante for example, is remarkable.*

One should not speak like that; these things are pleasures, as if someone were speaking about chocolate or ice cream. They are things which make you feel good. Say you are walking casually in front of a bar and you see a nice ice cream or you discover pistachio. Also it is not as if I know these things very deeply and completely. When you read a book it is like speaking with the author. When you cite an aphorism it is like saying that is what I wanted to say but he said as well as it could possibly be said therefore I will say it like he said it. They help us.

I recall the great Russian writer, Leskov[2] who described the artist, which could also be a film director, with this beautiful aphorism. One day he was walking in the woods and he saw some peasants who wanted to move a tree trunk out of the road and but it was so heavy that they could not move it. At a certain point one of them climbed on top of the trunk and began to sing and even with the extra weight of the man they were able to move it because he was singing. Leskov said that is what the artist is: a burden for society, a parasite. With the strength and will and value of dreams things can be moved that were impossible before. It is a beautiful metaphor, the artist who helps us. So there are things that we get from artists, the sense of dreams, lightness, and poetry that trouble us because they dig so deeply. They are like miners who pull things out, pieces of coal or pieces of gold deep within us that we have never seen before that frighten us, truly frighten us.

## BENIGNI ON *LA VITA È BELLA/LIFE IS BEAUTIFUL*

*Conducted by Vanina Pezzetti*

La vita è bella *presents the story of a family of Tuscan Jews, actually a mixed family, deported to a concentration camp. How did you become interested in a subject so different from the ones you have done previously?*

Even if it might seem like an outrageous statement, this film is not any different from my previous ones. I think that a comedian should always be involved with stories that are startling. All of the plots of the films of great comedians are born from things that are tragic. Just think about Chaplin, whose stories are all tragic. This film was not planned. It just came to me. I wanted to let myself go into something that would take me over completely. In this moment the thing that I feel the most is the Holocaust. My family is not Jewish, although my father was in a work camp, not a concentration camp. In his stories he did not make me relive it as a trauma. He always told me about it gently and that stayed with me. When I was looking for a story this ogre came out who existed, even if my father did not let me see it. Anyway, I speak about it in my own way, not like a clown or minstrel,[3] because I too have a certain degree of sensitivity. You know, what scares me the most about the Holocaust is the lack of an explanation.

*What is your character in the film like?*

I am an antifascist, not only in my heart, but even physically. One understands this from my appearance. I cannot be a fascist because of my eyebrows, my buckteeth, my belly are all antifascist. So I represent complete liberty, the chaos of being and generosity. Anyway, I did not go overboard with a posthumous criticism of fascism which would have been too easy, rhetorical, and ugly.

*I understand that you have read a lot of Yiddish literature. Do you think that Guido, the character you play, comes close to the figure of the "schlemiel"?*

No, it's not like that. I wanted to create a character who would not be recognizable as a Jew because of obvious clues but who ultimately would be just like me. I wanted the spectator to ask himself, "Why did they go after Benigni?" As if he could ask the same question for himself. My character is a Jew who lives in his city, who is not involved in politics. He does his job and then all of a sudden this ax comes down which splits his life apart, just as it happened in reality. That is the reason why I wanted to create a character that everyone could identify with. Anyway, he is like all the Jews I know.

*So Guido does not have a Jewish identity?*

No. Guido represents total liberty, the sparkle and the shine in life. He is someone that you would never like to see get hurt. That is how I see Jews as well as all people in the world. There is a sense of Hebrew tradition, especially in the second part of the film, but he is an assimilated Jew.

*Chaplin in* The Great Dictator, *Lubitsch in* To Be or Not to Be, *Brooks in* The Producers *were able to create highly comical situations, even while speaking about Hitler and Nazism. How were you able to reconcile the comic and tragic tones of the film, especially in the last part of the film set in the concentration camp?*

This is a question that I often asked myself, from the time the story was born. The story was born from the idea of being alone in a concentration camp with a five-year-old child. This child finds out that the Jews are killed and burned in the ovens and in order to protect him, the father tries to joke about the absurdity of this thing, which is so unfathomable. Yet this film does not become a farce or a parody, even if Chaplin, Lubitsch, and Brooks were poetic. It is a realistic film, even if it does not have a realistic style.

*Can* La vita è bella *be considered a fable?*

Yes. It is a realistic fable. The story of this Jewish family is realistic. But I constructed a camp that is the idea of a camp, a den of iniquity and an imperial Italy, which was all a shine, all invented. For example, I did not do a caricature of the German soldiers; I used German actors instead. Terror is always present but never shown directly. It is evoked. There is nothing more powerful and terrible than an evoked terror. Anything that you can see directly will never have the same impact as something that you cannot see. Anyway, from everything that I have read, seen, and heard from the statements of deportees, I realized that nothing could come close to the reality of what actually happened. There was nothing that I could have done to repeat what has already been done to show things that I did not even have the courage to mention. It is better to evoke it, to have it be imagined. Anyway, I did not want to explain the Holocaust. I just showed some of the most defenseless people of the world in their everyday lives.

*Guido protects his son Giosué from the horrors of the camp. Do you think that this was really possible?*

This did happen, as told in *The Child from Buchenwald,* an extraordinary story, even if the child was younger (he was three years old) and the camp was not a death camp. In my case, my son is five years old, an age in which one can understand some things but not everything. When Guido realizes that the idea of the tank could save the child's life, he never abandons it, even when he is being destroyed. So in a certain sense, this story is close to the one of the child from Buchenwald. On the other hand, nothing was made up, even the most paradoxical things. Think, for example, of the scene in the film where my non-Jewish wife follows me of her own will on the deportation train. Marcello Pezzetti from the Centro di Documentazione Ebraica of Milan has confirmed that this really happened.

*You worked with a large group of children in Ferreri's film* Chiedo asilo/Seeking Asylum. *Was it difficult directing a five-year-old child?*

Oh, certainly! I chose this boy, Giorgio Cantarini, because he looks like Nicoletta and me. Also, his face had this innocence, beauty, knavery, and cleverness. He had never acted before. I had some trouble getting him to do strong emotions. He saw the screams, the tortures, and guns for the first time. He did not even know what the word "Hebrew" meant. He only understood the difference between good guys and bad guys. So he identified the Jews as the good guys and others as the bad guys. What really struck me was how he came to understand what really happened. The boy became a historian!

*As you must know almost all of the Italian Jews were deported to the extermination camp of Auschwitz-Birkenau. You show an idealized camp. What type of camp were you trying to make? What models from film and literature did you refer to for the construction of the camp?*

I saw almost all of the films on the subject. I knew that the Jews had been transferred from Fossoli to Auschwitz and I knew about the existence of the rice storehouse of San Sabba. I reconstructed an archetype of a camp with brick buildings, without the wooden barracks. For the sets I was able to count on the input of Donati, Nedo Faiano, an Auschwitz survivor [who] supplied precious advice on the clothing of the deportees, and for the cinematography—Delli Colli. With Donati it was decided to build a set which would give the idea of a fable and at the same time of the horror of the concentration camp. However, the image of the camp is never farcical. That is the reason I did not introduce the image of a sidecar. I did not want to because it is funny. Just think a little: the sidecar from *Duck Soup* to Lubitsch and Brooks is a classic gag.

*In order to do the scene, in which the Jews undress before being murdered, you were helped by Schlomo Venezia, the only Italian survivor who worked as a* Sonderkommando *[he was forced to work in the death chambers]. You also decided to get help from Marcello Pezzetti, a historian at the Centro Documentazione Ebraica of Milan. What made you require such precision?*

In order to be less hampered, more creative, and to avoid large mistakes, I had to learn, read, and research. To do otherwise would have been a terrible mistake as well as a lack of respect. The research was vital because we were dealing with a wound that has remained open. What drove me was not necessarily a philological reconstruction but the idea of a sense of totality. When Venezia came on the set he must have thought: "Benigni is making a film in a concentration camp, he has to be stopped." But he was moved by the scene of the undressing and told me not to let it be seen all the way through. I had to do this film because no other topic could compare to something so powerful.

*Do you want people to think about it?*

Yes. We must never forget and I don't want this to become an advertising slogan. We must "not forget" as if that "not forget" was being said now for the first time. Above all, we must remember the conditions that led to the deportations. When the film begins, two student types play a prank on Guido's uncle. This event is accompanied with the same musical theme that we hear in front of the ovens. From that prank, from such often-dismissed nonsense, my character is deported. Those are the sort of stupidities that lead to barbarism. Primo Levi said that man should never lose his dignity.

*How did you feel when Schlomo Venezia came on the set?*

I couldn't wait to see him. It was a generous surprise from Marcello. It was like touching Abraham. I was very moved. I was struck by the look in his eyes, but above all his voice, the way he spoke, as if he was still in that gas chamber. Scholmo's voice is not something that I will easily forget. He did not tell me anything. I knew his story because I had seen that marvelous film, *Memoria.*

*Speaking of the film* Memoria *by Ruggero Gabbai, is Guido's character like Romeo Salmoni (one of the survivors who related his experiences) in the combination of tragedy and humor?*
Romeo is very funny and lively; he has a desire to live. He is wonderful and marvelous. My character is a little different. He is an intellectual. He is not able to pretend and make the others happy. He is only happy when he is with the boy. He is so affected by what happens that he cannot make it. He is overcome by this madness, by something that he does not understand. For me Guido is a combination of all the deportees. I would like the public to identify my character with all deportees.

*After the success of your previous films in this period when comedies do not have much social consciousness, are you afraid that the public will not be interested in a story like this one?*
It's just the opposite. Even if they don't follow me anymore, I would still be convinced that I gave them something. It is like a carpenter who gives the most beautiful thing that he knows how to make. I have given the most beautiful thing that I have at this time. I could have been concerned about box-office receipts or producers. If I tell a producer, "I am going to do a film on a deportee," he'd answer, "Forget about it." But I have to do what interests me most and I would have felt guilty if I had chosen to do something else out of fear. Even cinematographically, this is an extraordinary story.

*Do you have any contact with the Jewish world?*
I was lucky enough to be introduced to Jewish literature through Sholom Aleichem and Singer, who has been my favorite for a long time. And then there is Jewish humor in general, which is the best in the world and from which I have stolen many things, above all in terms of self-deprecating humor. I always wanted to meet Singer and once I actually met him in New York. However I knew from his books that he does not like to be bothered. He looked just like Geppetto. I observed him for an hour but I did not approach him. I would like to do many of his stories, for example "Gimpel the Idiot." My film *The Little Devil* has a bit of Singer. As Walter Matthau said, he is a *dibbuk,* a playful devil.

*Have you ever been to Israel?*

Yes, I have been there a couple of times. Some interesting things happened when I was there. When I arrived at the Tel Aviv airport I was paged by the public address system. They put me in a Mercedes with three rabbis who were speaking in Hebrew and who took me to my destination; they knew exactly where I had to go. Then I read the announcement of my arrival in the *Jerusalem Post*. I think I finally understood the reason for the fine treatment I received. In Rome there was an attack on the synagogue, and I declared my indignation to a couple of journalists. I was the only show business figure to do so. They did not forget about it. This really made an impression on me.

*Does your wife, Nicoletta, like this film?*

It is absolutely her favorite film. Her character is extraordinary. Then above all it is a love story. My character loves her and always thinks about her. He is so much in love with this woman that he is lost, forever.

## NOTES

1. *Inferno*, XXXIII, 1.
2. Nicolai Leskov (1831–1895).
3. The word in Italian is *giullare*.

# Bibliography

Ambrogi, Silvano. "Le antiche radici di un comico moderno," in *Quando Benigni ruppe il video.* Turin: Nuova ERI, 1992.

Apih, Elio. *Mostra storica della Risiera di San Sabba.* Trieste: Comune di Trieste, 1989.

Bakhtin, Michail. *Rabelais and His World.* Cambridge, Mass.: MIT Press, 1971. Italian translation, Bachtin, Michael. *L'opera di Rabelais e la cultura popolare riso, carnevale e festa nella tradizione medievale e rinascimentale,* trans. Mili Romano. Turin: Einaudi, 1995.

Baldassarre, Angela. *The Great Italian Directors: Interviews with Filmmakers of Italian Descent.* Toronto: Guernica, 1999.

Baudrillard, Jean. *Simulations,* trans. P. Foss, P. Patton, and P. Beitchman. New York: Semiotext(e), 1983.

Baudry, J. L. *L'effet cinéma.* Paris: Albatros, 1978.

Bencistà, Alessandro. *I bernescanti.* Florence: Edizioni Polistampa, 1994.

Ben-Ghiat, Ruth. "*La vita è bella* (review)," *The American Historical Review,* 104(1) (February 1999): 298–299.

Benigni, Roberto. *E l'alluce fu,* ed. M. Giusti. Milan: Einaudi, 1996.

————. "A lezione da Benigni," *L'espresso* (June 24, 1999): 78.

————. "Babele Benigni," RAI 3, dir. Belli, May 30, 1993.

————. *E l'alluce fu monologhi e gag.* Turin: Einaudi, 1996.

————. *Quando Benigni ruppe il video.* Turin: Nuova ERI, 1992.

————. "Roberto Benigni . . . Fare il buffone oggi . . . meglio il medioevo," *L'Unita'* (January 15, 1981): 15.

Benigni, Roberto, and G. Bertolucci. *TuttoBenigni, Berlinguer ti voglio bene, Cioni Mario di Gaspare fu Giulia.* Rome: Theoria, 1992.

Benigni, Roberto, G. Bertolucci, and Massimo Troisi. *Non ci resta che piangere,* with Anna Pavignano. Milan: Mondadori, 1994.

Benigni, Roberto, and V. Cerami. *La vita è bella.* Torino: Einaudi, 1997.

————. *Johnny Stecchino.* Rome: Theoria, 1991.

Bergson, Henri. *Laughter.* New York: Doubleday, 1956.

Berlinguer, Enrico. "Riflessioni sull'Italia dopo i fatti di Cile," *Rinascita* 5 (October 9, 1973).

Bernardinelli, Alfonso. "Benigni, la nuova estetica di sinistra ha fatto splash," *Corriere della Sera* (January 7, 1997).

Bertolucci, Giuseppe. "Vi presento Benigni," in *Si fa per ridere, ma è una cosa seria . . .,* vol. 6, ed. S. Bernardi, pp. 103–106. Florence: Casa Usher, 1985.

Bianchi, Paolo. *Avere 30 anni e vivere con la mamma.* Milan: Bietti, 1997.

Bieber, Margrete. *The History of the Greek and Roman Theater.* 2nd ed. Princeton, N.J.: Princeton University Press, 1961.

158 *Bibliography*

Bondanella, Peter. *The Cinema of Federico Fellini*. Princeton, N.J.: Princeton University Press, 1992.

Bottoni, Luciano. "La scena di Caino e la sua metamorfosi: Da Alfieri a Benigni," *Rivista di letterature moderne e comparate,* 50(1) (January–March 1997): 21–41.

Brunetta, Gian Piero. *Storia del cinema italiano. Dal miracolo economico agli anni novanta 1960–1993.* 4 vols. Rome: Editori Riuniti, 1993.

Bruni, Francesco. *L'italiano: elementi di storia della lingua e della cultura.* Turin: UTET, 1987.

Calhoun, John. "La not so dolce vita," *Interiors* (April 1999): 85–86.

Canby, Vincent. "Bus Driver and Mafioso in a Comedy of Errors," *The New York Times Current Events Edition* (October 9, 1992): C8.

Cartwright, Justin. "Why the Holocaust Is No Laughing Matter," *The Guardian* (May 29, 1999): T9.

Casella, Paola. *Hollywood Italian gli italiani nell'America di celluloide.* Milan: Baldini & Castoldi, 1998.

Celli, Carlo. "Interview with Marcello Pezzetti of the CDEC (Centro Documentazione Ebraica Contemporanea di Milano)," *Critical Inquiry,* 27 Autumn 2000, 149–157.

———. "The Representation of Evil in Roberto Benigni's *La vita è bella/ Life is Beautiful,*" *Journal of Popular Film and Television.* 28:2, Summer 2000, 74–79.

———. "Roberto Benigni and the *Cioni Mario di Gaspare fu Giulia* monologue." *Italica,* 77(2) (Summer 2000): 171–186.

———. "Federico Fellini's Anti-Intellectualism," *Romance Languages Annual,* 8 (1997): 168–171.

Cerami, Vincenzo. "La scrittura creativa," in *L'officina del racconto,* ed. G. Francesio, pp. 119–134. Forlì: Nuova Compgnia editrice, 1996.

———. *Consigli a un giovane scrittore.* Turin: Einaudi, 1996.

Ciment, M. "*La vita è bella* (review)," *Positif,* 449–450 (July/August 1998): 99–100.

Cosentino, Andrea. *La scena dell'osceno. Alle radici della drammaturgia di Roberto Benigni.* Rome: Oradek, 1998.

Cremonesi, Lorenzo. "Benigni laurea ad honorem Israel lo incorona filosofo," *Corriere della sera* (June 7, 1999).

Denby, David. "Darkness Out of Light," *The New Yorker* (November 16, 1998): 114–116.

———. "In the Eye of the Beholder," *The New Yorker* (March 15, 1999): 96–99.

Eco, Umberto. *Apocalittici e integrati.* Milan: Bompiani, 1984.

Ferrara, Giuliano. "Olocausto Show," *Panorama* (January 22, 1998): 30.

Fofi, Goffredo. "La vita è una furbata," *Panorama* (January 15, 1998).

Forsyth, Douglas J. "The Peculiarities of Italo-American Relations in Historical Perspective," *Journal of Modern Italian Studies* 3(1) (1998): 10–25.

Frankl, Viktor. *Man's Search for Meaning.* New York: Washington Square, 1984.

Frondon, Jean Michel. *La projection nationale: cinema et nation.* Paris: O. Jacob, 1998.

*Garzanti atlante storico.* Milan: Garzanti, 1982.

Gehr, Richard. "*The Monster* (review)," *The Village Voice* (April 23, 1996): 69.

Gil, J. A. "The Camera As the Eye of God: Conversation with Roberto Benigni," *Positif* 452 (October 1998): 34–38.

Giraldi, Massimo. *Giuseppe Bertolucci.* Milan: Il Castoro, 1999.

Girlanda, Elio. "Il cinema delle nazioni," in *Gillo Pontecorvo. La dittatura della verità*. Assisi: ANNCI, 1998.

Gorin, Francois, and Vincent Remy. "La comique peut rendre compte de l'horror," *Telerama* (May 27, 1998).

Goudet, S. "*La vie est belle* (review)," *Positif*, 452 (October 1998): 32–33.

Gramsci, Antonio. *Gli intelletuali e l'organizzazione della cultura*. Turin: Einaudi, 1949.

Grassi, Giovanna. "Benigni: Moretti ha già vinto l'ulivo d'oro," *Corriere della sera* (May 18, 1998).

Grasso, Aldo. *Storia della televisione*. Rome: Garzanti, 1992.

Greene, Naomi. *Landscapes of Loss: The National Past in Postwar French Cinema*. Princeton, N.J.: Princeton University Press, 1999.

Guerrera, Guido Guidi, and P. Ceccatelli. *Benigni ragazzo di Prato*. Florence: Loggia de'Lanzi Editori, 1999.

Hinson, Hal. "Benigni's 'Monster' Won't Carrey You Away," *The Washington Post* (May 31, 1998): D6.

Hoberman, J. "Nazi Business," *Village Voice* (October 27, 1998): 98.

———. "Dreaming the Unthinkable," *Sight & Sound*, 9(2) (February 1999): 20–23.

Holt, Linda. "If All This Were Nothing but a Joke, '*La vita è bella*' (review)," *Times Literary Supplement*, 5006 (March 12, 1999): 20.

Jacobsen, Kurt. "Roberto Benigni's *Life Is Beautiful*," *New Politics*, 7(3) (Summer 1999): 192–195.

Jameson, Fredric. "Postmodernism or the Cultural Logic of Late Capitalism," *The New Left Review*, 146 (1984): 53–92

Jousse, Thierry, and N. Saada. "Roberto Benigni," *Cahiers du Cinema*, 421 (June 1989): 39.

Kaufmann, S. "Changing the Past," *New Republic* (November 23, 1998): 26–27.

Kelly, Christopher. "*The Monster* (review)," *Premiere* (August 1999): 95.

Kezich, Tulio. *Dizionario del cinema italiano. I film dal 1980 al 1989 A/L*, vol. 5, ed. R. Poppi (Rome: Gremese, 2000), p. 331.

Kinkielkraut, Alain. *Une voix vient de l'autre rive*. Paris: Gallimard, 1999.

Klarsfeld, Serge. *The Auschwitz Album, Lili Jacob's Album*. New York: The Beate Klarsfeld Foundation, 1980.

Kracauer, Siegfried. *From Caligari to Hitler*. Princeton, N.J.: Princeton University Press, 1966.

Landy, Marcia. *Italian Film*. Cambridge: Cambridge University Press, 2000.

Leibman, Stuart. "If Only Life Were So Beautiful," *Cineaste*, 24(2–3) (1999): 20–22.

Lemon, Lee T. *Russian Formalist Criticism: Four Essays*, ed. Lee T. Lemon and Marion J. Reis. Lincoln: University of Nebraska Press, 1965.

Lerner, Gad. *Pinocchio RAI 2*, dir. Andrea Soldani with Roberto Benigni, Vincenzo Cerami, Marcello Pezzetti, and Ishayahu Nir, February 9, 1999.

Leroux, H. "Le petit diable," *Cahiers du Cinema*, 421 (June 1989): 48–49.

Levantesi, Alessandra. "Benigni e Troisi: due incontri d'epoca," in *Una generazione in Cinema. Esordi ed esordienti italiani 1975–1988*, ed. L. Miccichè, pp. 409–421. Venice: Marsilio, 1988.

Levi, Primo. *Survival in Auschwitz: The Nazi Assault on Humanity*, trans. S. Woolf. New York: Macmillan, 1958.

Lyotard, Jean François. *The Postmodern Condition,* trans. G. Bennington and B. Massumi. Minneapolis: University of Minnesota Press, 1984.

McCabe, Colin. *"Life Is Beautiful* (review)," *Sight & Sound,* 9(2) (February 1999): 46.

Machiavelli, Niccolò. *La mandragola,* trans. Mera J. Flaumenhaft. Prospect Heights, Ill.: Waveland Press, 1981.

Maltin, Leonard. *"Life Is Beautiful* (review)," *Playboy* (December 1998): 22.

Manicotti, Mauro. *La resistenza nel cinema italiano 1945/1995.* Turin: Istituto Storico della Resistenza in Liguria, 1995.

Manin, Iuseppina. "Il presidente della giuria: La Rossellini mi parlò di lui," *Corriere della sera* (May 26, 1998).

Martinelli, Massimo. "Un uomo e una lampadina," in *Benigni Roberto di Luigi fu Remigio.* Milan: Leonardo arte, 1997.

Martini, Giulio. "La grande depressione dell'Emilia e il trionfo della risata etrusca," in *Patchwork Due geografia del nuovo cinema italiano,* ed. Giulio Martini and Guglielmina Morelli, pp. 46–52. Milan: Il castoro, 1997.

Martini, Paolo. *TV Sorrisi e milioni.* Milan: Rizzoli, 1985.

Masi, Stefano. *Roberto Benigni.* Rome: Gremese, 1999.

Mereghetti, Paolo. *Dizionario dei film 1996.* Milan: Baldini & Castoldi, 1996.

Metz, Christian. *Langue et cinéma.* Paris: Larousse, 1971.

Miccichè, Lino. *Cinema italiano degli anni '70. Cronache 1969–1979.* Venice: Marsilio, 1980.

Mitry, Jean. *Esthétique et psychologie du cinéma. Les structures.* Paris: Edition Universitaires, 1963.

Mollica, Vincenzo. *Segni Benigni.* Perugia: Di, 1997.

Morandini, M. *"La vita è bella* (review)," *Cineforum* 37(10) (December 1997): 4–5.

————. "Benign(i)ly Speaking (Some Quotations from the Italian Press on Roberto Benigni's Oscar Awards for '*La vita è bella*')," *Cineforum* 39(3) (April 1999): 35.

Morandini, Orlando. "Giuseppe Bertoluccci: dietro i segreti," in *Una generazione in cinema Esordi ed esordienti italiani 1975–1988,* ed. Franco Montini, pp. 59–72. Venice: Marsilio, 1988.

Moscati, Massimo. *Benigniaccio con te la vita è bella.* Milan: BUR, 1999.

Nassini, Carla. *Benigni Roberto di Luigi fu Remigio.* Milan: Leonardo Arte, 1997.

Neumann, L. *"La vita è bella* (review)," *Histoire* 225 (October 1998): 12.

Parigi, Stefania. *Roberto Benigni.* Naples: Edizioni Scientifiche Italiane, 1988.

Pascal, Blaise. *Pensees.* Paris: Bordas, 1966.

Pasolini, Pier Paolo. *Heretical Empiricism,* trans. Ben Lawton and Kate L . Barnett. Bloomington: Indiana University Press, 1988.

————. "La scomparsa delle lucciole," *Corriere della sera* (February 1, 1975).

Paton, P. A. *The Greek Anthology,* vol. 5. Cambridge, Mass.: Harvard University Press, 1953.

Petrolini, Ettore. *Bravo! Grazie! Antologia petroliniana,* ed. Vincenzo Cerami. Rome: Theoria, 1992.

Pezzetti, Marcello. "Considerazioni sulla rapprentazione della Shoah ad opera del cinema," in *Storia e memoria della deportazione,* ed. Paolo Momigliano Levi, pp. 131–135. Milan: Giuntina, 1996.

————. "Rappresentare la Shoah, trasmettere la memoria," in *Il racconto della catastrofe. Il cinema di fronte ad Auschwitz,* ed. Francesco Monicelli and Carlo Saletti, pp. 27–33. Verona: Cierre, 1998.

Pezzetti, Vanina. *Kapo',* Unpublished thesis. Dipartimento Arte Musica e Spettacolo, 1998.

Picard, Max. *The World of Silence.* Chicago: Gateway, 1952.

Putnam, Robert. *Making Democracy Work: Civic Traditions in Modern Italy.* Princeton N.J.: Princeton University Press, 1997.

Quadri, Franco. *L'avanguardia teatrale in Italia 1960–1976.* Turin: Einaudi, 1977.

Quaglietti, Lorenzo. *Storia economico-politica del cinema italiano 1945–1980.* Rome: Editori Riuniti, 1980.

Radiotelevisione italiana. *Storia della RAI I. 30 anni di televisione Date Momenti personaggi 1954–1983.* Rome: RAI Documentazione e studi, 1983.

Regazzoni, Enrico. "La mia risata è una donna nuda," *La Repubblica* (November 17, 1992).

Rivette, Jacques. "De l'abjection," *Les cahiers du cinema,* 120 (1961): 75–79.

Rondi, Gian Luigi. "Il riso amaro del nuovo Chaplin," *La rivista del cinematografo* (December 1997): 7–15.

Rooney, David. "*Life Is Beautiful* (review)," *Variety* (December 22, 1997): 61.

———. "*The Monster* (review)," *Variety* (October 13, 1994): 89.

Rossi, M. "The Nazi Extermination Camps and Benigni's Movie," *Ponte* 55(4) (April 1999): 5–6.

Rothstein, Edward. "Using Farce to Break the Spell of Fascism," *New York Times* (October 18, 1998): 2, 28.

Roux, Herve. "*Il piccolo diavolo* (review)," *Cahiers du Cinema,* 421 (June 1989): 48–49.

Saada, N. Josset. "Roberto Benigni," *Cahiers du Cinema,* 421 (June 1989): 39.

Sabourand, Frederic. "Interview with Roberto Benigni," *Cahiers du Cinema,* 393 (March 1987): 10.

———. "*Tu mi turbi* (review)," *Cahiers du Cinema,* 434 (July/August 1990): 68–69.

———. "Eloge du bouffon," *Cahiers du Cinema,* 393 (March 1987): x.

Samueli, Anna. "Entretien avec Roberto Benigni," *Cahiers du Cinema,* 431–432 (May 1990): 23–25.

Sander, Gilman. "Is Life Beautiful? Can the Shoah Be Funny? Some Thoughts on Recent and Older Films," *Critical Inquiry,* 26(2) (Winter 2000): 279–308.

Schickel, R. "Fascist Fable," *Time* (November 9, 1998): 116–117.

Schopenhauer, Arthur. "The Christian System," trans. T. B. Saunders, in *Religion: A Dialogue and Other Essays,* pp. 103–118. Westport, Conn.: Greenwood Press, 1973.

Simon, John. "Lies Are Unbeautiful," *National Review* (February 22, 1999): 54–55.

Simonelli, Giorgio, and Gaetano Tramontana. *Datemi un Nobel! L'opera comica di Roberto Benigni.* Alessandria: Edizioni Falsopiano, 1998.

Socci, S. "Benignamente," in *Si fa per ridere, ma è una cosa seria . . . ,* vol. 6, ed. S. Bernardi, pp. 107–111. Florence: Casa Usher, 1985.

Steiner, George. *The Portage to San Cristobal of A.H.* New York: Simon and Schuster, 1981.

Stubbs, T. "Pick Up Your Bats ('Life Is Beautiful' and the Holocaust)," *Sight & Sound,* 9(5) (May 1999): 64.

Tesson, Charles. "L'enfance de la memoire a propos de *La vie est Belle,*" *Cahiers du Cinema,* 529 (November 1998): 46–48.

Tugend, Tom. "Can Humor Shed Light on the Holocaust?" *Los Angeles Times* (September 26, 1999).

Viano, Maurizio. "*Life Is Beautiful:* Reception, Allegory, and Holocaust Laughter," *Film Quarterly,* 53 (Fall 1999): 1, 26–34.

————. "*Life Is Beautiful:* Reception, Allegory, and Holocuast Laughter," *Annali d'italianistica,* vol. 17 (1999): 155–172.

Vogelmann, Daniel. "*La vita è bella* (review)," *Il tirreno* (December 18 1997): 1.

Waits, Tom. "Roberto Benigni (interview)," *Interview* (January 1993): 26–27.

Wills, Gary. *John Wayne's America.* New York: Simon & Schuster, 1993.

Young, Deborah. "*Johnny Stecchino* (review)," *Variety* (November 11, 1991): 54.

Zagarrio, Vito. *Cinema italiano anni novanta.* Venice: Marsilio Editori, 1998.

Zavattini, Cesare. *Neorealismo ecc.* Milan: Bompiani, 1979.

Zizek, Slavoj. "Camp Comedy," *Sight & Sound* 10(4) (April 2000): 26–29.

# Theatrical Work

*Una favola vera*

Teatro Metastasio, Prato, 1971; From: *Il re nudo* di Eugenij Schwarz; Cast: Loris Toso, Paolo Santangelo, Giampiero Bucci, Pamela Villoresi, Roberto Benigni; Director: Paolo Magelli

*I burosauri*

Teatro dei Satiri, Rome, 1972; Cast: Remo Foglino, Anna Montinari, Giancarlo Sisto, Carlo Monni, Roberto Benigni; Director: Donato Sannini

*Le fiabe del Basile*

Teatro S. Genesio, Rome, 1972; By Lucia Poli; Cast: Lucia Poli, Roberto Benigni; Director: Lucia Poli

*La contessa e il cavolfiore*

Teatro dei Satiri, Rome, 1973; Text: Mario Moretti and Lucia Poli; Cast: Donato Sannini, Roberto Benigni, Carlo Monni, Anna Montinari, Yuki Maraini; Director: Donato Sannini

*Bertoldo Azzurro*

Rondò di Bacco, Firenze; Teatro dei Satiri, Rome, 1973; Based on *L'angelo azzurro,* by Josef von Sterrnberg, and *Le storie di Bertoldo,* by Guilio Cesare Croce; Cast: Marco Messeri, Roberto Benigni, Graziella Porta; Directors: Marco Messeri and Paolo Poli

*Le metamorfosi*

Teatro S. Genesio, Rome, 1974; From Ovid; Cast: Lucia Poli, Roberto Benigni, Marco Messeri, Graziella Porta; Director: Lucia Poli

*La corte delle stalle*

Teatro Beat 72, Rome, 1974; By Franz X. Krotez; Cast: Roberto Benigni, Ornella Minnetti, Carlo Monni, Oscar Montini; Director: Donato Sannini

*Mi voglio rovinare*

Caserta, 1974; By Marco Messeri; Cast: Marco Messeri, Roberto Benigni; Director: Marco Messeri

*La Festa*

Teatro Beat 72, Rome, 1974; By Lucia Poli; Cast: Lucia Poli, Roberto Benigni, Gianfranco Varetto; Director: Lucia Poli

*Cioni Mario di Gaspare fu Giulia*

Teatro Alberichino, Rome, 1975; By Roberto Bengini and Giuseppe Bertolucci; Cast: Roberto Benigni; Director: Giuseppe Bertolucci

*Tuttobenigni*

Taranto, 1983; By Roberto Benigni and Giuseppe Bertolucci; Cast: Roberto Benigni; Director: Giuseppe Bertolucci

*Pierino e il lupo (Peter and the Wolf)*

Teatro Comunale, Ferrara, 1990; By Serge Prokovief; Featuring: Chamber Orchestra of Europe; Director: Claudio Abbado; Vocal recitation: Roberto Benigni

*Babele*

RAI 3, May 30, 1993.

*Tuttobenigni 95/96*

Rome, 1995; By Roberto Benigni and Vincenzo Cerami; Director: Roberto Benigni; Actor: Roberto Benigni; Musician: Nicola Piovani

# Filmography

## AS ACTOR

*Berlinguer ti voglio bene/Berlinguer I Love You*

Italy, 1977, 90 min.; Director: Giuseppe Bertolucci; Cast: Roberto Benigni (Cioni Mario), Alida Valli (Mother), Carlo Monni (Bozzone), Mario Pachi, Maresco Fratini, Donatella Valmaggia, Sergio Forconi, Patrizia Mauro, Chiara Moretti, Annalisa Foa, Donato Sannini, Rossana Benvenuti, Walter Fantini, Giovanni Nannini, Paolo Pieri, Luigi Benigni; Screenplay: Roberto Benigni, Giuseppe Bertolucci; Photography: Renato Tafuri; Music: Pier Farri and Franco Coletta; Sound: Raul Montesanti; Sets: Maria Paola Maino; Costumes: Luciana Morosetti; Editing: Gabriella Cristiani, Franco Arcalli; Producer: Gianni Minervini and Antonio Avati for A.M.A. Film

*Il comizio*

Italy, 1978, 22 min.; Written by Roberto Benigni, Carlo Monni; Directors: Paolo Brunatto, Mario Maglietti, Elio Rumma; Cast: Roberto Benigni, Carlo Monni; Photography: Piero Bargellini, Mario Gianni; Producer: Karma Film

*Chiaro di Donna/Clair de femme*

Italy/France, 1979, 110 min.; Director: Constantin Costa Gavras; Cast: Yves Montand (Michel), Romy Schnider (Lydia), Romolo Valli (Galba), Dieter Schiedor (Sven), Francoise Perrot (Alain), Lila Kedrova (Sonia), Gabriel Jabbour (Sacha), Roberto Benigni (bartender), Catherine Allgret (friend of Galba), Philipe Manesse; Story: Romain Gary; Screenplay: Costa Gravas; Photography: Ricardo Aronovich; Music: Jean Musy; Editing: Francios Bonnot; Producer: Parva Cinema/Les Films Gibe/Janus Films

*I giorni cantati*

Italy, 1979, 110 min.; Director: Paolo Pietrangeli; Cast: Paolo Pientrangeli (Marco), Mariangela Melato (Angela), Anna Nogaro (Anna), Roberto Benigni, Franco Bianchi, Alberto and Paolo Ciarchi, Ivan and Luiano Della Mea, Donatella Di Nola, Francesco Guccini, Susanna Javicoli, Claudio Lizza, Pasquale Malinconico, Giovanna Marini, Francesca Neonato; Screenplay: Giovanna Marini, Francesco Massaro, Paolo Pietrangeli; Photography: Dario Di Palma; Music: Ivan Della Mea, Francesco Guccini, Giovanna Marini, Pasquale Malinconico, Paolo Pietangeli, Franz Schubert, Antonio Vivaldi; Sound: Roberto Forrest; Sets: Elena Ricci Poccetto; Editing: Ruggero Mastroianni; Producer: Cooperativa Lunga Gitta

*Letti selvaggi / Tigers in Lipstick*
(Episode: Una mamma); Italy, 1979, 20 min.; Director: Luigi Zampa; Cast: Ursula Andress (traffic stopper), Laura Antonelli (wife/Giovanna), Silvia Kristel (Martucci/Giovanna), Monica Vitti (prostitute/Maria), Orazio Orlando (Fioroni), Michele Placido (Angelo/photo journalist), Roberto Benigni (the professor); Screenplay: Tonino Guerra, Giorgio Saovioni, Luis Castro; Photography: Giuseppe Ruzzolini; Editing: Franco Fratecelli; Producer: Zodiac/Corona

*La luna*
Italy/USA, 1979, 140 min.; Director: Bernado Bertolucci; Cast: Jill Clayburgh (Caterina Silveri), Matthew Berry (Joe), Fred Gwynne (Douglas), Bebetta Campeti (Arianna), Veronica Lazar (Mariana), Thomas Milian (Giuseppe), Alida Valli (Giuseppe's mother), Alessio Vlad (orchestra director at Caracalla), Carlo Verdone (director of Caracalla), Franco Citti (man in bar), Peter Eyre (Edward), Julian Adamoli (Julian), Jole Silvani (coat check at the Opera), Nicola Nicoloso (tenor of the *Trovatore)*, Fabrizio Poverini, Sarah De Nepi, Roberto Benigni (upholsterer), Francesco Mei (bartender); Story: Bernardo Bertolucci, Franco Arcalli; Screenplay: Bernado Bertolucci, Giuseppe Bertolucci, Claire Peploe; Photography: Vittorio Storaro; Music: Giuseppe Verdi; Sound: Mario Dallimonti; Sets: Gianni Sivestri, Maria Paola Maino; Costumes: Lina Nerli Taviani; Editing: Gabriella Cristiani; Producer: Giovanni Bertolucci for Fiction Cinema

*Chiedo asilo / Seeking Asylum*
Italy/France, 1979, 112 min.; Director: Marco Ferreri; Cast: Roberto Benigni (Roberto), Dominque Laffin (Isabella), Chiara Moretti (Irma), Carlo Monni (Paolo), Girolamo Marzano, Franco Trevisi, the children from the kindergarden P.E.E.P. Bentini di Bolognia, Luca Levi; Story: Marco Ferreri; Screenplay: Marco Ferreri, Gerad Brach, with Roberto Benigni; Photography: Pasquale Rachini; Music: Philippe Sarde; Sound: Jean Pierre Ruh; Sets: Enrico Manelli; Costumes: Nicoletta Ercole; Editing: Mauro Bonanni; Producer: 23 giugno/A.M.S. Production, Pacific Business Group, Ettore Rosboch

*Il Pap'occhio / Pope in Your Eye*
Italy, 1980, 101 min.; Director: Renzo Arbore; Cast: Renzo Arbore (director), Roberto Benigni (Judas), Silvia Annichiarico (director's secretary), Diego Abantuono (Father Gabriela), Luciano De Crescenso (voice of God), Le Sorelle Bandiera, Andy Luotto, Mario Marenco, Otto and Barnelli, Michele Pergolani, Isabella Rossellini (Isabella), Alessandro Vagioni, Fabrizio Zampa, Manfred Freyberger (pope), Graziano Giusti (Richelieu), Milly Carlucci (the nun, Buonasera), Mattero Salvadore (Gallo), Mimma Nocelli, Cesare Gigli (Italian teacher), Ruggero Orlando, Nando Murolo (leader of the Bronx cheer chorus), Martin Scorsese (television director), Mariangela Melato (unwanted actress); Story: Renzo Arbore; Screenplay: Renzo Arbore and Luciano De Crescenzo; Photography: Luciano Tovoli; Music: Renzo Arbore; Sound: Carlo Palmieri; Sets: G. F. Ramacci; Costumes: Lia Morandini; Producer: Mario Orfini for Eidoscope, RAI2, with Emilio Bolles

*Il minestrone*

Italy, 1981, 165 min. television, 105 min. theatrical release; Director: Sergio Citti; Cast: Roberto Benigni, Franco Citti, Ninetto Davoli, Franco Javarone, Daria Nicolodi, Fabio Traversa, Alvaro Amici, Giacomo Assandri, Adriana Citti, Cuerrino Crivello, Franco Diogone, Antonio Faa di Bruno, Giulio Farnese, Giulia Fossa, Carlo Monni, Cristina Noci, Sebastiano Nardone, Olimpia Carlisi; Story: Sergio Citti; Screenplay: Sergio Citti and Vincenzo Cerami; Photography: Dante Spinotti; Music: Nicola Piovani; Sound: Mario Bramonte; Sets: Dante Ferretti; Costumes: Mario Ambrosino; Editing: Nino Baragli; Producer: RAI/Medusa

*F.F.S.S. ovvero che mi hai portato a fare sopra Posillipo se non mi vuoi piu bene?*

Italy, 1983, 98 min.; Director: Renzo Arbore; Cast: Renzo Arbore (Onilu Caporetto), Pietra Montecorvino (Lucia Canaria), Gigi Proietti, Isabella Biagini (Madonna Sofia), Cesare Gigli, Stella Pende, Luciana Turina, I Fatebenefratelli, Bobby Solo, Isabel Russinova, Pippo Baudo, Gianni Mina, Renato Guttuso, Lory Del Santo, Severino Gazzelloni, Nando Martellini, Riccardo Pazzaglia, Nino Frassica, Massimo Troisi, Maria Giovanna Elmi, Domenico Modugno, Maurizio Costanzo, Lello Bersani, Don Lurio, Raffaella Carra, Lino Banfi, Luciano De Crescenzo, Andy Luotto, Maio Marenco, Nando Mureolo, Roberto Benigni; Screenplay: Renzo Arbore and Luciano De Crenzo; Photography: Renato Tafuri; Music: Renzo Arbore; Sound: Franco Borni; Sets: Franco Vanorio; Costumes: Adriana Spadaro; Editing: Anna Napoli; Producer: Mario Orfini, Emilio Bolles for Eidoscope

*Tuttobenigni*

Italy, 1986, 87 min.; Director: Giuseppe Bertolucci; Cast: Roberto Benigni; Photography: Renato Tafuri; Sound: H. Nijhuis; Sets: Maria Paola Maino; Costumes: Luciana Morosetti; Editing: Jannis Christopulos; Producer: Ettore Rosboch for Best International Film

*Down by Law*

USA, 1986, 110 min.; Director: Jim Jarmusch; Cast: Tom Waits (Zack), John Lurie (Jack), Roberto Benigni (Roberto), Nicoletta Braschi (Nicoletta), Ellen Barkin (Laurette), Billie Neal (Bobbie), Rockets Redglare (Gig), Vernel Bagneris (Preston), Timothea (Julie), L. C. Crane (L.C.), Joy Houck Jr. (Detective Madino), Richard Boes (detective), Dave Petitjean (Cajun detective), Adam Cohen (the graduate), Alan Klienberg (corpse), Archie Sampier (prisoner), David Dahlgreen (first police officer), Alex Miller (second police officer), Elliot Keener (third police officer), Jay Hilliard (fourth police officer); Screenplay: Jim Jarmusch; Photography: Robby Müller; Music: John Lurie, Tom Waits, Naomi Neville; Sound: Drew Kunin; Costumes: Carol Wood; Editing: Melody London; Producer: Alan Klienberg with Thomsa Rothman and Jim Stark for Blake Snake/Grokenberger

*Coffee and Cigarettes*

USA, 1986, 6 min.; Director: Jim Jarmusch; Cast: Roberto Benigni, Steven Wright; Screenplay: Jim Jarmusch, Roberto Benigni, Steven Wright; Photo-

graphy: Tom Dicillo; Editing: Melody London; Producer: Jim Stark for Blake
Snake

*La voce della luna/The Voice of the Moon*
Italy, 1989, 100 min.; Director: Federico Fellini; Cast: Roberto Benigni (Ivo
Salvini), Paolo Villaggio (Gonnella), Nadia Ottaviani (Aldina), Marisa Tomasi
(Marisa), Susy Blady (Susy), Angelo Orlando (Nestore), Dario Ghirardi (jour-
nalist), Dominique Chevalier (Micheluzzi brother one), Sim (Flautist), Nigel
Harris (Micheluzzi brother two); Story: based upon the *Il Poema dei lunatici,* by
Ermanno Cavazzoni; Screenplay: Federico Fellini, Tullio Pinelli, Ermanno
Cavazzoni; Photography: Tonino delli Colli; Music: Nicola Piovani; Sets: Dante
Ferretti; Costumes: Maurizio Millenotti; Editing: Nino Baragli; Producer: Mario
and Vittorio Cecchi Gori for C.G. Group Tiger

*Night on Earth*
(Episode: Rome) USA, 1992, 22 min.; Director: Jim Jarmusch; Cast: Roberto
Benigni (Gino), Paolo Bonacelli (priest), Gianni Scettino (first transvestite),
Antonio Ragusa (second transvestite), Nicola Facondo (lover), Camilla Begnoni
(lover), Romolo Di Biasi (upset driver), Donatella Servadio (dispatcher's voice);
Screenplay: Jim Jarmusch and Roberto Benigni; Photography: Frederick Elmes;
Music: Tom Waits; Producer: Jim Stark for Blake Snake

*Il figlio della pantera rosa/Son of the Pink Panther*
USA/Italy, 1993, 93 min.; Director: Blake Edwards; Cast: Roberto Benigni
(Jacques), Herbert Lom (Dreyfus), Burt Kwouk (Cato), Robert Bavi (Hans),
Anton Rodgers (Chief Lazar), Jennifer Edwards (Yassa), Debra Farentino
(Princess Yasmin), Shabana Azmi (Queen), Claudia Cardinale (Maria), Nicoletta
Braschi (Jacqueline), Graham Stark (Dr. Auguste Balls); Story: Blake Edwards;
Screenplay: Blake Edwards and M. S. Sunshine; Photography: Dick Bush;
Music: Henry Mancini and Bobbie McFerrin; Sets: Peter Mullins; Editing:
Robert Pergament; Producer: Tony Adams for United Artists in collaboration
with Filmauro (Italy)

*Asterix/Asterix and Obelix Take on Caesar*
France, 1999, 109 min.; Director: Claude Zidi; Cast: Christian Clavier (Asterix),
Gerard Depardieu (Obelix), Roberto Benigni (Lucius Detritus), Michel
Galabra (Panoramix), Daniel Prevost (Prolix), Pierre Palmade (Assurancetorix),
Latetita Casta (Falbula); Story/Screenplay: Gerard Lauzier and Claude Zidi;
Cinematography: Tony Pierce-Roberts; Editing: Herve de Luze and Nicole
Saunier; Producer: Claude Berri

## AS DIRECTOR

*Tu mi turbi*
Italy, 1983, 87 min.; Director: Roberto Benigni; Cast: Roberto Benigni (Benigno),
Carlo Monni (Saint Joseph), Nicoletta Braschi (Mary), Olimpia Carlisi (Angel),

Giacomo Piperno (bank director/prison guard/real estate agent), Claudio Biagli (the bersagliere), Alesso Marconi, Nicoletta Amodio, Tamara Triffez, Serena Grandi, Mariangela D'Abbraccio, Daniele Costantini, Eugenio Masciari, Fabrizi Corallo; Screenplay: Roberto Benigni and Giuseppe Bertolucci; Photography: Luigi Verga; Music: Paolo Conte; Sound: Remo Ugolinelli and Corrado Volpicelli; Sets: Giorgio Luppi and Silvia Polidoria; Editing: Gabriella Cristiani; Producer: Ettore Rosboch for Best International Film

*Non ci resta che piangere/Nothing Left to Do but Cry*
Italy, 1984, 111 min.; Director: Massimo Troisi and Roberto Benigni; Cast: Roberto Benigni (Saverio), Massimo Troisi (Mario), Iris Peynado (Astriah), Amanda Sandrelli (Pia), Carlo Monni (Vitellozzo), Livia Venturini (Parisiana), Elisabetta Pozzi, Jole Silvani, Loris Bazzocchi, Nicola Morelli, Mario Diano, Peter Bloom, Fiorenzo Serra, Stefano Gragnani, Galliano Mariani, Ronaldo Benacchi, Paolo Bonacelli (Leonardo da Vinci); Story: Massino Troisi and Roberto Benigni; Screenplay: Roberto Benigni, Massimo Troisi, Giuseppe Bertolucci; Photography: Giuseppe Rotunno; Music: Pino Donaggio; Sound: Francesco Frigeri; Sets: Francesco Frigeri; Costumes: Ezio Alitcheri; Editing: Nino Baragli; Producer: Ettore Rosboch for Best International Film and Mauro Berardi for Yarno cinematografica

*Il piccolo diavolo/Little Devil*
Italy, 1988, 110 min.; Director: Roberto Benigni; Cast: Roberto Benigni (Giuditta), Walter Matthau (Father Maurizio), Nicoletta Braschi (Nina), Stefania Sandrelli (Patrizia), John Laurie (Cusatelli), Paolo Baroni (novice), Franco Fabrizi (monsignor), Giacomo Piperno (man on train), Flavio Bonacci (ticket taker), Annabella Schiavone (Giuditta, the possessed woman), John Karlsen (confessor), Mirella Falco (mother of the young priest), Bruno Vetti (father of the young priest), Massimo Bianchi (the doctor), Roberto Corbiletto (hotel manager), Vito Passeri (maitre d'), Lim Hodi Hwa (young priest), Bianca Borracio (public relations), Toto Onnis (the carabinere), Stefano Antonucci, Giulia Borghini, Paola Batticciotto, Benedetto Fanna, Barbara Giommi, Mariella Minnozzi, Renato Pacotti, Monica Peracino, Enzo Saturini, Giuseppe Todisco, Fortunata Trapassi; Story: Giuseppe Bertolucci, Vincenzo Cerami, Roberto Benigni; Screenplay: Vincenzo Cerami and Roberto Benigni; Photography: Robby Müller; Music: Evan Lurie; Sets: Antonio Annichiarico; Costumes: Aldo Buti; Editing: Nino Baragli; Producer Mario Berardi (Yarno), Mario and Vittorio Cecchi Gori (C.G. Group Tiger) in collaboration with Reteitalia

*Johnny Stecchino*
Italy, 1991, 121 min.; Director: Roberto Benigni; Cast: Roberto Benigni (Johnny/Dante), Nicoletta Braschi (Maria), Paolo Bonacelli (D'Agata), Franco Volpi (minister), Ivano Marescotti (Dr. Randazzo), Alesandro De Sanctis (Lillo), Ignavo Pappalardo (Cozzamara), Loredana Romito (Gianna); Story: Vincenzo Cerami and Roberto Benigni; Screenplay: Vincenzo Cerami and Roberto Benigni; Photography: Giuseppe Lanci; Music: Evan Lurie; Sets:

Paolo Biagetti; Costumes: Gianna Gissi; Editing: Nino Baragli; Producer: Guido and Aurelio de Laurentiis for Filmauro

*Il mostro / The Monster*

Italy/France, 1994, 118 min.; Director: Roberto Benigni; Cast: Roberto Benigni (Loris), Nicoletta Braschi (Jessica Rossetti), Michael Blanc (Paride Tacconi), Domique Lavanant (Jolanda Tacconi), Jean-Claude Brialy (Rocarotta), Franco Mescolini (Chinese professor), Laurent Spielvogel (Frustalupi), Massimo Girotti (elderly resident), Ivano Marescotti (Pascucci), Luciana Pieri Palombi (Claudia), Vittorio Amandola (antique dealer), Rita Di Lernia (antique dealer's wife), Vincenzo Vitagliamo (renter), Gennaro Morrone (newspaper vendor); Screenplay: Vincenzo Cerami and Roberto Benigni; Photography: Carlo Di Palma; Music: Evan Lurie; Sets: Giantito Burchiellaro; Costumes: Danilo Donati; Editing: Nino Bargli; Producer: Roberto Benigni and Yves Attal for Melampo, Iris Film UGC Images

*La vita è bella / Life Is Beautiful*

Italy, 1997, 130 min.; Director: Roberto Benigni; Cast: Roberto Benigni (Guido Orefice), Nicoletta Braschi (Dora Orefice), Horst Bucholz (Dr. Lessing), Giustino Durano (Uncle Eliseo), Sergio Bustric (Ferruccio), Giorgio Cantarini (Giosué Orefice), Amerigo Fontani (Rodolfo), Pietro De Silva (Bartolomeo), Marisa Paredes (Dora's mother); Screenplay: Vincenzo Cerami and Roberto Benigni; Photography: Tonino Delli Colli; Music: Nicola Piovani; Sets and Costumes: Danilo Donati; Editing: Simona Paggi; Producer: Elda Ferrari and Gianluigi Braschi for Melampo Cinematografica

# Index

# About the Author

**Carlo Celli** earned his doctoral degree from the University of California Los Angeles. He has also pursued studies at the Universities of Virginia, Firenze, and Bologna. He currently divides his time between Crema, Italy and Bowling Green State University, Ohio where he is associate professor of Italian and Film Studies.